ARTHUR
THE KING IN THE WEST

R.W. Dunning

ALAN SUTTON PUBLISHING LIMITED · Stroud

ST. MARTIN'S PRESS · New York

First published in the United Kingdom in 1988
Alan Sutton Publishing Limited
Phoenix Mill · Far Thrupp · Stroud · Gloucestershire

First published in the United States of America in 1988
St. Martin's Press · Scholarly and Reference Division
175 Fifth Avenue · New York · N.Y. 10010

Paperback edition first published 1990
Reprinted 1995

British Library Cataloguing-in-Publication Data

Dunning, R.W. (Robert William) *1938–*
   Arthur: King in the west.
   1. Legends. Characters: Arthur, King
   I. Title
   398.352

ISBN 0-7509-0994-3

*Cover illustration: Arthur and his knights setting out on the quest for the
Holy Grail (Bibliothèque Nationale de France, Paris, MS Fr 343 f. 8v
Italian c. 1370–80).*

Designed by Richard Bryant and Martin Latham.
Typesetting and origination by
Alan Sutton Publishing Limited.
Printed in Great Britain by
WBC Limited, Bridgend.

INTRODUCTION

THE story of King Arthur and the Knights of the Round Table has a fascination which is universal. It has attracted sculptors and painters, poets and writers of fiction, printers and typographers, musicians and dramatists, philosophers and scientists. Product of the Celtic world, it embraced in the Middle Ages the Romance of France and Italy and the Teutonic themes of Northern Europe. It was the inspiration of the Gothic Revival in 19th-century England, and its following is as strong today in California as it is in Western Europe.

But the story is not only popular; it is controversial. Historians take diametrically opposed views on its central figure, Arthur, for the written sources are few and difficult to interpret with certainty. Archaeologists are inclined to be tentative about the significance of the artefacts from the Dark Ages. Both depend on legends whose age is often unknown, whose importance is often uncertain, whose veracity cannot as yet be tested by traditional disciplines.

Yet because the story is so popular, it suffers from being over-simplified. 'Did Arthur really exist?' is a common question, but one that cannot and should not be answered simply. The story is both too important and too complex for that. It is important because it has provided an ideal to which generations have aspired, the ideal of chivalry which has had such a profound effect on our social code.

Henry III's Round Table at
Winchester, Edward I's per-
sonal interest in Arthur,
Edward III's Order of the
Garter and Edward IV's
magnificent rebuilding of St
George's Chapel, Windsor,
are all products of the story.

The story is also complex,
for in its full flowering it
embraces some elements
which can be traced back to pagan Celtic mythology,
some which lead through Joseph of Arimathea to the
heart of the Christian Faith, some which derive
from literary and poetic themes of courtly love. The
modern blacksmith and the metallurgist both recognise the intensely practical elements in the apparently magical forging of Excalibur; yet to search for
an armour-clad knight or many-towered Camelot in
a Dark Age landscape is to search in vain, to be
entirely misled.

But in the West of England there is a real
landscape in which stands a fortress of obvious
strength. Legends told about it at the end of the
Middle Ages declared it to be Camelot, legends
perhaps fostered by its owners, whose political
traditions during the Wars of the Roses and later
were at the heart of a revived and reviving nation-
alism. Modern archaeology has interpreted the site
as having been refortified and reoccupied by a
military leader of wealth and power. This is not
'proof' of Arthur, but is a clear indication of the
importance of the legend, both as a tool to be
manipulated for political ends and a guide for
modern archaeologists. This book is the story of

how King Arthur, the Arthur of Legend, was brought to the West Country. It is the story of its manipulation.

Some elements in this story were firmly rooted in Cornwall from the beginning; the Welsh bards were in no doubt that Arthur's 'capital' at Kelliwic lay in the land where later writers placed Tintagel and Camlann. Somerset's role in the Dark Ages is obviously of considerable significance, but the 'Somerset' Arthur of the written sources was introduced with a clear political purpose in the 12th century, ironically through the agency of several writers from Wales whose 'ownership' of Arthur had for so long gone unchallenged.

This, then, is an attempt to trace how and why; a story of some mystery and much imagination, brilliant publicity and serious purpose. To see it as gross deception is to mistake the age and the men, for at its heart was the need to establish the Abbey of Glastonbury as the undisputed cradle of Christianity in England, in terms and in a language which the age could understand. Where other monasteries used saints to attract support, Glastonbury finally and successfully chose a popular hero and then allied him with the mystery of the Grail. It was a potent combination which kept the abbey at the forefront of English monasticism until the Dissolution, and keeps it still as a popular centre for pilgrims of all religions and of none.

But it is not simply Glastonbury whose sites –

Head of King Arthur from 13th century Germany

View from Glastonbury Tor down to Chalice Hill and Glastonbury and then across the ancient marshes to Brent Knoll and Wales

abbey, Tor, Wearyall Hill and Beckery — attracted visitors even in the otherwise depressing days just before the Dissolution in 1539. Its rival, Wells, may have inspired a story of Arthur on or near their land at Carhampton in West Somerset, and hence a notion that Arthur's court was near at hand, perhaps at Dunster. Brent Knoll, a Glastonbury outpost, inevitably had its tale to tell — of giants and a brave knight from Arthur's court. Further south was there not Camelot? Surely not just a notion of a friend of Sir Thomas Malory, companion in arms in the Yorkist cause. And further west are Tintagel and Camlann, the beginning and the end of the Arthurian story. The West of England is thus a treasure-house for those on the quest for the Once and Future King; and in the mysterious, misty marshes of Somerset is that sacred spot which is for many the Isle of Avalon.

THE REALM
OF THE
HERO KING

'But when did Arthur chance upon thee first?' Tennyson:
THE COMING OF ARTHUR, IDYLLS OF THE KING

SOUTH-Western Britain, the tribal lands of the Dobunni, the Durotriges and the Dumnonii, was an important part of the Roman province of Britannia, a significant fragment of the Roman Empire. Lead and silver from the Mendips and tin from Cornwall contributed to the general Imperial wealth; the healing properties of the waters of Aquae Sulis (Bath) were known far beyond Britain's shores; the corn grown and the stock reared on the larger villa estates of central Somerset were doubtless sold in distant urban markets and stored in garrison granaries. Into that same countryside, along the great Fosse Way and its offshoots, came the benefits of Rome: military protection, ordered government and the sophisticated and exotic products of Gaul and the Mediterranean.

Roman rule was, in a sense, a veneer. The native people still lived on the land accepting, some more, some less, the benefits of Empire, worshipping their native deities, some of whom acquired new names to set with the old, like Sulis Minerva at Bath; practising their traditional arts and crafts; going about their trade and commerce. The way they lived and farmed the land probably had as much to do with long-cherished social patterns as with the lie of the land and external demands.

The influence of Empire was all-pervading, the products of Empire everywhere to be seen and used. Roman coins and pottery, found even beyond the Cornish coast in the Scillies, indicate the penetra-

Above: Durotrigian coin

Opposite:
A gold Dubunnic stater

tion of Roman commerce and culture. But other Roman characteristics were alien to the far west. In the 2nd century there were only six places of significance, not necessarily even towns, in the whole country west of Bath, and none further west than the legionary fortress of Isca Dumnoniorum (Exeter). By late Roman times there were four places of importance besides Exeter, but none seems to have survived even as a village today, and their sites are not certainly known. One, Nemestatio, seems to have been in North Devon near the present Nymet place-names west of Crediton. Deventiasteno may have been somewhere in south Devon, Tamaris near the Tamar, and Durocornavis, perhaps the Rumps hillfort in North Cornwall.

Further east some of the traditional hilltop sites were abandoned. The Durotrigian strongholds of Hod Hill and Maiden Castle in Dorset were evidently attacked and destroyed by the Second Augustan Legion under Vespasian in AD 44, but two others in their territory, Cadbury and Ham Hill in Somerset, were left unharmed.

Life carried on at Cadbury almost as before, although a few people were bold enough to move outside the defences, protected by the Roman Peace, and started up a settlement at the foot of the hill which became the village of South Cadbury. Up on the hilltop business flourished: the entrance roadway was well worn, jewellery and tableware were imported from abroad, a shrine was rebuilt and

The 'Christ' roundel from the
Hinton St. Mary mosaic

visited. But two generations later there was another tale to tell, a tale of evident brutality. The Roman government probably demanded the removal of the people from their ancestral stronghold and when they tried to resist, by strengthening the rampart and barricading the south-west gate, the army took a hand. Defenders were cut down at the gate and were left where they fell; survivors were perhaps resettled in the lowlands at Catsgore or Ilchester. Cadbury's defences were destroyed, and for two centuries the site was under the plough.

In the peaceful conditions created by Rome, traders penetrated the south-west, establishing roads along the northern edge of Dartmoor and along Cornwall's spine to exploit her mineral deposits. They established river ports, in Somerset at Ilchester, Crandon and Combwich; Isca could be served as well by sea as by land. Roman technology drained the Somerset marshland around Brent Knoll and near Cheddar, and protected the low-lying pastures beside the Yeo around Yatton and Nailsea; quarried stone at Dundry and Ham Hill, mined iron ore on the Brendons; worked pewter, even made glass.

THE END OF EMPIRE

The famous letter of the Emperor Honorius of AD 410 effectually withdrawing the protection of

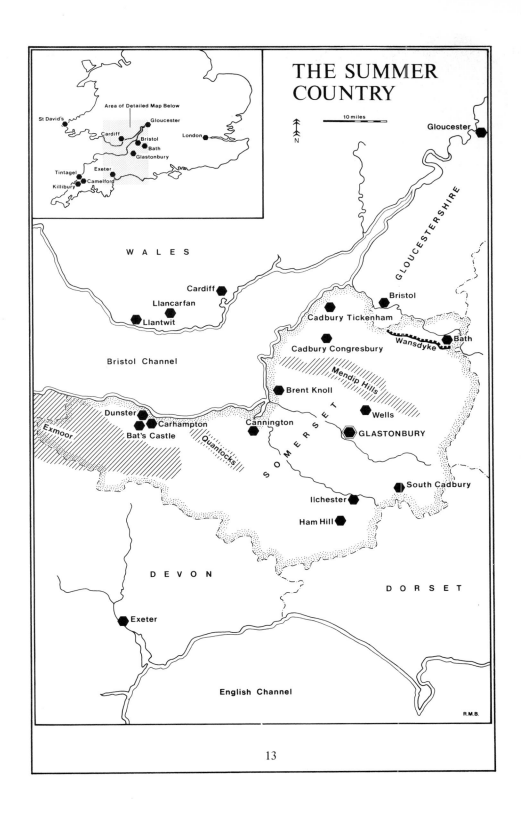

THE SUMMER COUNTRY

10 miles

N

St David's
Gloucester
Area of Detailed Map Below
Cardiff
Bristol
Bath
London
Glastonbury
Tintagel
Exeter
Killibury
Camelford

Gloucester

WALES

GLOUCESTERSHIRE

Cardiff

Llancarfan

Llantwit

Bristol

Cadbury Tickenham

Bath

Cadbury Congresbury

Wansdyke

Bristol Channel

Mendip Hills

Brent Knoll

Wells

Dunster

Carhampton

Cannington

GLASTONBURY

Exmoor

Bat's Castle

S
O
M
E
R
S
E
T

Quantocks

South Cadbury

Ilchester

Ham Hill

DEVON

DORSET

Exeter

English Channel

R.M.B.

Magnus Maximus, proclaimed emperor by the army in Britain in 383. He withdrew vital troops from Britain for his European campaign

the Roman army from Britannia did not mark the sudden end of a civilisation. Roman army units had been withdrawn before by, for example, the usurper Magnus Maximus in 383. Rural settlements like Trethurgy in Cornwall and small towns like Ilchester were still occupied, but parts of Isca in the 4th century were already turned over to agriculture, and after AD 400 some of the walled city became a graveyard. The drainage system of the baths at Bath collapsed and the area became waterlogged. But the countryside still needed defence, and the answer in the West Country was either a return to the ancient hilltop strongholds like Chun Castle in Cornwall and South Cadbury in Somerset or, at High Peak near Sidmouth, an entirely new fortification. The rebuilt or revived fortresses and other defences like the great embankment of Wansdyke were the work of a sophisticated and efficient body of men prepared to defend a cherished way of life.

One characteristic of that way of life, eagerly sought by archaeologists, is the use of imported pottery from the eastern Mediterranean. Another, and probably more important characteristic, is Christianity. The traditions of South-Western Britain are deeply imbued with the missionary activities of a host of men and women with Welsh, Irish or Breton connections to which a later age looked back with awe. The saints of western Somerset, of North Devon and of Cornwall are not to be found by strictly archaeological means, and there is little trace of the survival of Roman Christianity into the 5th century in the West.

Yet St Alban had been executed for his faith as long ago as AD 209 and four bishops represented the British Church at a Continental council a century later. The shrine at Henley Wood near Congresbury in

The central motif from a 6th century North African bowl

Somerset may, perhaps, have been destroyed by Christians; and the latest, late 4th century, building at the old shrines on Brean Down and Lamyatt Beacon, not many miles away, may have been Christian. There is more than a suspicion, however, that Christianity was predominantly urban, at least until the remarkable visit to Britain of Victricius, Bishop of Rouen, at the invitation of some British bishops, in AD 396.

Victricius brought with him, and successfully preached, the dangerous doctrines of Ambrose and Martin; he advocated the veneration of martyrs who had suffered against unjust authority; he encouraged monastic renunciation of society; he even preached to peasants and barbarians. His success was immediate. A shrine of St Alban was established at the place of his martyrdom, a church of St Martin was built at Canterbury 'while the Romans yet inhabited Britain'; and Ninian, a disciple of Victricius, preached to the barbarians in the North and built another church in the name of St Martin at Whithorn in Galloway. Here were the beginnings of a Church on the fringes of power, a Church of the countryside.

15

A mounted patrol returns to the fortress at South Cadbury

A tumbled mass of stone from the destruction of the Roman temple of Sulis
Minerva at Bath

About the year 540 a middle-aged man from the North – perhaps Lancashire or even Ninian's own Borderland – wrote a famous sermon. That man was called Gildas and he had been trained in his youth by a tutor who himself had a Classical education. As a man Gildas wrote for an audience of his own kind, people who could appreciate both his language and his learning and could remember what life had been like in the youthful past they all shared. Scholars are still not agreed about Gildas, though they agree about his crucial importance. Some think that he wrote in South Wales, for he was later looked upon as the founder of monastic life there. Others believe he wrote in the North-West. And where he wrote is important, for it helps to interpret what he wrote and to explain what he left unwritten.

The central motif from a 6th century North African bowl

What he wrote, a famous work called 'The Ruin of Britain', is probably the closest thing to a written history for the important century and a half after the end of official Roman rule – the Dark Ages. It was not meant to be history; it was an impassioned appeal that the civilisation and culture of his youth, and the past of which he was spiritually a part, might yet be revived by the warlords who in his time ruled the land.

Gildas saw the past as a sad decline from the civilised and ordered rule of Rome. In a 'history' written without mentioning dates, he told of invasions from the North when the Roman armies were

Amphora from the Mediterranean

withdrawn; of civil war and famine; then of a British revival and victory over the barbarians, followed by peace and the beginnings of kingship. After that came more barbarian invasions and an invitation to some Saxon mercenary troops to assist in their removal. The Saxons themselves revolted against their masters after initial successes; there was war, civilised city life was destroyed, and many of the British nobility retreated to Gaul. But gradually the Britons were reorganised and revived under a single leader, Ambrosius Aurelianus, who achieved a series of victories against the Saxons, culminating – and this may well have been within Gildas's own lifetime – in the Battle of Mount Badon. But, great victory that it was, it did not bring peace and the revival of culture which Gildas hoped.

Ambrosius, for Gildas, was a great warrior, 'perhaps the last of the Romans to survive', a man with an identity; no other warrior of his time was worth a name. Where, then, was Arthur, for surely Gildas, even with a northern bias, was not ignorant of the rest of Britain? Did he not denounce the petty tyrants of the West and Wales; the wicked Constantine of Dumnonia, the warlike Conan of Gloucester, the three dreadful kings of Wales? Surely he knew more of the campaigns which ended at Mount Badon than he is prepared to record? Does he name Ambrosius only to attack his descendants?

Reading Gildas alone, Gildas the near-

A Dark Age war leader

Nennius's *Historia Britonum* describes the twelve great battles of Arthur contemporary, Gildas the passionate preacher, that is the end of the story. But there remains ample evidence that, long before they were committed to writing, epics were sung, not just in Britain but in Ireland and Britanny, telling of another hero. Only two of these epics now survive, neither in their

A 3rd century armoured horseman from Dura Europos in the valley of the Euphrates

original form nor very near in date to their origins. One is a poem called the 'Elegy for Geraint' and the other a 'history' usually known as Nennius. The Elegy describes in vigorous language a battle (very probably at Portchester and not, as used to be thought, at Langport) where Geraint, the ruler of Dumnonia, was slain fighting in the campaign against the invaders:

> 'In Llongborth, I saw the clash of swords,
> Men in terror, bloody heads,
> Before Geraint the Great, his father's son'.

And for whom was he fighting, who was the leader who was masterminding the campaign?

> 'In Longborth I saw Arthur's Heroes who cut with steel;
> the Emperor, ruler of our labour'.

Nennius, written in Welsh about the year 800, tells much more about this ruler, this battle leader. He describes Arthur as the man who co-ordinated the British attack in twelve battles, leading the British chieftains not simply as military supremo,

23

An early Anglo-Saxon brooch

but even perhaps as a Christian standard bearer. At the battle of Castellum Guinnion, the eighth battle, 'he carried the image of the holy Mary, the everlasting virgin, on his shield'; and in the twelfth and last, Mount Badon, 960 men fell at a single charge.

Now where do we place this 'history' in time and space? A book of annals, compiled from the late 8th century onwards at St David's and known as the Annals of Wales, mentions Arthur twice. Under the year 72 it records the battle of Mount Badon in which (but this phrase may have been added later) Arthur carried his shield with the Cross of Our Lord Jesus Christ for three days and three nights and was afterwards victorious; and under the year 93 the battle of Camlann in which Arthur and Medraut perished. That is not helpful, but at least corroborates the other references to Arthur and Badon. Modern scholars, concerned to make the matter fit into the context of conventional history, date Badon between 480 and 520 and, with less confidence, place it somewhere in southern England, mentioning as possible sites Solsbury Hill near Bath, the earthworks at Badbury Rings in Dorset, or Liddington Castle near Badbury in Wiltshire.

Yet there are still some doubts. Some doubt the very existence of an individual Arthur, preferring some personification of Celtic opposition. Some see him as a figure from another time, when the struggle against the barbarian was in its infancy long before

The Welsh Annals record the battles of Mount Badon and Camlann

Gildas's time. Some even suggest a later period when the struggle continued on the fringes of the Saxon kingdoms. And there is, and can be, no absolute proof.

TRADITION AND ARCHAEOLOGY

Tradition and the evidence of archaeology between them plead strongly for what cannot be proved, an Arthur of the West Country and Wales, an Arthur who co-ordinated the power of hillfort chieftains, an Arthur who led fast-moving cavalry to military success, an Arthur who could have known Glastonbury. Tradition takes us to the mysterious 'king-lists', royal genealogies which play such an important part in Welsh historical studies. One of these was compiled in South-East Wales to demonstrate the long royal descent of Morgan ap Owain, King of Morgannwg, another traced a line of princely saints. And in both, far back at a time when the memory of man ran not to the contrary, was the royal line of the kings of Dumnonia: Constantine of Cornwall, father of Erbin, father of Geraint, father of Cadwy. Was this the Constantine denounced by Gildas? Was this the Geraint who brought his men east to fight for Arthur against the barbarian and lost his life? Was this the Cadwy who ruled with Arthur at Dindraithou?

King-lists and the many other Welsh literary sources, some of them known to Geoffrey of Monmouth and some still surviving, are not strictly

history. By the time they were written down they had long been part of an oral tradition, and their Dumnonian origins can only be dimly discerned within the Welsh tradition. By the 9th century Constantine, Geraint and Cadwy had become Welsh folk heroes. So is there nothing left of Dumnonia, nothing more solid than sagas and vague stories? Is there no trace of a hero in the Land of Summer, no chieftain fighting from his hilltop stronghold?

If there are historical doubts about the heroes of Dumnonia, there is no doubt about a stone monument that stands near Castle Dore in southern Cornwall. The stone bears in Latin the words 'Here lies Drustan, son of Cunomorus' which, being interpreted is 'Here lies Tristan, son of Cynfawr'; and Cynfawr (who might also be Mark) is in the king-list of Dumnonia, the father of Constantine of Cornwall. And real enough, on Cornwall's north coast, was the monastery on the headland once called by the Irish Rosnant and now Tintagel. This was a school for saints in the Irish tradition, a centre of both religion and culture. And there have been found those fragments of pottery which are in many ways the key to the Dark Ages in the West. Those fragments are the remains of vessels for wine, oil, and perhaps even fruit from the far Mediterranean, the wine and oil bespeaking ritual use as well as sophisticated palates. Heroes and saints there were indeed in Dumnonia.

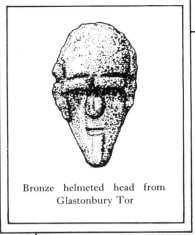

Bronze helmeted head from Glastonbury Tor

But Cornwall was, for many years to come, far from the front line in the struggle for survival. The real challenge was further east and there, in the Land of Summer, Somerset, sophistication and Christian culture seem to go hand in hand with organised and powerful regional government, and a military force able to stand up successfully to the Saxon threat.

Archaeologists have found the same Mediterranean pottery and high quality metalwork at Cadbury–Congresbury, on Glastonbury Tor, and on the great hillfort of South Cadbury. It is likely that other Iron-Age strongholds were re-occupied like them – notably Brent Knoll, Cadbury–Tickenham and Bat's Castle, the last one of a triumvirate of forts around the later site of Dunster Castle. Two more such hillforts, Maes Knoll and Stantonbury, are integral parts of the massive linear earthwork called Wansdyke which may well have marked the frontier of a British Kingdom against the Saxon enemy. And such a vast undertaking as Wansdyke involved considerable administrative organisation as well as military expertise. Another hillfort, at Cannington, is associated not only with some sort of permanent settlement, but with a cemetery, part pagan and part Christian, in which some graves were placed as if in deference to a single tomb, the tomb of a youth. Was he, like the nephew of Caratacus named on the stone of Winsford Hill, the offspring of a noble Christian house, a ruler, the

The Caratacus Stone, Winsford Hill, Somerset

Wansdyke snakes its way across Wiltshire and North Somerset, a frontier boundary of a British Kingdom

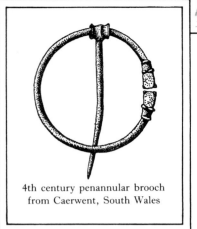

4th century penannular brooch
from Caerwent, South Wales

like of whom may have occupied the hilltop strongholds further east?

Perhaps supreme above all these leaders was he who ruled from the height of South Cadbury, he whose men crowded into the great timber hall on its summit. Cadbury is on a scale requiring vast resources, constructed for an army large by the standards of the time. It occupies a site of strategic importance, a base for action deep into Saxon-held territory, in a country within striking distance of the acceptable sites for the great victory of Mount Badon. Could Cadbury have been the springboard for the final triumph of the leader of battles?

GEOFFREY OF MONMOUTH AND THE GROWTH OF ROMANCE

The earliest written sources which refer to Arthur are themselves evidence of his continuing and increasing popularity. Nennius and the Annals of Wales were part of a growing body of writing, of which nothing else now survives, which by the late 8th century had made Arthur a Welsh hero. He became, naturally enough, a popular figure in Welsh literature; his name is found in the Welsh Triads, the titles which served as aides memoires which the bards used to remember the stories they told. Arthur's followers by the end of the 11th century people the stories known collectively as the Mabinogion, stories part mythological, part drawn from the French Romances.

Arthur appears, too, by the late 11th century in those peculiar literary devices known as Lives of Saints. Four survive, all probably written by Welshmen in praise of Welshmen, two from the monastery of Llan-

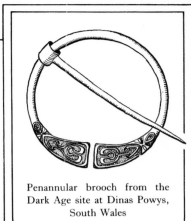

Penannular brooch from the Dark Age site at Dinas Powys, South Wales

carfan. They tell of the holy behaviour and remarkable deeds of Cadoc and Padarn, Carantoc and Gildas. The saint is, of course, the hero of each, but one character is common to all, Arthur. In all four Lives, he is something of a rogue and petty tyrant, converted to higher deeds and attitudes by the influence of the saint in question. St Cadoc found him as a quarrelsome ruler of easy morals, dicing on a hilltop with his companions Kay and Bedivere; St Padarn met him as a man who laid covetous eyes on the saint's tunic. St Carantoc encountered him as a ruler unable to subdue a dragon which was devastating his realm and as a petty thief who tried to convert the saint's portable altar into a domestic table. St Gildas found him as a ruler who could brook no opposition but a husband whose wife had been taken to Glastonbury by Melwas, King of the Summer Country.

It is clear that the stories of Arthur were known and established by the early 12th century throughout the Celtic world and beyond. Some canons of Laon, visiting the West Country in 1113, were shown Arthur's Chair and Arthur's Oven, probably on Dartmoor in Devon, and in Cornwall

Arthur defeats King Lucius

they nearly provoked a riot at Bodmin by refusing to believe a local who asserted that Arthur was not dead. William of Malmesbury, the 'official' historian of Glastonbury Abbey, knew an Arthur of history and an Arthur, as he devastatingly described him, of 'lying fables'; he accepted the evidence of Nennius as accurate, but he was less than happy with the literary embroidery which seemed by his time to have overtaken it.

And that literary embroidery reached its full flowering in the work of Geoffrey of Monmouth, who between about 1130 and 1136 or 1138 wrote his greatest work, the 'History of the Kings of Britain'. Geoffrey, Cornishman, Breton or Welshman, was a cleric rather by accident; by choice he was a scholar and a romantic, and the learning of Oxford for once found popular expression in his literary genius. But was it all embroidery? William of Newburgh, writing about 1190, declared: 'It is quite clear that everything this man wrote about Arthur and his successors . . . was made up, partly by himself, or for the sake of pleasing the Britons'. That is one opinion. Geoffrey himself claimed that he based part of his book 'The Prophesies of Merlin' on stories he had heard from his friend Alexander, Bishop of Lincoln; and he stated more than once that his source for his History was 'a certain very ancient book written in the British language' given to him by another friend, Walter, Archdeacon of Oxford.

Scholars argue a good deal about Geoffrey's sources, but there is general agreement that his work owes something to his own scholastic background (he knew the works of Gildas, Bede and Nennius); something to the traditions of the Celtic world to which he belonged; and very much to

Arthur defeats King Lucius

his own fertile imagination and literary bent. And it owes something, too, to his own desire for advancement. Geoffrey dedicated his History jointly to Robert, Earl of Gloucester, illegitimate son of Henry I, and to Waleran, Count of Mellent, son of Robert de Beaumont. They were powerful men.

Geoffrey's work was a literary success, a best seller in medieval terms; more than two hundred copies still survive. William of Newburgh was one of the few who considered it unreliable at the time. For almost six centuries afterwards it was accepted as actual history; but more than that, it created the Arthur most people still recognise: a larger-than-life figure possessed of a wonderful sword, protected by the magic of Merlin, ruling over a splendid court, conquering an empire beyond the sea. There was just enough history in Geoffrey's work to make it acceptable; and just enough reality to make it entirely plausible. Part of that reality was to give Arthur a topographical base. He was no longer vaguely Welsh, as the older sources had implied; he was South-Western and particularly Cornish. He was the successor to a kingdom sometimes almost independent, successor to a Cornish dynasty which

Camlann

had once ruled the whole of Britain. First and last, Arthur was Cornish; he was conceived at Tintagel, and his final battle, Camlann, was fought by the river Camel. Perhaps Geoffrey's own origins suggested Caerleon on Usk as the site of Arthur's court, but that was almost an aberration.

Tintagel was the significant choice. Its importance in the history of the Celtic South-West may well still have been remembered in the 12th century; and its owner in Geoffrey's day was none other than Reginald, another illegitimate son of Henry I, half-brother to Robert, Earl of Gloucester, who was married to a Cornish heiress and was soon to hold the Cornish earldom. And here about 1141 – could it have been inspired by Geoffrey himself? – Reginald built a castle.

Geoffrey has been credited with political flattery, implying that the Norman kings were the true successors of the great kings of the British past, and that the Norman nobility were the modern mirrors of their faithful followers. Was it, therefore, a continuation of that flattery to suggest that Arthur had been saved from a mortal death? Might he not still live on in the good deeds of the House which now ruled the land? But if so, where did he rest? Geoffrey was not at all specific; Arthur went to Avalon for the healing of his wounds. Of course Geoffrey knew of Glastonbury; it was not Glastonbury.

THE CLAIMS
OF THE
PAST

'. . . but it lies deep-meadow'd, happy, fair with orchard-lawns
and bowery hollows crown'd with summer sea. . .'
Tennyson: MORTE D' ARTHUR

Ring-knot from an Anglo-Saxon
stone cross at Glastonbury

A T the time of the
Norman conquest, the
Abbey at Glastonbury was
the richest monastery in the
land. As the Saxon kings had
established their rule down
the western peninsula the
abbey had been favoured so
that its lands stretched far
from its home in the central
lowlands of Somerset. King
Cynewulf had given land at Culmstock in Devon
about 670 and his successor, Ine, after his victory
over Geraint of Cornwall, had given an estate
further west, between the Tamar and the Lynher.
Another large estate, in the Torridge Valley of
Devon, was the next addition, about 729, and King
Egbert, in about 855, gave more land in north
Devon, the old minster at Braunton. By the time of
Domesday, however, these lands had slipped from
Glastonbury's grasp: Braunton had passed to the
Crown, Culmstock to the bishop of Exeter. The
abbey's sole estate in Devon by 1086 was Uplyme;
in Cornwall it possessed nothing at all.

GLASTONBURY UNDER PRESSURE

The abbey remained vulnerable to the jealous eyes
of its new neighbours, the men from across the
Channel who came with the Conqueror to supplant
the Anglo-Saxon landowners, once the abbey's good
friends and benefactors. Abbots Aethelweard and
Aethelnoth, if later historians are to be believed, had
led their house into decline even before the Con-

queror came, and it was unable to withstand the demands of the new land-lords. Aethelweard was remembered by the abbey's historians because he exhumed the remains of King Edgar and crammed them into a casket with the relics of St Vincent and St Apollinaris. Aethelnoth sold

Ring-knot from an Anglo-Saxon stone cross at Glastonbury

some of the abbey's treasures, including gold and silver ornaments which had been given by Bishop Brihtwold of Ramsbury fifty years earlier.

The reward of these profligates was fitting. Aethelweard went out of his mind and not long afterwards broke his neck as he left the abbey church. Aethelnoth, who gave the abbey estate at Batcombe to his own mother, much to the annoyance of the monks, withdrew to Normandy with the Conqueror and stayed there until 1077–8, when he was deposed and retired to Canterbury Cathedral Priory. For Glastonbury monks that fate might well have been accounted madness.

Beyond these ancient memories of decline from the high standards of St Dunstan's time, there is the factual record of Domesday Book. In 1066, while Edward the Confessor was still alive, Glastonbury's estate in Somerset alone amounted to over 473 hides of land. Twenty years later the abbey had lost over 67 hides, mostly to the Bishop of Coutances and the Count of Mortain, a loss greater than the whole estate of the neighbouring monastery of Muchelney. The historian William of Malmesbury, writing fifty years later, was still conscious of the grudge felt by

Anglo-Saxon ring-knot

the community at such treatment: the house, he declared, had been 'almost stripped' of its estates by the 'hostile assaults and violent oppression', first of the Danes and then of the Normans. That was a fair reflection of Glastonbury feeling; to Saxon monks, Norman and Dane were much the same.

The removal of Aethelnoth did not end the trouble. In his place the king and Archbishop Lanfranc appointed Thurstan, a monk of Caen. At first he proved himself a worthy successor to Dunstan, establishing not only the abbey's supremacy over the little Benedictine houses of Muchelney and Athelney but also its independence of the bishops of the diocese. At a meeting before Lanfranc, sometimes called the Council of the Parrett, Thurstan argued 'with great and steady eloquence' on behalf of his house, quoting royal charters from Centwine and Ine to prove Glastonbury's liberties against the counter claims of the Bishop of Wells. It was a great victory; Wells, so Thurstan's supporters claimed, 'departed without glory or honour'.

But it was for Thurstan a temporary victory. Soon afterwards he was involved in a dreadful incident which profoundly shocked contemporary opinion. Behaving more like an autocrat than a caring pastor, he first proposed a more strict rule of life than the monks had been used to, and then demanded the introduction of a foreign chant for the liturgy. Glastonbury monks were nothing if not traditiona-

Glastonbury Tor, from the South-West

The Somerset Levels in flood.
When the waters receded the
land appeared as the Summer
Country.

The Magna Tabula, the late-14th century Glastonbury guide book

St. Dunstan kneels at the feet of Christ: a page from 'St. Dunstan's Classbook'.

lists, and finally their opposition drove Thurstan to action. He called in a group of soldiers to compel obedience. Norman knights fought Saxon monks as the religious retreated into their church and barricaded themselves in the choir. Hiding behind benches and armed only with candlesticks, they were no match for arrows fired from a gallery above. Two, and perhaps three, monks were killed and a dozen or so wounded.

When the king heard of the incident, Thurstan was quickly taken back to Normandy; many of the monks, too, were moved away and kept under guard in other monasteries. Norman could not condone such opposition, even against brutal Norman. Glastonbury, almost in defiance, retained a relic of that dreadful time. During the fighting an arrow pierced a crucifix held by one of the monks and the figure of Christ was damaged below the knee. A miraculous stream of blood from the wound actually brought the attack to an end, and the soldier who fired the arrow immediately went mad. The crucifix was thereafter venerated, and still in the 14th century, according to John of Glastonbury, the trace of the wound was clearly visible.

Most of Glastonbury's losses to the new Norman landowners must have occurred when Thurstan was abbot (c 1077/8–1096–+). His successor, Abbot Herluin (1100–18), another Caen monk, was remembered as a great builder and benefactor, and some of the lost land was recovered. The next abbot,

The West Front, Wells Cathedral, consecrated 1239

Seffrid Pelochin (1120/1–
1125), a monk of Seez and
brother of Archbishop Ralph
of Canterbury, gave away at
least three manors to a rela-
tive, thus undoing much of
the work of his predecessor.
The task facing the next
abbot was considerable.

But the man was equal to
the task. A young monk from
Cluny, under thirty years of age, able and well
connected, Henry of Blois was a nephew of King
Henry I and brother of Henry's successor, King
Stephen. A man of undoubted financial and administrative flair and wide cultural sympathies, Henry was
appointed Abbot of Glastonbury in 1126, and three
years later also became Bishop of Winchester. He
held both offices until his death in 1171.

As soon as he arrived at Glastonbury, Henry set
about the restoration of the abbey's finances and the
creation of a splendid group of monastic buildings.
Recent excavations at the abbey exposed the massive
wall footings of Abbot Henry's 'palace', south-west
of the present Lady Chapel, and finely carved
stonework in the Abbey Museum is witness to the
high quality of the work in the cloister, chapter
house, refectory, dormitory and infirmary.

But in order to pay for this work the lost estates
had to be recovered, and even with Abbot Henry's
power and influence the task was not easy. The
Glastonbury chroniclers record that he won back the
manors of Mells, Uffculme, Camerton and Damer-
ham, several villages along the Polden ridge, the
island of Nyland, and pieces of land in Brent Marsh.

To make sure that these and
its other estates were protected for the future, the
abbot secured the approval
of three popes, who issued
formal charters confirming
ownership to the abbey:
Pope Innocent II in 1137,
Pope Lucius II in 1144, and
Pope Alexander III in 1168.
In the eyes of the Church

Wells Cathedral

Universal, Glastonbury's lands were secure.

Yet still there were threats to the abbey's independence. Bishop Giso of Wells had tried unsuccess-
fully in Abbot Thurstan's time to question
Glastonbury's privileges, and his successors would
doubtless try again. From another direction, the
monks had recently been challenged most rudely by
Osbern of Canterbury, who, in his Life of St
Dunstan, had dismissed Glastonbury's claim to be
an ancient foundation by suggesting that the saint
had been its first abbot! Eadmer, another Canterbury monk, had gone further by contradicting the
Somerset claim that Dunstan's bones had been
rescued from Canterbury to save them during
Viking raids.

THE ATTRACTIONS OF SANCTITY

So in face of these pressures the monks of Glastonbury, English to their fingertips, determined to
re-establish their traditions. They were themselves
in no doubt that the history of their house reached
back beyond the time of written record. Each

45

generation of monks had passed to the next the belief that the wattle church at the heart of their monastery was, of a truth, the earliest Christian shrine in the land. But there was nothing to prove it. Now this belief must be established beyond doubt. The saints of Glastonbury must be recorded, both to raise the spirits of a depressed community and to encourage recruitment. And, perhaps, more generally, to raise the level of public interest in a house which needed the support of patrons and pilgrims.

The monks turned, therefore, to two men to lead them out of their difficulties. They were men of very different talents, the one a hagiographer, that is a writer of saints' lives, the other an historian. Caradoc of Llancarfan, the hagiographer, who had already written a Life of Cyngar for the canons of Wells as well as Lives of St Cadoc and probably St Illtud for his own house of Llancarfan in Wales, compiled for Glastonbury a Life of St Gildas. Hagiographers by their very calling had a special purpose, namely to tell the story of their subject not in strictly historical terms, but rather with the object of creating a sense of devotion. Caradoc, like many of his kind, wove the few known facts about Gildas with tales from other sources about other saints and the products of his own imagination into a narrative quite unacceptable as history.

There is, for example, no doubt that Gildas was venerated at Glastonbury in the 11th century; and it is at least possible that he spent some time there. But

The chapel of St. Gildas near Carhaix – Plouguer, Britanny

it is quite clearly nonsense for Caradoc to claim that Gildas died at Glastonbury and was buried there before the altar. The traditions of the saint in Britanny are not only earlier but essentially more likely. The saint lies buried behind the high altar of the church of St Gildas-de-Rhuis in Morbihan. But, historically accurate or not, one element in Caradoc's Life of Gildas above all others is of the greatest interest. It appears to be the first time that Glastonbury and Arthur were linked together in writing.

This story may well have been told at Glastonbury before Caradoc gave it some respectability, and there is no doubt that he used it to advantage in his tale. He recounted how Gildas, coming to the abbey, found that Melwas, King of the Summer Country, was in conflict with King Arthur, having abducted Guinevere and held her at his stronghold. Gildas, as might be expected, mediated between the rivals, Guinevere was returned to her lord, and the two chieftains, promising always to follow Gildas's counsel, gave much territory to the Church.

A year or two before Caradoc came to Glastonbury the monks invited William of Malmesbury to perform a similar service. He came to the abbey about 1129, commissioned to write Lives of four Glastonbury saints, Patrick, Benignus, Indracht and Dunstan. Now William was an historian and something of an archaeologist rather than a hagiographer, and his Lives were not exactly what the monks expected. William found, for instance, no proof that Glaston-

William of Malmesbury's 'History of Glastonbury'

bury had ever recovered the bones of Dunstan from Canterbury, and he could not bring himself to pretend otherwise. He felt much the same about other tales the monks told him; but reluctant to reject anything so dear to his hosts, he carefully distinguished what he believed from what he did not.

So the results were a disappointment to the monks. In his preface to his more famous history of Glastonbury, William explained how he had submitted his Lives to the community 'so that if anything unreasonable had been said it could be properly corrected'. The monks deliberated at length and finally assessed the works favourably, agreeing that 'nothing in them gave offence to religious eyes or lacked graciousness'. But their judgement clearly lacked enthusiasm.

So William embarked on a much more important task, nothing but the complete story of Glastonbury from its foundation. He was, of course, faced again with the problem of fact versus legend; and again he made it clear that he believed some of the monks' traditions and not others. But he endeavoured to tell the story in all its richness from the very beginnings: the story of twelve disciples sent by the Apostle Philip, the story that the first Christian converts found at Glastonbury an ancient church 'prepared by God himself for human salvation . . . consecrated to himself and to Mary, the Holy Mother of God'. History or not, it was a bold claim.

FIRE

AND

VAPOUR OF SMOKE

'And truth is this to me, and that to thee; and truth or clothed or naked let it be' . . .' Tennyson: THE COMING OF ARTHUR, IDYLLS OF THE KING

HISTORY, however, was evidently not enough; that must be the inference. For within a very few years of the appearance of William of Malmesbury's 'De Anti-quitate Glastoniensis Ecclesia', his history of the Church of Glastonbury, other hands had added what William himself had not chosen to include, others claimed as history what William had barely recognised as respectable legend. And the reasons for such alterations were the same as those which had prompted the monks to invite him and Caradoc a generation earlier. Glastonbury was under pressure again.

In the 12th century there was a great extension of monasticism as the new Orders – the Cluniacs, the Cistercians and the Augustinians – established themselves. They were, consciously or unconsciously, the rivals of the long-established Benedictines, competing for both patronage and recruits. In Somerset, Glastonbury thus found itself with popular new monastic neighbours, some like Montacute or Witham offering a stricter and more simple Rule, others such as Taunton, Bruton and Keynsham a more relaxed discipline.

And the claims of the bishops of Bath became more pressing. The end of the rule of Abbot Henry of Blois in 1171 was followed first by a vacancy of well over a year, and then by the election of Robert, until then Prior of Winchester. John of Glastonbury, the abbey's historian writing in the 14th century, recorded that Robert was 'adorned with the

flower of all virtues and a special lover of the poor' but he had to admit that 'with rather less wisdom' the abbot had been outwitted by Bishop Reginald of Bath. Robert had been induced to become a member of the Chapter of Wells, and thus the bishop's subordinate. And, in establishing that his control of the central churches on the abbey's estate was secure, the abbot was obliged by the bishop to give up the church of South Brent as compensation to the Archdeacon of Wells. The first arrangement was soon repudiated, but the churches of Pilton and Ditcheat were permanently lost to Wells.

There was a nine-year vacancy following Abbot Robert's death in 1180, nine years of crisis and tragedy. For four years from 1189 Glastonbury was ruled by Henry de Sully, formerly prior of the Cluniac house at Bermondsey. Abbot Henry's great success was to obtain from Pope Celestine III in 1191 the right for himself and his successors to wear the mitre, ring and other trappings of a bishop. John of Glastonbury, writing in the 1340s but incorporating contemporary material, marvelled how a man like Abbot Henry could make such efforts on behalf of his house, but at the same time could contemplate leaving his flock to the teeth of a wolf. That wolf was Savaric FitzGeldewin, Bishop of Bath, who engineered the removal of Abbot Henry to the bishopric of Worcester and contrived his own appointment as Abbot of Glastonbury in 1193. For the next seven years or so the monks made concerted efforts to rid

The North Doorway of the Lady Chapel, Glastonbury Abbey

themselves of their unwanted abbot-bishop. There was violence, and for a short time the house lay under an interdict; the monks were divided among themselves and their spiritual state was at a very low ebb. Yet the community survived not only these troubles, but a still greater tragedy.

The Lady Chapel, Glastonbury

DISASTER AT GLASTONBURY

On the feast of St Urban (25 May) 1184 a devastating fire destroyed the monastic buildings at Glastonbury, leaving only a chamber and chapel built by Abbot Robert and the bell-tower built by Abbot Henry of Blois. Gold, silver, silks, books, ornaments and other furnishings were reduced to ashes and formless lumps of metal; the holy relics of the past were either charred or hopelessly confused. There was no abbot to take a lead; moans, tears and lamentations were to be heard on all sides.

Soon after the fire the king, who had hitherto been enjoying the income of the abbey in the absence of an abbot, appointed his chamberlain, Ralph FitzStephen, to take charge of the work of rebuilding. And so efficiently did Ralph carry out his task that, apparently within a year or two, the Lady Chapel, built on the site of the old church, was finished in the 'most attractive workmanship' which can still be enjoyed today. Ralph also began the restoration of the conventual buildings – presum-

ably some of the walls had been left standing – and, using the stone from Abbot Henry's 'palace' and the precinct wall, laid out the massive foundations of a new abbey church.

But there was more to recovery than renewing buildings. The abbey's precious relics had to be put in order and more widely publicised if Glastonbury was to keep pace with the rival attractions of Abingdon and Ely, Westminster and especially Canterbury. The first stage was to exhume the bodies of St Patrick, St Indracht and St Gildas from near the altar in the Old Church and place them in suitable shrines. The second stage was the remarkably fortunate discovery of an ironbound wooden chest containing the bones of St Dunstan, complete with his episcopal ring on one finger. The painted initials S and D at each end of the chest left no-one in any doubt of their authenticity, whatever Canterbury might claim. A special gold and silver shrine was made to contain the bones in proper state, a shrine which was later to be shared with the shoulder and forearm of St Oswald.

Building work, of course, continued and 'a large part' of the abbey church was finished when Henry II died. Work then seems to have come to a halt until the appointment of Henry de Sully as abbot; and he, it seems, had little enthusiasm for building. The monks, therefore, had to take matters into their own hands, carrying relics and indulgences around the country to raise funds. Their success, on their

own admission, was only moderate. Something more effective had to be done. It is not certain where the idea of King Arthur at Glastonbury first came from. There may well have been folk tales relating to the place in Celtic mythology, for the topography of the area and its often mysterious weather pattern must have given rise in a more impressionable age to many flights of fancy.

THE DISCOVERY OF ARTHUR

Caradoc of Llanfarcan is the first, apparently, to claim an historical connexion as early as the 1130s when he brought Arthur to the place in search of Guinevere. But William of Malmesbury in his comprehensive history did not mention Arthur, and for sixty years the monks looked to other methods to support their cause. Yet the relics of St Gildas, St David, St Patrick and the rest proved neither convincing nor popular. The discovery of the relics of King Arthur was a masterstroke.

Apparently, no doubts were raised about the discovery until the 20th century but there is no surviving eye-witness account of such an important event, and the near-contemporary sources do not agree on many points. Therein, if for no other reason, lies the suspicion.

Evidently the earliest version of the story comes from Wales, from a chronicler at the abbey of Margam who may well have had before him Glaston-

Glastonbury Abbey:
the crossing, looking east

bury's official report in the form of a circulated newsletter. The Margam chronicler describes how one of the monks had 'begged and prayed' to be allowed to be buried in the ancient cemetery, at a spot between the two ancient cross shafts which bore a series of names in almost indecipherable writing. So when the monk died, about 1191, a grave was dug in the place he had chosen. First the diggers came upon a coffin containing the bones of a woman, with the hair still intact. Beneath it they found a second coffin containing the bones of a man; and below that they found a third, on which a leaden cross was fixed which was inscribed with the words in Latin 'Here lies the famous King Arthur buried in the isle of Avalon'. Inside this third coffin were the bones of a large man. The first tomb, declared the chronicler, was that of 'Guinevere, wife of the same Arthur; the second, that of Mordred, his nephew; the third that of the aforesaid prince'.

The second record of the discovery is by another Welshman (why were the Welsh so keen to give Somerset the credit?), the popular writer and publicist Gerald of Wales – a sensible choice if the monks wished to broadcast their success. Gerald visited Glastonbury within a fairly short time of the discovery and described both the leaden cross, which he actually handled, and a thigh bone and a skull, both of remarkable size, which Abbot Henry de Sully showed him. But by the time of his visit the story had significantly changed.

Gerald prefaced his description with a swipe at 'popular stories' about Arthur which had the 'fantastic' ending that the king was 'carried away to a remote place and was not subject to death'. Of course there was a body. Gerald declared that records of the abbey contained 'signs' of the body's

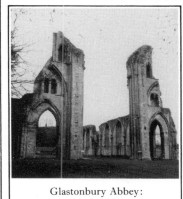
Glastonbury Abbey:
the crossing, looking east

presence in Glastonbury, and the letters inscribed on the cross shafts in the cemetery, although 'almost obliterated by age' suggested the same. Further, 'visions and revelations' had been seen by 'holy men and clerks'; and, finally, King Henry II himself had been told by a Welsh bard (the Welsh again) that Arthur's body would be found sixteen feet down in the earth in a hollow oak, all rather different from the accidental discovery recorded by the Margam chronicler.

What was found had changed, too. The actual discovery was accompanied by 'wonderful and miraculous signs', perhaps necessary to encourage the diggers. Deep down, so Gerald declared, there was first a stone, under which the leaden cross was fixed. And then the coffin, only one, but divided; two thirds at the head contained the bones of a man, one third at the foot the bones of a woman, together with a tress of golden hair which turned to dust when touched by an eager monk. There was no third coffin, no third body. And the words on the cross were not as the Margam chronicler reported: 'Here lies buried the famous King Arthur with Guinevere his fortunate wife in the isle of Avalon'.

A third chronicler, Ralph of Coggeshall, writing about 1193, mentioned the discovery briefly. For him, as for the Margam chronicler, it was accidental, the result of the wish of the dying monk. And the words on the leaden cross made no mention of Guinevere. The two later Glastonbury chroniclers, Adam of Domerham and John of Glastonbury, added their own details, declaring that there were two tombs, and that during the excavations curtains had been placed around the site.

Doubts have reasonably been raised, even on the evidence of these sources. Two facts are not open to question. One is that a hole was dug between the two cross shafts in the monks' cemetery; traces of that excavation were clearly seen during the excavations in the 1960s. The other is that the cross was real. John Leland in Henry VIII's time held it in his hands. It measured, he wrote, nearly a foot in length, and the words it bore were those reported by the Margam chronicler. The antiquary William Camden published a drawing of it in 1607, the only clue to its characters, and it has been lost to sight since the 18th century. It cannot thus be submitted to scientific study which might prove it a 12th century forgery or a genuine product of the 6th century. But genuine or not does not now matter. The cross 'proved' Glastonbury to be Avalon and the bones to be Arthur's. That was enough.

But just in case the bones were not entirely convincing, the Margam chronicler, presumably

William Camden's drawing of the Arthur Cross (1607)

briefed by the Glastonbury monks, indulged in a little etymology. Glastonbury must be the Isle of Avalon for it used to be an island surrounded by marshes, and 'aval' in the British language meant apple. Gerald of Wales went further into the matter: one of the old names for Glastonbury was Inis Avallon, the applebearing island; another name was Inis Gutrin (otherwise Yniswithrin), the Isle of Glass, hence the Saxon name Glastingeburi, 'for in their tongue glas means glass and a camp or town is called buri'. Modern place-name experts would not accept such a specious explanation.

THE TOMB OF THE KING

Once found, the bones of Arthur and Guinevere were translated into the (presumably still unfinished) abbey church and placed in a tomb in the centre of the choir, at the heart of the liturgical life of the community. Not much less than a century later the tomb was opened, the high point in an event stage-managed to perfection by the able Abbot John of Taunton.

John of Glastonbury tells in detail how in 1278 the young Edward I and Queen Eleanor, accompanied by Archbishop Kilwardby of Canterbury, came to spend Easter at the abbey. Three times during those few days the abbot pointedly maintained the privileges of his house in the Liberty

The site of King Arthur's Tomb, Glastonbury Abbey

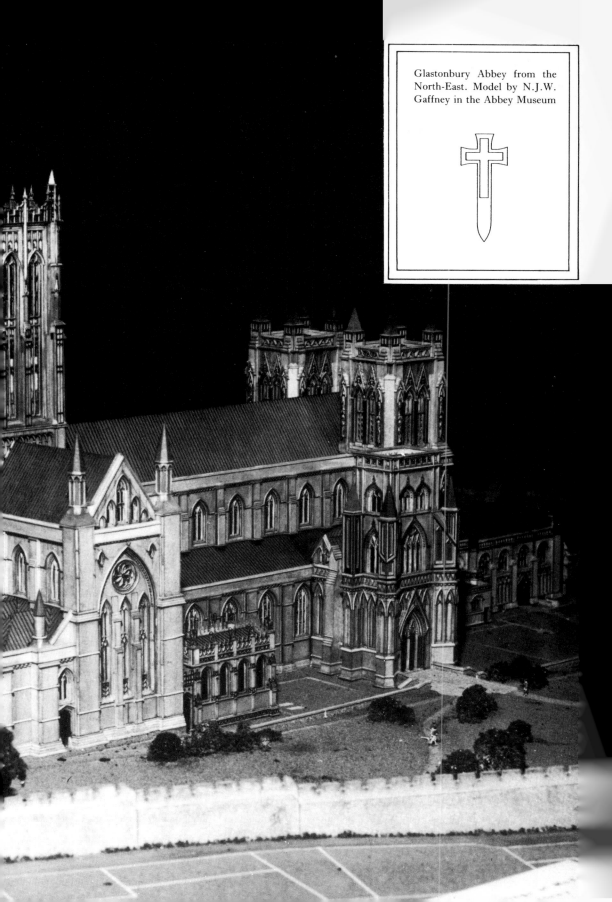

Glastonbury Abbey from the
North-East. Model by N.J.W.
Gaffney in the Abbey Museum

of the Twelve Hides, first by refusing the Earl Marshal's claims to take lodgings for the royal retinue; second by taking an offender against the king into his own custody; and third by successfully resisting the suggestion that the king's judges should hold the Assizes within the Liberty. They were therefore held outside, at Street. And – John of Glastonbury could not resist recording – the canons of Wells were put in their place by the Archbishop when they claimed a major role in the blessing of the Holy Chrism. They had no such claim, Kilwardby decided, since their bishop was far away and since the ceremony took place in the abbey church.

So the king paid his own expenses until the last day of his stay and then, on Easter Tuesday, King Arthur's tomb was ceremonially opened. Within were found two separate bones of the king of 'wonderful' size and the delicate and beautiful bones of the queen. Next day the living king and queen wrapped most of the bones in precious palls, marking them with their seals, keeping out only the heads and knee-joints 'for the people's devotion'. The tomb was then closed again, leaving on the inside an inscription recording the event which had been witnessed by the whole of the English Court including the Earl of Lincoln and the Count of Savoy. Abbot John had proved himself a great defender of Glastonbury's liberties and a great promoter of Glastonbury's hero.

Exactly two hundred years later William Wor-

The church of The Holy Trinity, Street

cestre visited Glastonbury. Curiously, he recorded the hollow between the two stone crosses where the bones had been found, but his surviving notes make no mention at all of the tomb. But it was still there: Hugh Forester, the abbey almoner in 1446–7, paid the sacrist the sum of 2 shillings for 'scouring the tomb of Arthur', and his successors paid similar sums until the Dissolution. The last visitor to record the tomb in position was John Leland. In the choir, he noted, were three tombs: King Edward the Elder on the north, King Edmund Ironside on the south, and in the centre 'Arcturus'. 'Here lies Arthur, the flower of kings, the glory of the kingdom', he quoted from the inscription on one side of the tomb, 'whom custom and learning commend by constant praise'. And below, at the foot: 'here lies buried the fortunate wife of Arthur whose virtues merit the promise of heaven'.

Leland's brief notes suggest that at the head of the tomb was carved a crucifix with two lions and some words recording the part Abbot Henry de Sully had played in bringing the bones from the abbey churchyard. At the foot were a figure of Arthur and two more lions. And on the top of the tomb was a cross, presumably the leaden cross which had been found in the grave in the churchyard. Archaeologists examining what they presumed to be the site of the tomb in 1931 found a substantial ashlar base, quite empty.

THE CULT
OF
ST JOSEPH

'For what are men better than sheep or goats that nourish a
blind life within the brain, if, knowing God, they lift not hands
of prayer.' Tennyson: MORTE D'ARTHUR

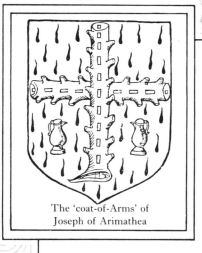
The 'coat-of-Arms' of
Joseph of Arimathea

ABOUT the middle of the
13th century, when
King Arthur had been firmly
established at Glastonbury,
the History written first by
William of Malmesbury was
given a new and final addition. This was the story of
how Joseph of Arimathea,
placed at the head of twelve
disciples by the Apostle
Philip, was sent over to Britain. Here, at the bidding
of the Archangel Gabriel, he built the first church at
Glastonbury. A note in the margin beside this
addition added that Joseph had come with his son
Josephes and that he had died at Glastonbury.
Readers were referred to a book of 'the deeds of the
famous King Arthur', to 'the Quest of Lancelot de
Lac' and to 'the Quest of the vessel which there they
call the Holy Grail'.

A century later John of Glastonbury told a much
more detailed story, beginning with a statement
that, according to the 'Book of Melkin', Joseph was
buried in a marble tomb at Glastonbury 'on a two
forked line next the south corner of an oratory
fashioned of wattles', and that in his tomb were
placed two silver cruets, filled with the blood and
sweat of Our Lord. Then, using a popular book
called the 'Gospel of Nicodemus', John recounted
some of the earlier activities of Joseph: how,
arrested for burying the body of Jesus, he had been
miraculously rescued from his prison cell by angels;
how he and his son became disciples of the Apostle
Philip; how he witnessed the Assumption of the
Virgin. And then how, at Philip's request, he had

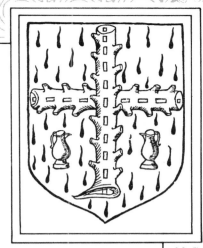

come to Britain and to Glastonbury.

And now John of Glastonbury added a marvellous story from another source, from a book called 'The Holy Grail'. It was a story which told that 600 and more men and women, following Joseph and Josephes, took vows of chastity until they should have come to a land appointed for them. All but 150 broke their vows, but a faithful remnant crossed the sea on the shirt of Josephes on the night of Our Lord's resurrection. When the rest repented they were collected by a ship made by King Solomon and preserved for just that purpose. And so Joseph and Josephes and their disciples finally reached Yniswithrin, the Glassy Isle.

Now at this point John of Glastonbury has to be followed very carefully. He says that the death of Joseph of Arimathea is recorded in the 'book of the deeds of the glorious King Arthur', and in that part of the book which describes a search by the companions of the Round Table for a famous knight called Lancelot de Lac. In the same part of the book, so John records, there is mention of a mysterious fountain which changed taste and colour (so a hermit told Gawain), and a story of the White Knight who explained to Galahad at the beginning of the quest for the Holy Grail the mystery of his miraculous shield.

Joseph of Arimathea was thus firmly established at Glastonbury, but to make quite sure of his 'historical' credibility he was made the ancestor of

71

King Arthur himself. So runs the geneaology: Helains, Joseph's nephew, begat Josue, and Josue Aminadab, and from Aminadab in five generations to Ygerna 'of whom King Uther Pendragon begat the noble and famous King Arthur'. And, to make doubly sure, Peter, Joseph's cousin and king of Organia, begat Erlan and so in four generations to Loth, who married Arthur's sister and was the father of Gawain.

Joseph was thus both founder of Glastonbury and ancestor of her most famous son. But no connexion was made between the abbey and the Holy Grail. The Grail itself was a Christian form of the magic healing cup of Celtic legend. It had become the sacred dish of the Last Supper, begged by Joseph from Pilate to catch the drops of Our Lord's blood from the Cross; and hence for some it was the Cup of the Last Supper. The High Romances tell how Joseph brought the Grail with him to Britain; the Grail sought by King Arthur and his knights on their Quest. In the Romances Avalon is occasionally mentioned but – and this is important – Glastonbury never claimed to have anything to do with the Grail. Instead it substituted the tradition of the cruets. That claim gave Glastonbury a direct place not only in the first Christian mission to Britain, but also with the events of the Crucifixion itself.

That was a claim which not even Canterbury could answer. It gave the Abbot of Glastonbury precedence among his brethren in England; and at international

The Holy Thorn and St. Patrick's Chapel, Glastonbury

The east end of the Lady Chapel Undercroft, Glastonbury, once the shrine of St. Joseph of Arimathea

St. Joseph of Arimathea, Langport church

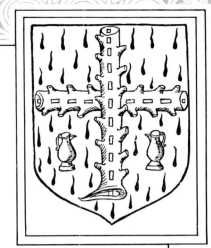

national Councils in the 15th century, when the French claimed seniority on the strength of St Mary Magdalene, Martha and Lazarus, whom they said had preached in Provence, and the Spanish because of their conversion by St James. Glastonbury's tradition of St Joseph gave the English the victory.

At home in Glastonbury by the end of the 14th century there was more physical evidence of the cult of St Joseph. In 1382 Abbot John Chinnock rebuilt a chapel in the cemetery, and in it placed the images of Joseph, Nicodemus and of Our Lord being taken down from the Cross. By about 1500 there was more to be seen. A poem called 'the Lyfe of Joseph of Armathia' written about 1502 and printed (so popular had it become) in 1520, recorded how miraculous cures were being performed in a crypt chapel of St Joseph, apparently under the eastern end of the Lady Chapel, its position still marked by the words JESUS, MARIA on the wall outside. This chapel was, it seems, extended under the whole Lady Chapel as the cult grew in popularity. Thus was unwittingly destroyed the best archaeological evidence of Glastonbury's origins!

William Good, who died an exiled Jesuit in Naples in 1586, remembered serving as an altar boy in St Joseph's chapel about 1535 when he was eight years old. He remembered, too, seeing the chapel destroyed when the abbey was dissolved. By that time, thanks to the devotion of Abbot Richard Bere (abbot 1493–1524) who may well have created the

crypt chapel, St Joseph's 'arms' could be seen in several places outside Glastonbury. A green cross raguly with the two cruets and a background of blood drops, can still be seen in painted glass in the chancel of St John's, Glastonbury. A cross and the cruets record Abbot Bere's work inside and outside St Benignus's church, Glastonbury, and at the rear of his house at Sharpham. The same coat of arms is carved on a pew at North Cadbury and the saint himself is pictured in glass in Langport church and in the screen at Plymtree (Devon).

The image of St Joseph and the chapel in which it stood were destroyed with the rest of the abbey in 1539 but the story of the Grail and the Quest was still remembered. In the 18th century the special properties of the water springing from the sandy beds of Middle Lias limestone in the valley below Tor Hill were recognised. A spa was established in Magdalen Street and for a time people flocked to Glastonbury again. Early in the 20th century those same waters took on a new phase in their persistent story.

Malory told at the end of his Le Mort D'Arthur how Lancelot had retired to a valley between the hills near Glastonbury, the valley described but not named in the great Romances of the Grail. Might this not, indeed, be the place where lies the Chalice of the Last Supper? Are not the stones in the well shaft at Chalice Well still stained red?

That well shaft has been studied by archaeo-

The Chalice Well

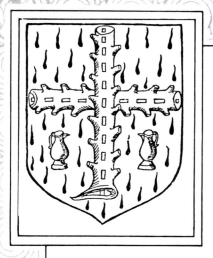

logists, who are generally agreed that its squared lias blocks are similar to pieces used in the abbey in the 12th century. It is therefore possible that the shaft was designed to improve the abbey's water supply after the fire of 1184, and that it was built about 1220. Whether the shaft was a free standing building at that time, forming a well-house, or was more as it stands today has yet to be established.

The well has borne the name Chalcwelle or a variant since at least 1210; and Chilkwell Street, so called at least since 1265, is named after it. The name presumably comes from the limestone source of the water. But the name Chalice Well is so close; and the mystery of the water has had a profound effect on many. For much of the 20th century the well has formed the focal point of a shrine, and its modern lid symbolises the Bleeding Lance and the interlocking Visible and Invisible worlds. So does the magic of the Glastonbury Legend span the centuries.

PILGRIMS
TO
AVALON

'What record, or what relic of my lord should be to after time but empty breath and rumours of a doubt?' Tennyson: MORTE D'ARTHUR

THERE is no doubt that pilgrims came in their thousands to Glastonbury before the Reformation. Ever since the 2nd century saints had been publicly venerated; church dedications from the 7th century and liturgical calendars from the 8th show how cults were established in England, their growth encouraged from the late 7th century by writers of saints' Lives such as the Venerable Bede, who aimed to foster the devotion of the people by stories of miraculous deeds. By the early 11th century a list of about fifty English shrines was compiled, but Glastonbury did not then appear. Another such list survives from the 14th century, and by that time Glastonbury had a prominent place.

William of Malmesbury and Caradoc of Llancarfan in different ways established Glastonbury as a shrine, and the claims of the monks in defence of their abbey had made a collection of relics and records sometimes of doubtful veracity. Royal patronage from Saxon times had brought it an estate which made it the largest landowner in Somerset, arguably the richest monastic house in Britain. Glastonbury's liberties had been established, and the bishops of Bath and Wells were effectively excluded from the Twelve Hides, the heart of the abbey's lands. But, above all, its magnificent buildings occupied the holiest site in the land, holy because it held the bodies of saints whose witness took the history of Christianity back to its very

beginnings in Britain and beyond.

According to the fantastic charter of St Patrick, Glastonbury offered to her pilgrims greater privileges of indulgence; ten or even thirty years exemption from purgatory gained by St Phagan and St Deruvian from Pope Eleutherius, twelve years through St Patrick from Pope Celestine, and thirty more, again through Phagan and Deruvian, for those who would actually attempt to climb the Tor.

In 1247 a scribe working among the muniments made a list of Days of Indulgence offered by charters which had been lost but which had been accepted and confirmed by Pope Innocent III between 1198 and 1216. The earliest of the 17 charters, quite probably a forgery, was a grant of 100 days indulgence by St Dunstan. Archbishop Lanfranc gave 30 days, Bishop Reginald 100 (probably at the dedication of the new Lady Chapel after the fire), Bishop Savaric 100 days, Bishop Jocelin 30 days. Forgeries or not, the attraction of a pilgrimage to Glastonbury was apparent.

And when pilgrims came, there was plenty to see: 'the stone pavement, the sides of the altar, and the altar itself are so loaded, above and below, with relics packed together that there is no path through the church, cemetery, or cemetery chapel which is free from the ashes of the blessed', wrote John of Glastonbury. The abbey was, par excellence, the resting place of saints. Here lay St Patrick, St

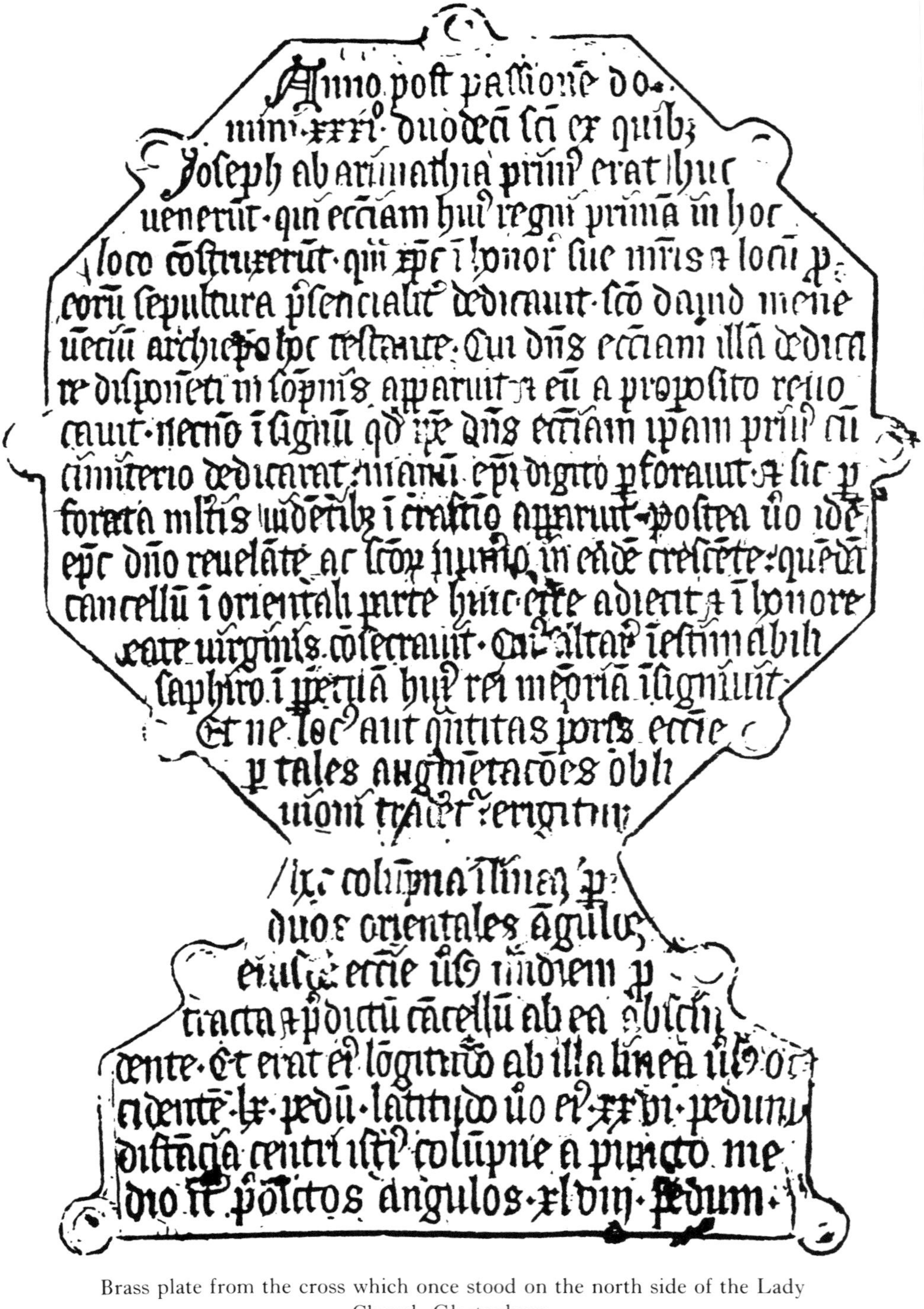

Anno post passione do-
mini xxxi duodecim sci ex quibz
Joseph ab arimathia prim' erat huc
uenerut qui ecciam hui' regni prima in hoc
loco construxerut qui xps i honor' sue mris et loci p'
coru sepultura psencialit dedicauit sco dauid mene
uectu archiepo hoc testante Cui dns ecciam illa dedica
re disponeti in sopnis apparuit et eu a proposito reuo
cauit memo i signu qd ipe dns ecciam ipam priu' cu
cimiterio dedicarat manu epi digito pforauit et sic p
forata mltis uidetibz i crastio apparuit postea uo ide
epc dno reuelate ac scor numio in eade crescete quedam
cancellu i orientali parte huic ecce adiecit et i honore
eate uirginis colecrauit Cui altar iestimabili
saphiro i perpetua hui' rei memoria isigniuit
Et ne loc' aut quntitas ipius' ecce
p tales augmetacoes obli
uioni tradet' erigitur

/ix columpna illinea p'
duos orientales angulos
eiusq; ecce us9 indiem p'
tracta et pdictu cancellu ab ea obliquan
cente et erat ei logitudo ab illa linea us9 oc
cidente lx pedu latitudo uo ei xxui pedum
distancia centru isti' columpne a pucto me
dio ir postctos angulos xlui pedum

Dunstan, St Gildas and others inextricably bound up with Glastonbury's past. Here, too, were the bodies of saints collected by Saxon kings and nobles and given to the abbey from Ine's time onwards, including Aidan, Paulinus, the Venerable Bede, Benedict Biscop, and the Abbess Hilda of Whitby, all the flowers of northern Christianity. Here were St David (brought by a noble matron) and St Illtud, flowers of Wales. And, lest these possessions might seem a little parochial and narrowly nationalistic, there were representatives of the Church Universal: the disciples of the Apostle Philip, including St Joseph of Arimathea; St Urban, pope and martyr; St Apollinaris, disciple of the Apostle Peter; St Vincent, protomartyr of Spain. And, of course, from a different kind of universality, King Arthur and Queen Guinevere.

Relics could be, as it were, circumstantial as well as personal. There were from Old Testament times parts of the rods of Moses and Aaron, some manna from the wilderness, and a piece of the tomb of Isaiah. And from the New Testament, fragments of the swaddling clothes and the manger from Bethlehem, part of a jug from Cana whose contents had been changed from water to wine, many fragments of Our Lord's clothing and relics of his Passion, including part of the Crown of Thorns and some of the hole which the Cross made on Calvary. There were personal relics of the Virgin, of the Apostles, Martyrs, Confessors and Holy Virgins; the list was

almost endless. So Glastonbury was holy ground, a place chosen by kings and princes: 'the chief personages of the country . . . would rather await the day of resurrection in the monastery of Glastonbury . . . than anywhere else'. So holy, indeed, was the church and cemetery that sinners could not rest there for fear of apparitions; animals and hunting birds were known to drop dead there, and those facing trial by ordeal praying there leapt for joy at their salvation. So well known was Glastonbury abroad, John of Glastonbury claimed in the 14th century, that foreigners sent for samples of its holy earth against the time of their own burials, and could not understand why English pilgrims travelled across the sea to foreign shrines when they had such a holy place at home. Even the Sultan (of which land is not stated) knew something of the place and demanded of an imprisoned pilgrim to the Holy Land a glove filled with the soil of the cemetery where Joseph of Arimathea was buried. 'Those who live there', declared the Sultan, do not know 'what virtue there is in that earth'. The Sacristan of Glastonbury publicised the story 'so that, as the fame of the spot's sanctity grew, those who dwelt there might become holier, while those who lived elsewhere might be more inclined to honour the place in the future'.

Is there just a suspicion of special pleading in these marvellous stories, and is it possible that the abbey was still not achieving its maximum visitor

potential? There had clearly been visitors there, but perhaps not enough. Henry III in 1243 gave the abbey a charter to extend the fair on the Tor from two to five days, and surely some of the buyers and sellers would spend some time in the holy places? The heads and knee joints of Arthur and Guinevere were deliberately kept out of the great tomb in the choir in 1278 for public display. People would surely be interested to see the crystal cross given by the Virgin to Arthur at the Mass at Beckery, which was carried every year in procession on Wednesdays and Fridays in Lent. In the late 1340s even 'the common people' knew the crucifix from which blood had flowed when it was damaged during the attack on the monks in Abbot Thurstan's time.

But if there is some doubt about the success of Glastonbury's publicity in the 14th century, it is clear that by the beginning of the 16th a change had come about. In the 1380s or a little later a visitors' guide was produced. It was made from folding wooden boards and was probably fixed to a pillar in the abbey church. It summarised, remarkably briefly, the story of the monastery as told by John of Glastonbury, mentioning at the end the rebuilding of the cemetery chapel by Abbot Chinnock in 1382. This guide would have formed the starting point of a pilgrim tour, first of the abbey church and its precinct and then of various sites in and around the town where the story of Arthur and Joseph might be brought more fully alive.

Inscription on South Wall of Lady Chapel, Glastonbury

In the choir of the abbey church, to begin with, was the tomb of Arthur and Guinevere, on which lay the leaden cross by which their bones had been recognised, and through which Glastonbury had been identified as Avalon. Next, beneath the Lady Chapel at the western end of the great church, was the crypt chapel of St Joseph, small at first but extended by Abbot Bere about 1500 to cope with the sick who flocked there – from Wells, Doulting, Banwell, Ilchester, Yeovil, Milborne Port, Compton and Pilton for certain, and surely from many other places beyond Somerset as well.

Outside, to the north of the Lady Chapel, a stone cross marked the eastern end of an old chapel which had stood there before the fire. The cross bore a metal plate telling the story of the coming of St Joseph of Arimathea, the dedication of the first church, and the buildings and gifts of St David. On the south side of the Lady Chapel was the abbey's ancient cemetery. The visitor coming through the carved and painted south doorway might first look at the JESUS MARIA inscription on the wall, marking the former entrance to the little crypt chapel of St Joseph. And then, looking across the hallowed plot, the pilgrim could see, as William Worcestre saw in the 1480s, the two ancient cross shafts bearing the names of the ancient abbots, and the hollow between them whence the bones of Arthur and Guinevere had been taken. And 'harde by', as the visitor was told about 1500, grew a new marvel: a walnut tree, protected by a wall, which did not come into leaf each year until St Barnabas's day, 11 June.

Inscription on South Wall of Lady Chapel, Glastonbury

From the precinct of the abbey church the pilgrim could go out by the main entrance into High Street. Passing to the top of the town and then along Chilkwell Street, the road skirted the barton of Glastonbury manor, including the great barn, and then the well at the foot of Tor Hill. After that came a sharp climb through the rabbit warren to St Michael's chapel on the summit.

From there the next leg of the circuit could be seen; back past the barton again and then westwards, up the gentler slope of Wearyall Hill, above the abbot's park. There, so the story went, was once a nunnery where Arthur often stayed. And there, for all to see, according to the 16th century author grew 'thre hawthornes also . . . (which) do burge and bare grene leaves at Christmas as freshe as other in May'.

From Wearyall the route led down to the edge of the moors, to Beckery, once the home of St Bridget. Here stood the chapel, or rather its successor, where Arthur had witnessed the Mass of the Virgin and where he was given the crystal cross by the Virgin herself. And after that, perhaps, across the Brue by the Pons Perilous, to yet another part of the Arthur story. When Abbot John of Taunton had stood up for the liberties of his house during the royal visit in 1278 and packed the king's justices out of the Twelve Hides into Street, some of the cases

The George and Pilgrims Inn, Glastonbury

were heard before the king himself. And they were heard in the chapel of St Gildas. Could this be the place where Gildas had retired from the community across the river, as Caradoc of Llancarfan had written? Well, perhaps not exactly; for the church Gildas built was dedicated to the Holy

The ancient Market Cross, Glastonbury

Trinity. But still in 1545 there was a chapel of St Gildas in Street; and still, near the river and curiously isolated from the modern town, stands the parish church of the Holy Trinity.

Back into Glastonbury, passing the newly built meat market and stalls and Abbot Bere's Tribunal, might not the weary pilgrim return to his lodgings? The better-off would surely choose the George Inn, completely rebuilt by Abbot John Selwood about 1473 when the new tenants, David and Edith Adam, paid the large sum of £7 6s 8d for a lease of the 'great hospice'. The annual rent was only 12d, the value of the site and not the business, but somehow by 1500 John Stowell, then the host, was in arrears for that small sum and more besides.

So Glastonbury offered many attractions to its visitors, but what did the abbey receive in return? Its financial records have not survived well, but the accounts of two Receivers mention alms. Brother Alexander Colyns accounted for gifts amounting to £4 5s made in the abbey church in 1503–4, and Brother Thomas Dunstan, Receiver in 1525–6, recorded the sum of £10 9s 9d received as alms in the church and a further £17 4s 10d passed on to him by

The Tribunal, Glastonbury

Brother John Milton for alms received elsewhere. Such sums were insignificant in the abbey's great financial machine, but it was not simply a matter of money. The prayers of the faithful, too, still counted for something at Glastonbury in the decades before the Dissolution.

Those years witnessed a remarkable revival in the number of men entering the community, a revival probably inspired by Abbot Richard Bere (1493–1525). Bere himself had come into the community in the 1470s. He was a man of wide sympathies: 'good, honest, virtuous, wise and discrete', said a contemporary, a man fully aware of his additions to their already magnificent church: the chapel of Our Lady of Loretto, whose cult he had encountered in 1504 when he headed an embassy to Pope Pius III in Rome; the chapel of the Holy Sepulchre, where he was later to be buried; and the enlarged crypt of St Joseph under the Lady Chapel. This last addition, together with the work on the magnificent Edgar chapel which he began, showed Bere's awareness of how Glastonbury's glorious past could be exploited.

It was in this same spirit that the old argument with Canterbury over the remains of St Dunstan was revived in 1508. Abbot Bere made a new shrine and placed there the precious relics of his great predecessor. When the monks of Christ Church heard of it they protested to Archbishop Warham and opened their own shrine to make sure the bones were intact. Inside the inner leaden coffin they discovered a

The Bishop's Throne, Glastonbury Pilgrimage

Glastonbury Tor from the top
of Wearyall Hill

tablet with the inscription 'Here lies St Dunstan, archbishop'. Glastonbury monks knew all about inscriptions in coffins and were quite unmoved. Abbot Bere excused himself on the grounds of ill health from visiting Canterbury to inspect the evidence in person and the matter was dropped.

Bere's contribution to revival was apparent in one further way. From 1505 onwards recruits to the community took new names in religion, names of the holy men who had long been revered in the abbey. John Phagan and John Deruvian, Martin Indracht and John Patrick covered the whole span of Glastonbury's history. They adopted the names of Saxon kings whose contributions to Glastonbury's greatness were much less open to doubt. And among them were John and William Joseph, Robert and John Armathy or Abaramathia, Robert Gylde, Robert Yder and John Arthur. Glastonbury in the years before the Dissolution was as aware of its glorious past as it had ever been.

THE TOR

The Tor is a landmark for miles, a constant reminder in medieval times of the far-seeing eye of the Abbot of Glastonbury. And it stands out in the story of King Arthur and Glastonbury for here, according to Caradoc of Llancarfan, was the stronghold of Melwas, King of the Summer Country.

To this lair Melwas brought Guinevere, whom he had abducted from her lawful spouse; and King Arthur came here with an army from Devon and Cornwall to retrieve her. The Abbot of Glastonbury and Gildas brought peace between the warring parties, Guinevere was restored, and the grateful king gave much land to the Church.

Some unknown writer produced a different story, amazing in its boldness and ingenuity. This story is the concoction known as the 'Charter of St Patrick'. It was probably not dreamed up until the early years of the 13th century, but it purported to be written by the saint himself in the 5th. It tells how Patrick, having finished his work in Ireland, came to Glastonbury. Here he found twelve brethren living as hermits (one called Wellias, just to show that Wells was subordinate to Glastonbury even then). These twelve, 'imbued with the rudiments' of the Catholic faith and of 'pious conversation', were the successors of two holy men, saints Phagan and Deruvian. Patrick was soon elected abbot of the community, and was then inducted into the secrets of their foundation, contained in the writings of the two saints. These writings declared that the Old Church had actually been built in honour of the Virgin by disciples of saints Philip and James on orders from the Archangel Gabriel, and that 'the Lord from Heaven' had dedicated the church himself.

And there was more. The 'Charter' goes on to describe how, some time later, taking with him only

Wellias, Patrick climbed up
through the dense wood to
the summit of the Tor.
There they found an ancient
oratory, almost in ruin but
somehow imbued with so
sweet an odour that they
thought themselves already
in Paradise. On searching
the oratory they discovered a
book, badly damaged but
still partly legible, which included the Acts of the
Apostles and the Acts and Deeds of Phagan and
Deruvian. At first they could just make out a passage
which described how the oratory had been built by
the two saints under Divine inspiration and
dedicated to St Michael the Archangel. The book
also told how Phagan and Deruvian had lived there
for nine years.

Patrick and Wellias stayed on the Tor, fasting, for
three months; and then, after learning in a vision
that his left arm would wither until Patrick told the
rest of the brethren the whole story, they returned
to Glastonbury. Thereafter two monks, beginning
with the Irishmen Arnulf and Ogmar, were to live
permanently on the Tor.

A third story of the Tor completes a remarkable
trilogy. St Collen, according to a Life written in the
12th century, came to Glastonbury, but he
quarrelled with the monks and took himself off,
alone, up the 'mountain'. There he was confronted by
the King of the Underworld who tempted him with a
vision of a castle, musicians, and dishes of dainties.
Not, of course, to be tempted, the saint sprinkled the
ground with holy water and the vision vanished.

If all these fantasies failed to encourage visitors to mount the steep slope to the chapel on the summit, the 'Charter' offered ample inducement. Patrick himself promised 100 days pardon to all who would cut down the trees which had made his climb so difficult; and the abbey's historians recorded that Phagan and Deruvian had offered 30 years for all visitors.

Now what is the evidence of sober history? Professor Rahtz' excavations there revealed both significant dark-age Mediterranean imports and some fascinating later finds. Most important, as far as medieval visitors were concerned, was the chapel of St Michael. In fact, the remains of two chapels were found, the first of which was evidently destroyed in the earthquake of 11 September 1275. The second chapel, on the same site, was built a few years after that disaster, for fragments of floor tiles of 1290 or later were unearthed, together with stained and painted glass of the 14th century.

It was a simple, one cell building with a west tower, but only the tower now survives. Among the many finds near the chapel were a small bronze badge of the Virgin and Child and a fragment of a Purbeck marble portable altar – proof that there were visitors at the chapel in the Middle Ages, and that Mass was said there, though perhaps not often. And, splendidly, an account of one of the abbey precentors, the monk-official in charge of services, bears all this out. In 1538–9, the last full year of the

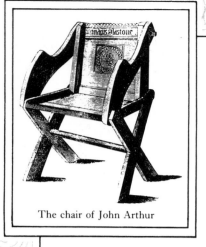
The chair of John Arthur

abbey's life, the precentor paid 16d for candles in the chapel, 1s for repairs, 1s for cleaning, 1s for a chest for the chapel's valuables and 6d for a lock and key (were the visitors stealing the ornaments?). And the precentor paid himself a fee of 6s 8d for saying Mass there on St Michael's day. One final charge was the sum of 1s for cutting nettles there, a rather easier task than felling the trees in St Patrick's time.

Finally, the Tor was the scene of a tragedy, for there on 15 November 1539, the last Abbot of Glastonbury, Richard Whiting, and the two monk-treasurers, John Arthur and Roger Wilfred, were hanged on a charge of robbery for hiding the abbey's plate and ornaments from the King's commissioners. They died, wrote an eye-witness, 'very patiently'. While he lived, John Arthur, bearer of a noble name, had occupied a chair, still to be seen in the Bishop's Palace at Wells. It bears his name and style, John Arthur, monk of Glastonbury.

BECKERY AND POMPARLES: 'The Chapel Right Adventurous and the Dangerous Bridge'

Down below Wearyall Hill beyond the abbot's deer park, where the River Brue flows into the great moor, lies a little island of higher ground called Beckery or Little Ireland. William of Malmesbury recorded the monks' belief that this was a holy place, where the Blessed Bridget of Kildare had stayed for a time, from

The tower arch of St. Michael's Chapel, Glastonbury Tor

St. Mary Magdalene's Chapel, Beckery, excavated in 1967–8. The foundations have now been covered again

the year 488. When she returned home to Ireland she left behind some relics of her stay, namely a bag or wallet, a necklace, a small bell and weaving implements. And, claimed William, they were still preserved at Beckery in the 12th century in her memory.

In the minds of the monks the 'island' had thus been long set apart, but it only came into their possession in a formal way through a charter (probably forged but with truth behind it) granted to them by the Saxon King Cenwalh in the later 7th century.

But what really was at Beckery? Two excavations, one in the 19th century and one in the 20th, have found some answers. First, there was some kind of monastic settlement there in the mid-Saxon period, perhaps after Cenwalh's time. Sixty-three graves were found in association with fragments of wattle and daub, raising the possibility of a timber chapel or tomb shrine, surrounded by a defensive ditch.

Later in the Saxon period, or even after the Conquest, a stone chapel was built there, with other stone and timber buildings nearby. Later still, during the rule of Abbot John of Taunton (1274–91), the island was bought back by the abbot from some powerful tenants-turned-owners, and the chapel was 'lavishly' rebuilt.

Archaeologists agree with the Glastonbury historian, Adam of Domerham, about Abbot John's chapel, but there are still some problems about Beckery. After William of Malmesbury's time a new

The Well Cover, Chalice Well, Glastonbury

From Middlezoy across Sedge-
moor; the ruined chapel of St.
Michael, on Burrow Mump,
stands sentinel in the green
moors

The Tower of St. Michael's Chapel, Glastonbury Tor

story began to be told which gave the chapel something more than an odour of ancient sanctity. At some time in the later 12th century it was mentioned first that the oratory of Beckery had been dedicated to St Mary Magdalene; but this dedication had been changed to St Bridget after its then more popular erstwhile resident. And, to add a touch of the miraculous, there arose a belief among the 'common folk' that anyone who passed through an opening on the south side of the chapel would receive forgiveness of sins.

In the 14th century, John of Glastonbury told a new story; or rather he brought an incident from another source, the Persevaus, the High History of the Holy Grail, and planted it in Glastonbury. It was another story of King Arthur.

Arthur, according to John, often used to stay at the nunnery of St Peter at Wearyall. There, one night, an angel appeared, telling him to go to the hermitage of St Mary Magdalene at Beckery, at dawn. He took little notice and the angel appeared on the second night. Again, the king did not go, but ordered his servant to be ready if the vision should come again. During the next night the servant himself went to the chapel and found there a corpse on a bier, surrounded by candles, with two golden candlesticks on an altar. He stole one of the candlesticks but was wounded by someone as he left. Returning to the king, he confessed, showed his wound and died.

The king thus determined to go as he was bidden. He found the chapel doorway guarded by hands

The Tor and the old Pomparles or Pont Perilous bridge

holding swords, but having prayed to be worthy to enter, the swords disappeared. Inside he met an old, bearded man robed in black. As the king watched, the man began to put on priestly robes and was approached by none other than the Virgin herself, bearing her Son in her arms. The Boy took his place on the altar, was consumed and remained as before. In token of this appearance, the Virgin gave to Arthur a crystal cross, which was thereafter preserved in the abbey treasury. The Virgin and Child then disappeared from view. The old man explained to the king that the corpse his servant had seen was that of a brother hermit from Nyland or Andredesey. The king, for his part, made vows of contrition to the Virgin and changed his shield of arms in her honour. Kings from Brutus until his time had borne three red lions on a silver ground, but now he would bear the Virgin's cross in silver on a green ground, with the image of the Virgin and her Son over its right arm.

This was John of Glastonbury's version of the story; and one phrase from his source, the Persevaus, described the chapel and its site. 'The place is right perilous and the chapel right adventurous'. It was a phrase which John did not use, but which the many readers of the Persevaus would have remembered. John, of course, added other touches: Nyland lay at the western edge of the abbey's Twelve Hides, the core of its ancient holding; and the king's new coat of arms was none other than the arms of the abbey itself.

But the perilous place and the adventurous chapel

took visitors on to another scene in the story. There was a tale, known both to the French and the English, about a lad named Gingelain, son of Gawain. In English the tale appeared in the earlier 14th century as a poem called Libeaus Desconus. It told how Gingelain came incognito to King Arthur's court at Glastonbury. The king, dubbing him knight, called him the Fair Unknown, and offered him the next adventure going. A maiden and a dwarf appeared looking for a champion who would rescue a lady captured in an enchanted castle. Gingelain offered himself, but the maiden scorned him and the dwarf declared he would not be worth a farthing for there were three battles to be won, the first 'at the point perilous, be (by) the chapell auntrous'. Arthur, recalling his promise, blessed the youth and the three set off.

> Upon a faire cause,
> Be the chapel auntrous.
> The knight they gonne y-se
> In armes bright of ble (colour)
> Upon the point perilous.

So here, by the chapel adventurous, the chapel at Beckery, is the point perilous, subtly changed in later versions of the poem to 'pont perilous', the perilous bridge, and a causeway. It was, the monks would point out, the bridge and the causeway by which the road from Glastonbury crossed the moor and the

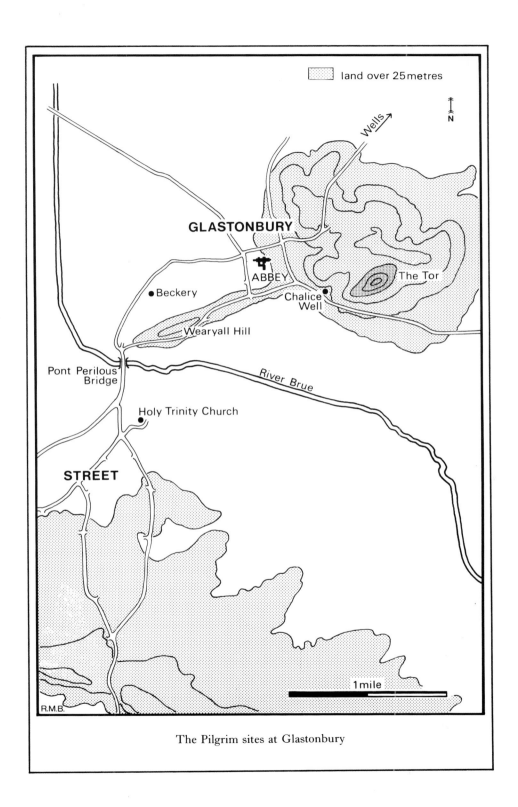

land over 25 metres

N

Wells

GLASTONBURY

ABBEY

The Tor

● Beckery

Chalice
Well

Wearyall Hill

Pont Perilous
Bridge

River Brue

Holy Trinity Church

STREET

R.M.B.

1 mile

The Pilgrim sites at Glastonbury

The old Pomparles or Pont
Perilous Bridge

River Brue into Street.

The bridge was real enough. In Abbot Michael of Amesbury's time (1235–52) it was under the charge of William *pontarius*, William the bridge man. No trace then of another name, simply a bridge. But in 1392–3, John Deor, collector of rents in Glastonbury manor, accounted for income from land 'near Pound perilous'. Another attraction had been created for the visitor. By the time John Leland visited the town in the 1540s its story had changed again. The stone bridge of four arches 'communely caullid Pont perlus' was 'wher men fable that Arture cast in his swerd'. 'Men fable', said Leland: surely local invention again.

The medieval bridge was pulled down in 1826 and its modern counterpart has little romance about it. No longer does the Brue swell to a lake as once it did, at least in winter. And how far is the scene from the bulrush-beds described by Tennyson where Sir Bedivere wheeled Excalibur above his head and closed his eyes and flung him with both hands into the deep!

STRONGHOLDS
OF THE
SUMMER COUNTRY

G LASTONBURY stands in the centre of that land which the Welsh have always called the Land of Summer. It stands overlooking a flat and mysterious basin, once tidal marsh but now an expanse of rich grassland where former islands stand out like stranded whales in a sea of green. Glastonbury Tor, Brent Knoll and Nyland, all later to be part of the abbey estate, or Burrow Mump and Fenny Castle in the hands of lesser lights, each bear significant traces of earlier occupation. And circling round this great green sea are hills to east and south and west, offering superb sites of natural strength, castles in earth and rock commanding wide views across the Summer Country.

BRENT KNOLL: THE MOUNT OF FROGS

A grassy hill 450 feet above sea level, Brent Knoll in ancient winters stood, like the Pillars of Hercules, at the mouth of the Somerset marshes. Before the Romans came the natives had recognised its value: they could see the fortress of Dinas Powis across the Severn Sea, and the Tor across the marshes at Glastonbury. And from there to Cadbury was an easy view. Thus might messages in fire be swiftly sent.

Brent Knoll was obviously, like the other hills, more than a beacon. Its ramparts defended a strong position which still preserves many of its secrets.

Roman debris and burials have been found, and walls were apparently standing in the middle of the 13th century, for Graecia de Meisi, widow of Richard de Cotele, one of Glastonbury Abbey's powerful tenants in Brent Marsh, held a *castellarium*, a little fort, there. And there too, in 1189, another Glastonbury tenant, Richard de Conteville, had land called Batelebergam, still remembered as Battleborough on the lower slopes of Brent Knoll. Was this, as some have said, the site of a battle between Alfred and the Danes, or maybe there is a different origin altogether?

Brent Knoll, its villages of South and East Brent, and the rich marshland around, were themselves pawns in the battle between Glastonbury and the bishops of Bath in the 12th century, and the monks had to marshal all their forces to their defence. That campaign involved the production of title to legal ownership or, perhaps more telling, evidence of long-standing possession.

William of Malmesbury knew that Glastonbury had owned Brent at the time of Domesday in the 11th century. He believed, further, that the land was named after Bregden, an ancient whose name appeared on the taller of the two cross shafts in the monks' graveyard. The abbey later produced a charter, copied into their Great Chartulary or register of title deeds, by which King Ine granted to Abbot Haemgils the land at Brent Knoll in the year 663. The date is obviously wrong, for Ine did not

113

Brent Knoll, the Mount of Frogs

become king until 688, but there was probably truth behind the forgery; and the careful William of Malmesbury corrected the date to 690.

But that was not sufficient title when the Bishop of Bath was snapping at their heels, so the monks perpetrated another forgery, known as the Great Privilege of King Ine, which the king is said to have given in 725. This document began by declaring Glastonbury's unique origin – 'the church which the great priest and highest bishop with the help of angels had once dedicated with many unheard of miracles to Himself and the perpetual Virgin Mary, as He revealed to the blessed David'. The charter continued by confirming the gifts of Ine and his Saxon predecessors, including Brent.

And then came the impudence of the forgers, for the Privilege went on to put the bishop in his place. Calling on 'the intercession of Almighty God, the perpetual Virgin Mary, the blessed apostles Peter and Paul and all the saints', the king forbade 'any bishop to presume, on any pretext at all, to establish his episcopal seat, or to celebrate solemn mass, or to consecrate altars, or to dedicate churches, or to confer holy orders, or to do anything at all in the church of Glastonbury itself, or in any of the churches subject to it . . . unless he be invited by the abbot or brethren'. And if 'in his swollen pride' he should fail to follow these instructions, his lands at Pilton and Greinton would be taken away. Episcopal power was brought to its knees.

The bishop of Bath remained totally unmoved by such a forgery, and Bishop Reginald's victory over Abbot Robert not only made a nonsense of the Great Privilege, its outcome left Glastonbury without the churches of South Brent and Pilton, the latter lost forever despite its holy and apostolic protection. So a second line of defence was clearly called for.

That line was to demonstrate that the abbey had held Brent long before Ine's time, given to the monks by a greater benefactor, none other than King Arthur. Where the story came from is not certain, but it was added to William of Malmesbury's History in the later years of the 12th century. By the 14th century, John of Glastonbury told a fuller version, incidentally showing it to have been borrowed from Wales.

John recounted that one Christmas at Caerleon, Arthur knighted young Yder, son of King Nuth, and sent him to the mountain of Areynes in North Wales where lived three giants, famed for their evil deeds. The mountain of Areynes in Latin is *mons arenarum*, that is the mount of spiders. The version of the name which crept into William of Malmesbury's work is *mons renarum*, the mount of frogs; and according to that version, the mountain was not in Wales but in Somerset, none other than Brent Knoll. The story might surely be used to Glastonbury's advantage.

The story was, on the face of it, a tragedy. The

brave young Yder, anxious to impress the king, took on the three giants and killed them 'in a marvellous slaughter'. Arthur and his companions, following later, found the young man unconscious, worn out by his exertions. Arthur returned home saddened that he had been the unwitting cause of the lad's death, although two versions of the tale say that Yder survived. What mattered to Glastonbury was not a doubtful death, but the consequence: that Arthur established a community of monks – one version says 24, another 80 – to pray for the young man's soul at Glastonbury, giving gifts and land for their support, including Brent Marsh and Polden. That was an ancestry of possession which could hardly be challenged.

DUNSTER AND CARHAMPTON: DINDRAITHOU AND CARRUM

The Severn Estuary was no barrier to the holy men of Wales. They could see the misty heights of Exmoor in the Autumn and the clear colours of the lower land in Spring. This lower land they called the Land of Summer, for then its floods and marshes gave way to lush green pastures for summer grazing. Over those few miles of treacherous sea the monks of Llantwit, that great Celtic Christian centre of learning, could look across to Watchet – their name for the little river inlet 'under the wood' – and could

Dunster Castle and Grabbist
Hill from the ramparts of Bat's
Castle

St Decuman's Well

pray for courage to face the pagan and unruly people on the other side.

Still today along that coast those holy Welshmen and Welshwomen are remembered: at Watchet itself St Decuman, who came over on a hurdle; at Timberscombe the great Cornish saint Petroc. And so westwards to St Brannoc's monastery at Braunton, and from there down the coast to the Camel Estuary, to St Petroc's monastery and last resting place at Padstow. In between the missions planted by the saintly sons and daughters of the Welsh king Brychan are still recalled: John at Instow, Nectan at Hartland, Morwenna at Morwenstow, Juliot at Tintagel, Endelient at St Endellion, Menfrede at St Minver.

Porlock and Carhampton have not forgotten their founders. Porlock's patron saint is Dyfrig, otherwise Dubricius, the great bishop of South Wales and the Welsh borderlands; the man who, according to Geoffrey of Monmouth, was the Dubricius from the 'City of the Legions' (Caerleon) who, having 'lamented the sad state of his country . . . bestowed the crown of the kingdom' upon Arthur.

Carhampton's saint is Carantoc or Carannog, a holy Welsh prince who, journeying first to Ireland, returned to his cave in Llangrannog, on the coast north-east of Cardigan, and then determined to preach the Gospel in the Land of Summer. Where he actually went was in the hands of the Almighty, so he threw his portable altar into the sea and prepared to follow wherever it led him. The altar

came to land at the mouth of
the river Guellit in the
district of Carrum, a land
ruled by Cadwy, son of Geraint, and by Arthur, the joint
rulers dwelling in a place
called Dindraithou. The
saint enquired of Arthur
whether any had seen his
altar, but Arthur preva-
ricated. He had a greater

St Decuman's Well

problem on his mind, a terrible dragon which was
plaguing the countryside. If Carantoc could possibly
bring it under control then the missing altar might
be discovered.

A dragon was as nothing to the saint. The dragon
came to Carantoc 'as a calf running to its mother'
and he, wrapping his stole around its bull-like neck,
led it into Cadwy's hall at Dindraithou. The people
threatened to kill the beast which had so terrified
them, but the saint saved its life and ordered it to
leave the district.

Carantoc's reward was two-fold. Arthur gave him
back his errant altar, very glad to be rid of it; he had
tried to use it as a table, but everything put upon it
had been thrown off. The other reward was the gift
of land at Carrum on which to build a monastery.

Now the life of St Carantoc, according to experts,
was probably put together from earlier sources in
south-east Wales about 1130, just at the time when
Caradoc of Llancarfan was describing how Gildas
had come with a host from Devon and Cornwall to
Glastonbury to make peace between Melwas and
Arthur. Whoever brought Arthur to Dindraithou
and Carrum will probably never be known, but it is

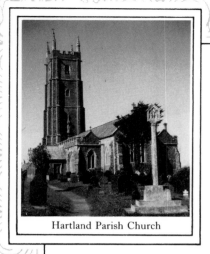
Hartland Parish Church

just possible that Glastonbury's arch-rival, Wells, had something to do with the identification of Carrum with Carhampton. Is it simply coincidence that about 1180, just about the time of Glastonbury's greatest crisis, two churches at Carhampton came into the possession of Wells Cathedral?

One of those churches, dedicated to St Carantoc, was still standing in the early 14th century, but even its site is not now known. The other was the present parish church of St John the Baptist, famous for its fine, late medieval screen. John Leland suggested in the early 16th century – but modern experts would not agree – that the place-name Carhampton is derived from 'Carentokes town'. It is no more accurate in strictly historical terms to suggest that Dindraithou is Dunster, though the Mohun family, owners of the castle in the 12th century, might well have been flattered to think that they were living where Arthur had trod.

Yet there is no doubt that Welsh missionaries came to West Somerset in the 5th and 6th centuries; that the words inscribed on the Caratacus Stone on Winsford Hill recall a land where a Christian chieftain once held sway; that the Christian graves found at Cannington were arranged around the final resting place of a youth in token, perhaps, of servitude, perhaps of fidelity; and that the three hillforts of Bat's Castle, Gallox Hill and Grabbist above Dunster, built in the same tradition as Cadbury and Brent Knoll, may yet reveal that they, a remarkable triumvate, were occupied by a Dark Age warrior chieftain.

CAMELOT

'a city of shadowy palaces and stately'. Tennyson: IDYLLS OF THE KING, GARETH AND LYNETTE

'Camallate . . . sumtyme a famose town or castelle, upon a very torre or hille, wunderfully enstrength-eid of nature . . .'. So wrote John Leland. Rising massively above the little village of South Cadbury, the hill's wooded crown now masks the ramparts of a great fortress. There was no doubt at South Cadbury in the early 16th century when Leland was there that the site was special. On the top were still to be seen the foundations of buildings, and during ploughing, gold, silver and copper coins of the Roman period with 'many other antique thinges' including a silver horseshoe had been found there.

The names of two nearby villages, West and Queen Camel, also suggested the identification, together with the river Cam that flowed beside them. The name, in fact, is not a satisfactory answer, although Camel may mean bare ridge or rim, certainly a good description of the hills behind South Cadbury today. Yet the name and the archaeology seem to have convinced Leland, or rather convinced the people whom he met there: 'the people can telle nothing ther but that they have hard say that Arture much resorted to Camalat'.

Could this green hill, fortified in times past, be

The ramparts of the Hillfort of South Cadbury. Could this be Camelot?

King Arthur enters Camelot

the centre of the Arthurian world? Camelot of the Legends was a castle surrounded by plains, with a forest and a river not far away; Camelot was the place where the quest for the Holy Grail began; Camelot was the desired resting place of Gawain; and Camelot was destroyed along with all the significant features of Logres when Mark invaded after the death of Lancelot. This is the Camelot of the High Romances, whose site was never named. Somewhere in Southern England, perhaps, until Sir Thomas Malory identified it as Winchester, home of the Round Table, ancient capital of England.

Did Malory's claim give rise to other notions; notions which might have been inspired by political motives? Malory, the Yorkist author, doubtless had Yorkist readers. South Cadbury belonged to the Lancastrian Hungerfords until about 1478 when their sole heiress, a child named Mary, came into the guardianship of the Lord Chamberlain of England. That most loyal of all Yorkists was William, Lord Hastings, Knight of the Garter, well-known retainer of knights. Hastings married the girl to his own son and heir Edward, and it was one of their descendants, the sober Puritan Sir Francis Hastings of North Cadbury, who wrote about 1583 describing Camelot in greater Arthurian detail than Leland even mentioned. Was this part of the Hastings' family tradition, originating perhaps in a piece of Yorkist propaganda, which prompted Sir Francis to describe the 'gallante hil where there hathe bene a

castel in times past called Camelot, wherein Sir Lancelot in King Arthur's time is fayned to have dwelled'? And what of the coat of arms of St Joseph of Arimathea, carved on a bench-end in North Cadbury church? Could that be another piece of Hastings-inspired tradition, linking the place within the popular traditions of Glastonbury?

From the 16th century to the early 20th local traditions have persisted. King Arthur's Palace, the highest point within the ramparts, was spoken of in the 1580s; King Arthur's Well may still be seen beside the footpath which runs below the defences. King Arthur's Hunting Causeway or Arthur's Lane is a notional trackway running northwards from the hill, perhaps towards Glastonbury (crossing the river Alam below Lamyatt Beacon by Arthur's Bridge). It is said that the king still sleeps in a cave within the hill, and once a year a pair of gates swings open for all to see him; and the king and his horsemen ride, either at Midsummer or at Christmas, their horses stopping to drink near Sutton Montis church.

Legend or history, the view across green Somerset to Glastonbury Tor and Brent Knoll is reward enough for the effort of the climb to the ramparts of Camelot. John Steinbeck stood there first on May Day 1959, a golden day, but promised himself he would 'go back over and over . . . at night and in the rain'. But that first day was 'noble gold . . . mystic, wonderful'.

KING ARTHUR
IN
CORNWALL

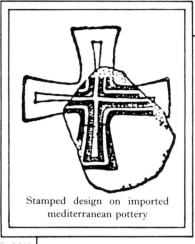

Stamped design on imported mediterranean pottery

T HERE are those who claim that the gentle green of the Land of Summer blends imperceptibly into its English neighbours, but there is no doubt that the granite land further west, across the Tamar, is a different world. Advancing Saxons, like the Romans before them, settled comfortably in Somerset and Devon, but found the land beyond less to their liking. The native Celtic people were allowed to keep their ancient ways, their language and their religious enthusiasm, outpost of a world they shared with Wales and Ireland and Brittany. Celtic strongholds still abound in Cornwall, Celtic placenames act as guides to the history of settlement and shrine. Yet of Arthur, the Celtic hero, the traces seem not Celtic, not ancient; rather, they belong to the realm of England, medieval but romantic.

TINTAGEL

'The castle of Tintagel . . . built high above the sea which surrounds it on all sides (with) . . . no other way except that offered by a narrow isthmus of rock'. That was how Geoffrey of Monmouth described the place where Gorlois, duke of Cornwall, sent his wife Ygerna to be safe (so he believed) from the roving eye of King Uther Pendragon. Geoffrey is often, perhaps deliberately, vague about the places he mentions in his history, but there

130

seems to be no doubt about
Tintagel. It is in Cornwall,
and from the 12th century
that curious headland in the
ancient parish of Bossiney
has borne the name that
Geoffrey used. Geoffrey was
the first, in fact, to use it in
surviving written records,
but that is not to say he
invented it. Indeed, the

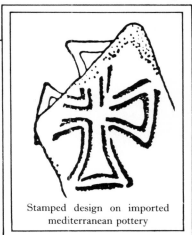

Stamped design on imported
mediterranean pottery

name may be formed in part from the ancient
Cornish word *din* or *dun*, meaning hill or fort. And
so it clearly is, a headland jutting out into the sea,
joined to the mainland by a narrow ridge of rock.

Ygerna, however, was not safe there. While Uther
Pendragon laid siege to Gorlois in Dimilioc, his
passion grew stronger. How could he reach her, for
he was assured that three armed men could defend
the lady at Tintagel against even the strongest army.
Merlin's potions solved the problem. With their aid
Uther was magically changed to assume the form of
Gorlois and was warmly received by a wife over-
whelmed to see her lord come to visit her at the risk
of his life. So there, at Tintagel, Arthur was conceived. Remarkably, neither the deception nor the
death of Gorlois seems to have upset the lady
unduly, and she and Uther 'lived together as equals,
united by their great love for each other'.

Was it simply its romantic situation which led
Geoffrey of Monmouth to place the events at Tintagel? What stood there in his day, or what tales
from the past surrounded it? Perhaps he found the
idea in the ancient stories of Tristan and Isolt; later
versions of the story made Tintagel the site of King

Mark's castle, the place to which Tristan was to bring Isolt as a bride for his uncle and king. There may have been practical reason, too, why Geoffrey used the name, for as he was writing Reginald, Earl of Cornwall, was building for himself a strong castle there. Reginald, an illegitimate son of Henry I, was clearly a man to be flattered by a cleric looking for a patron, as Geoffrey almost certainly was. Was not his whole book dedicated to Reginald's infinitely more powerful half brother Robert, Earl of Gloucester?

Curiously, John Leland, who spent a good deal of time in Cornwall and faithfully recorded Arthurian traditions elsewhere in the country, describes Tintagel castle as he saw it in the 1540s but makes no mention of Arthur. 'A mervelus strong and notable forteres, and almost situ loci inexpugnable', he declared, with a keep on the 'high terrible cragge' surrounded by sea but in his day the feeding ground for sheep and rabbits, approached only by a bridge made of long elm trees.

But if there was no Arthur – and no Mark – in 16th century Tintagel, still there was one thing which suggested a more ancient origin. This was the nearby chapel of St Juliot, one of the children of Brychan, a 5th century king from Wales whose progeny brought the Christian faith to the coasts of Devon and Cornwall. Juliot is, in fact, a somewhat elusive figure, for experts are unsure whether Juliot is male or female, and are divided on the number of

The Tristan Stone, Castle Dore

Mediterranean Amphora

probable brothers and sisters – anything between 11 and 62 have been claimed.

Archaeology has revealed something more certain. Excavations on the headland brought to light cell-like structures which have long been identified as part of a Celtic monastic site of the greatest importance, perhaps the Rosnant of ancient Irish tradition. How else could the clusters of primitive stone buildings with earth floors and thatched roofs be interpreted but as the cells of monks? And there was little doubt about the date, for scattered across the site were found fragments of pottery imported from the eastern Mediterranean from the later 5th century onwards. The site, it is agreed, was in use until the 8th century, when there are clear signs of decline.

But there are doubts, for as more and more sites have produced this special pottery, the more they seem to be associated with secular rather than with religious contexts. Was there at Tintagel a chieftain's stronghold before the monastery was founded? Was Geoffrey of Monmouth so wide of the mark after all? When Gorlois fled to Cornwall his army was too small to face King Uther in battle. Instead, he garrisoned his 'castles' and himself took refuge 'in a fortified camp called Dimilioc'. Can this be any place but Domellick, formerly Domeliock, a few miles south-west of Tintagel in the heart of Cornwall, the *din* or fortress of Mailoc in the parish of St Dennis? The farm of Domellick used to include the hill where the church of St Dennis

The rocky crag of Tintagel

Tintagel: the foundations of the early buildings over-look a boiling sea

Mediterranean Amphora

stands within the earthworks of an ancient fortress. And not St Denis, patron of France, of course, but *dinas*, a fortress. Mailoc's fortress, not the great stronghold of Gorlois; surely that lies a mile or two north, across Goss Moor, the great Castle-an-Dinas. Geoffrey of Monmouth was clearly no stranger to the traditions and topography of Cornwall.

KELLIWIC

There is another Cornish fortress, a fortress with a longer history than Tintagel, a longer tradition even than Caerleon, the City of the Legions. According to ancient Welsh tradition enshrined in the Triads, the aides memoires of storytellers, there were in the island of Britain in the days of Arthur three tribal thrones. Pen Rhionydd, somewhere in the north, and St David's were two seats of government. The third was Kelliwic, evidently in Cornwall, at once Arthur's home and his capital.

Where was this 'woodland fortress' which the name implies? Callington, Callywith and Barras Nose by Tintagel have had each their supporters, and so have Gweek Wood and Willapark. But the most convincing argument lies with Castle Killibury or Kelly Rounds, a hillfort north-east of Wadebridge, which overlooks the river Camel.

Two other Cornish place names reveal the depth

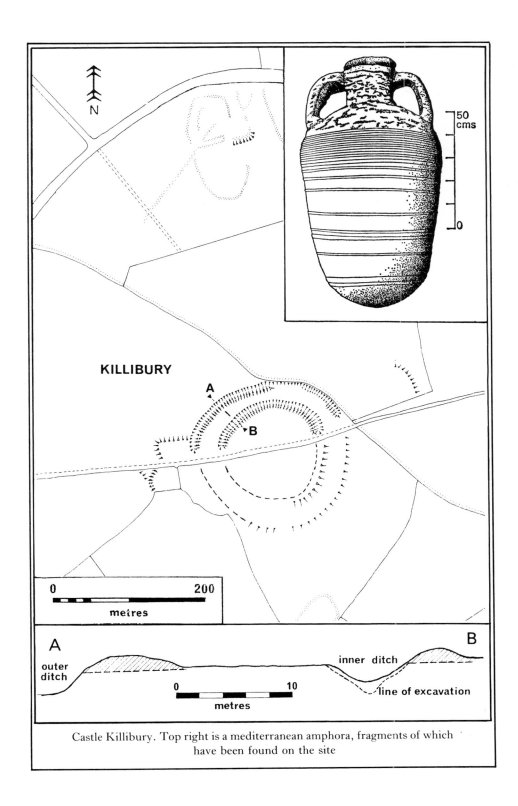

KILLIBURY

A

B

50
cms

0

0   200
metres

A   B

outer
ditch

inner ditch

line of excavation

0   10
metres

Castle Killibury. Top right is a mediterranean amphora, fragments of which
have been found on the site

of Arthurian tradition. Just by Castle Dore was a farm called Carhurles, 'very possibly', according to Cornwall's historian, Charles Henderson, meaning the fortress (caer) of Gorlois. And may not Tremodret in Roche and Carvedras in Kenwyn be echoes of a homestead and a fortress of Mordred?

CAMLANN

Two vast armies, 60,000 under Mordred, nine divisions under Arthur, faced each other by the river 'Canblam' and there was great slaughter. Mordred the traitor lay dead, Arthur mortally wounded. So said Geoffrey of Monmouth; for him 'Canblam' was without doubt in Cornwall and the Welsh tradition of the final battle they called Camlann was also in south-western Britain.

Leland in the 1540s told how locals near Camelford claimed to have ploughed up bones and harness from a battle where 'Arture fowght his last feld', so the tradition of the site there was very much alive. Yet 16th century archaeology hardly proves a Dark Age battle site, and a later battle in 823 when the Saxon Edgar was conquering the Cornish could be a more likely explanation of the remains. The name Slaughter Bridge, not far from Camelford is, indeed, a most suggestive name, and a site called Arthur's Tomb adds weight for the credulous, but the 'tomb' is actually an ancient funeral slab brought

fait le chief voler del bu en mi
la place. Ensi q̃ j grãt mortalite del
roi Artu ⁊ de Mordres son fil la v il
furent tout destruit.

vant li rois Artus voit
celui cop si dist trop do
lans. ha: dier por quoi
ne laissies vos tant abaissier de
proesce t̃iene. Et por lamor de
cestui cop veu ion a dieu qui co
ment ichi morir moi ou mordret
Il t̃nt j glaiue gros ⁊ fort ⁊ lais
se corre q̃sques il puet del cheual
traire vers mordret. Et mor
dret qui bien voit ine li rois ne
haiot salui non ochire nel refuse

The battle of Camlann from a 14th century French manuscript

from some distance in the 18th century which records not the grave of Arthur but the burial place of Latinus, son of Magarus. The worn letters led someone many years ago to see the name 'Atry' there, and perhaps wishful thinking did the rest.

There are more difficulties about Camlann; not with the site so much as with what actually happened. Geoffrey of Monmouth wrote of a great slaughter. Leland told of a single combat on a bridge between Arthur and Mordred in which Mordred first wounded Arthur with a poisoned sword before Arthur struck the fatal blow. Welsh sources, compiled much earlier than Geoffrey, record 'the battle of Camlann where Arthur and Mordred fell' and also make Mordred a hero fighting on Arthur's side. Is this the explanation of the first version of the discovery of the graves at Glastonbury, the version to be found in the records of Margam Abbey, where Mordred shares a grave with his king? Was this version for Welsh eyes only, leaving for West-country consumption the more tragic tale of treachery? Both traditions are, however, essentially agreed: Camlann was the end of an era. The resting, waiting king in Avalon could surely be no more than of spiritual significance.

THE PERSISTENCE

OF

ARTHUR

LEGENDS do not die by political decision or the hangman's rope; rather they flourish. The dissolution of Glastonbury Abbey and the execution of its abbot and two monks in 1539 did not destroy the Legend of Arthur. By the 17th century the three blossoming thorns on Wearyall Hill had become the descendants of Joseph of Arimathea's staff, brought from the Garden of Gethsemane and an offence in the eyes of a Puritan with an axe. That sober Puritan Sir Francis Hastings could write of Lancelot at Camelot without making any compromise to his religious sensibilities. King Arthur was, as he had been from the 12th century, a national, even an international figure. Cornwall may have been the place of his birth and of his final battle, Somerset the base for many of his activities, and Glastonbury his last resting place, but he belonged to the nation.

Several medieval kings had played their part in his 'nationalisation'. Experts now seem agreed that the Round Table at Winchester was made during the reign of Henry III. Edward I's interest in Arthur was clear enough from his visit to Glastonbury in 1278. Edward III's foundation of the Order of the Garter was evidently based on notions of the Round Table; and the extension of the Order by Edward IV reflected the interests of a king who probably knew the author of Le Mort d'Arthur. He was a king, besides, whose illegitimate son by Elizabeth Lucy, nee Wayte, was christened Arthur and bore

Arthur, Overlord of Thirty Kingdoms

many of the characteristics of his handsome, easy-going father. And why Arthur? Perhaps because Elizabeth's home was not far from Winchester, where Malory himself placed Camelot; but perhaps it was simply the king's own wish, another piece of Yorkist propaganda.

Henry VII, looking for 'a worthwhile figure from the British past to include among the pantheon of Tudor ancestors', had his first-born son, born at Winchester, christened Arthur, and placed a statue of the hero-king in the hall of his newly-built palace at Richmond in 1501. Henry's daughter, Margaret, wife of James IV of Scotland, called her second son Arthur in 1509, but buried him within a year. Margaret's son James V, had a son Arthur born and died 1541. Henry VIII, who owed his throne and his first wife to the death of his elder brother, Prince Arthur, had the Round Table at Winchester repainted to impress the Emperor Charles V in 1522. The figure of a Tudor-looking Arthur in the place of honour at the table, and a Tudor rose at its centre, are splendid examples of Tudor propaganda.

Another century but the same throne. Queen Victoria's third son was christened Arthur in 1850. He later became Duke of Connaught and passed his name to his son and his grandson. Arthur was one of the names Prince Albert, later King George VI, was given at his baptism in 1895; one of the names given to his grandson Prince Charles in 1948. The influence of Tennyson is far reaching.

The Round Table, Winchester Castle

And what of more common stock? The choice of a name is sometimes dictated by fashion, sometimes by family tradition. Was it politics or literature, the king or Malory, which influenced Humphrey Nevill of School Aycliffe in Weardale to name his son Arthur in the 1470s or 1480s, and that Arthur to name his son Lancelot? Loyalty to Glastonbury and its traditions obviously inspired John Brooke (d. 1522), the abbey's chief steward, to name his second son Arthur; and other Somerset gentry, like William, Lord Stourton (d. 1548), and Christopher Hadley (d. 1540) named sons after a hero-king. The St Albyns of Alfoxton went further. For several generations down to the end of the 18th century they favoured the name Lancelot, a tradition begun by John St Albyn (d. 1573), who named four sons Lancelot, Tristram, Arthur and George. The name Arthur appeared in the 16th century, too, in the Malet family of West Quantoxhead, the Blakes of Plainsfield, the Bluetts of Kittisford, all in Somerset; and in the Champernouns of Dartington in Devon, but curiously not among the gentry families of Cornwall, although the Trevelyans of St Veep and later of Nettlecombe in Somerset bore as their arms a horse rising from the sea, in recognition of their ancestor who alone swam his horse from St Michael's Mount to the mainland for a wager with other knights of Arthur's court.

Family connexions, and possibly even local politics maintained and spread the name among

Irish landowners from the 16th century onwards, but the source could not have been more English. He was none other than Edward IV's illegitimate son Arthur Wayte. Brought up at his father's court, Arthur was married first to Elizabeth, Baroness Lisle, and second to Honor, nee Grenville, widow of John Basset, the Grenvilles and the Bassets both of solid Devon stock. Arthur, the last Plantagenet, was created Viscount Lisle, served his king at Calais, but came under suspicion of treason. He died, it is said, from relief on hearing he was to be freed from the Tower in 1542.

Lisle's eldest daughter, Frances, married one of his stepsons, John Basset, and their son, Arthur Basset (1541–86) was the ancestor of the Bassets of Umberleigh and the Chichesters of Hall, both in Devon. And he was, very likely, the reason why John Chichester of Hall named his second son Arthur in 1563. That Arthur, 1st Baron Belfast, was the first of the Irish Chichesters, Viscounts Chichester and Earls and Marquesses of Donegall. Arthur Chichester, 1st Earl of Donegall (1606–75), was succeeded by his nephew, another Arthur, son of his brother Colonel John Chichester of Dungannon in County Tyrone. Viscount Dungannon was the title taken in 1662 by Mark Trevor (d. 1670), Governor of Ulster and Marshal of the Irish Army. Presumably he was a neighbour of the Chichesters, probably a friend; and his own family, from Brynkialt in North Wales, had several Arthurs in their pedigree.

And so the name Arthur continued, passing to a younger Trevor son and then through a marriage into the Hill family, one of whom also married a Trevor daughter. Arthur Hill-Trevor was created Viscount of Dungannon in 1766. His son Arthur succeeded him in 1771 and his daughter Anne married in 1759 Garret Wesley, Baron Mornington. Their fifth but third surviving son, born in 1769 was, almost inevitably, christened Arthur. He died in 1852 better known as the Duke of Wellington; saviour, surely, of his country against a darkness from across the sea; holder of a title and an estate without question in the Land of Summer.

THE ONCE
AND
FUTURE KING

THE concept of a sleeping king who lies ready to save his people at the hour of their greatest danger fulfills the need for certainty in an uncertain world. Arthur is not the only leader who rests until his country needs him, but the confidence he evidently inspired in northern Europe is reflected in claims for his dormant presence in places as far apart as the coast of Norway and the Celtic fringes of France. The heroic, sleeping or not, must never be allowed to die; it is the spirit of the nation.

For a thousand years and more Arthur has entertained and inspired. Each age in need of a hero, each nation in need of an inheritance to be proud of, and several monarchs in need of an ancestry have made of him what they would; have crowned him, clad him in armour, surrounded him with jousts and tourneys. Romances have introduced magic and the sins that flesh is heir to, poets have brought their dreams and artists their visions. The quest for the Grail and deeds of knightly valour have added a purpose and a moral force which have transcended the historic and have confused and obscured a distant reality. For too many people Arthur has become a myth and not a legend.

And the reasons for confusion and obscurity are obvious; the story has been manipulated. Geoffrey of Monmouth, the monks of Glastonbury and the canons of Wells ought not to be seen as the villains of the piece, for we cannot be sure how much they relied upon authentic sources not now surviving. We

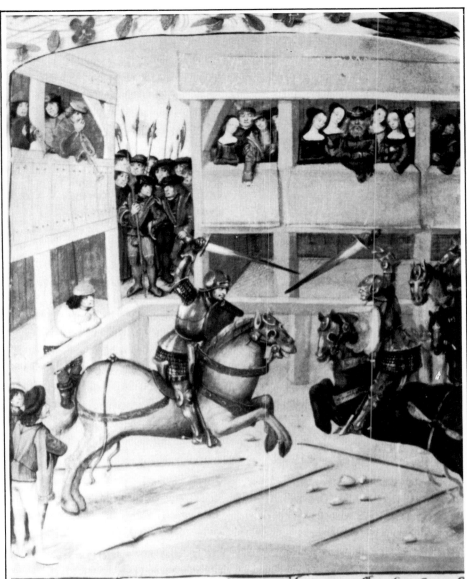

A tournament before King Arthur

A Vision of Arthur

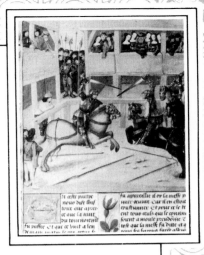

cannot be sure; but we may
be justified in our suspicions
that their motives had at least
something to do with private
or community advantage.
And yet, in archaeological
terms, what are the Dark
Ages to the 20th century may
well not have been so dark in
the 12th. The characters on
those cross shafts at Glaston-
bury were certainly confusing to William of Malmesbury, but they may not have been confusing to
some of his contemporaries.

The archaeological element is, indeed, crucial.
The sophisticated and organised society so clearly
revealed in the refortified hillforts of South-West
England must have been led not, to be sure, by a
king bearing the attributes of an age not his own, but
by one whose success was soon enshrined in the
consciousness of his people. Where he was conceived and where he lies was for a later age to decide,
for its own good reasons; that he lived and fought to
defend his nation is the essence of Arthur.

Acknowledgements

Anyone who studies the Arthurian Legends in Somerset owes a great debt of gratitude to Dean Armitage Robinson, whose little book *Two Glastonbury Legends: King Arthur and Joseph of Arimathea* (1926) began the critical study of stories which the monks of Glastonbury had claimed to be history. Professor R.F. Treharne's *The Glastonbury Legends: Joseph of Arimathea, the Holy Grail and King Arthur* (1967) built persuasively upon his arguments, and was my first introduction to the subject. The excavations carried out in recent years by Philip Rahtz at the Tor, Beckery and Chalice Well have subjected those sites to the kind of archaeological scrutiny not undertaken at the abbey itself, but paralleled on many Dark Age sites in the West of England. Geoffrey Ashes's *A Guidebook to Arthurian Britain* (1983) is a fair-minded and balanced commentary on the claims of Arthurian sites throughout the country. Richard Barber's *King Arthur: Hero and Legend* (1986) is his latest splendid work on the literary and historical versions of the Legend. James Carley's edition (now translated) of John of Glastonbury's *The Chronicle of Glastonbury Abbey* (1985) provides in its editorial notes and bibliography a rich vein of secondary, as well as primary, material. His notes have on a number of points inspired my bolder statements and suggestions. W.E. Hampton's vast knowledge of late-medieval England produced the skeleton around which the idea of a Yorkist cult of Arthur emerged. Steve Minnitt read a draft of the archaeological chapter and Richard Bryant has been archaeological adviser, artist and cartographer as well as sympathetic publisher.

I wish to acknowledge the following for the use of illustrations: Mick Aston (colour plate 1); Bodleian Library, Oxford, (colour plate 3, and plates on pp. 2, 41, 153); British Library (pp. 22, 25, 49, 126, 141, 145); Richard Bryant (13, 16–17, 21, 43, 67, 73, 90, 109, 124–5, 139); Professor Barry Cunliffe (18); Jeremy Dunning (119); Jim Hancock (30–31); Hampshire County Council (147); Martin Latham (154); Kevin Redpath (colour plate 4 and pp. 54, 63, 64–5, 74–5, 79, 102–3); Mick Sharp (6–7, 136–7); The Trustees of Glastonbury Abbey (64–5); Jean Williamson (colour plate 6 and p. 101). Other illustrations are by the author.

INDEX

BEAN .... DONE THAT

BY FORMER FA 'SLEAZEBUSTER'
GRAHAM BEAN

EMPIRE
PUBLICATIONS

EMPIRE PUBLICATIONS

1 Newton Street, Manchester M1 1HW

© Graham Bean 2022

ISBN: 978-1-909360-98-3

CONTENTS

INTRODUCTION

S O HOW DID A working class man from Barnsley go from being a hard-nosed detective with South Yorkshire Police, to a confidante and personal shopper for the greatest football manager of all time?

Graham Bean swapped fighting crime for fighting the corner of Sir Alex Ferguson, along with a host of other big name managers, players and clubs during a remarkable career as one of the sport's most infamous and respected football administrators.

From Manchester United to Macclesfield Town, Bean's story takes in some of the most well-known and compelling disciplinary cases of the last 20 years, including Fergie's fall out with 'unfit' Premier League referee Alan Wiley, Rafa Benitez's infamous clash with Phil Dowd, Duncan Ferguson's many misdemeanours, and the day QPR got involved in a kung fu style brawl, to name just a few.

Bean also lifts the lid on the mysterious and controversial inner workings of the Football Association, where he highlights their many failings while also recalling his time as the organisation's first ever 'Compliance Officer'. During four years in the role Bean travelled the world pursuing dodgy agents and questionable transfers, as well as taking to task many high-profile players, clubs, and agents for their behaviour on and off the pitch.

While representing the FA, Bean learned the dark arts of the prosecution process, laying the foundations for a new career on the opposite side of the fence. This saw him defending some of the biggest names and personalities in the game. Bean took on, beat and embarrassed his former employers on many occasions, while along the way forming close friendships and making bitter enemies with some of those he came across, including madcap former Leeds owner Massimo Cellino, which ended in an acrimonious dispute that led to the Italian being banned from football for 12 months.

This book charts his crazy path through the minefield of football disciplinary cases, combining the good, the bad and the ugly of the game.

Bean also reveals some amusing stories never told before that lie behind the headlines – and have remained secret until now. The big football names just keep on coming in what is a riveting, revealing and raucous read for any football fan.

In memory of my beloved mam, Janet Annie Bean
"Football jobs are no good lad"

JEREMY CROSS

DAILY STAR Chief Sports Writer Jeremy Cross assisted me in writing *Bean There, Done That*. A former *Yorkshire Post* sports journalist, he was appointed to his present role in 2012 and has covered some of the greatest events in world sport including the World Cup finals of cricket, football, and rugby union. He lives in Leeds with his partner Nicola and two children. He first met me shortly after I joined the FA in 1999 and we have remained close friends ever since.

FOREWORD

I FIRST MET GRAHAM in the late noughties when he had started working for Liverpool and helped me out on some disciplinary cases I found myself involved in. I spoke to a few people at the club who knew him already and they all spoke really highly of him, making it clear to me he would be a huge asset to Liverpool moving forward. I liked him straight away, we connected from the start and I knew we would go on to have a strong relationship.

Coming from Spain this was the first time as a manager I'd experienced the FA's disciplinary system and I needed someone I could trust to help me deal with it. Graham was the perfect person to do this, because his knowledge of the rules was second to none.

Not only did he have huge experience when it came to this side of the game, but the fact he was a Liverpool supporter made me realise it was good to have someone on my side who had so much passion for the club.

Graham was a fighter. He was also passionate about what he did and was always the ultimate professional. He made both myself and the players feel like we were all in good hands when it came to challenging the authorities.

Over the years I grew to trust him and we went on to become good friends. We would talk about football all the time and I valued his opinion greatly.

I remember once he even took the trouble to drive me to a disciplinary hearing – in Manchester of all places! I got to know his family, too, and his son Matthew was delighted when on one occasion he got invited to watch some of his heroes in a training session at Melwood. I know Graham really appreciated this.

When I was asked to contribute to his book, I was delighted to be given the opportunity, because I will always be grateful for the help Graham gave me down the years. It was a relief to have him on my side, instead of him being the opponent!

Congratulations on a great career Graham.

Rafa Benitez
July 2022

The Fall Guy

A TENNER... THAT'S ALL IT COST to get me into football. Police surveillance operations are nothing like you see on television, where all the action starts within 60 seconds of arriving at the scene. They're long and boring, so to pass the time you will read everything and anything, from the personal ads to the cartoons. By chance on one long stakeout, I stumbled on a discarded football magazine which drew me to an advert from the Football Supporters' Association ('FSA').

Back in the mid-nineties the FSA was viewed by the football authorities as a militant supporter campaigning organisation. Its roots were in Liverpool and it was formed by Liverpool supporters following the 1985 Heysel Stadium disaster, when 39 Juventus fans died in trouble at that year's European Cup Final between Liverpool and the Italian club. The FSA pressed the football authorities for better rights for fans and it seemed like an ideal fit for me. I was a left wing, staunch Labour-supporting bloke brought up in a working class family from the mining town of Barnsley who cared about how supporters were vilified and treated by the odious Margaret Thatcher government. The FSA were on a recruitment drive and I thought I was the perfect fit. As it turns out, sitting patiently on that surveillance operation, I was in the right place at the right time, just not in the way I ever dreamed of! Little did I know it then but answering that advert would change my life.

Within months I was at Everton's Goodison Park listening to supporters speaking about campaigning and the issues of the day at the FSA's annual conference when, keen to be more involved, I found myself being elected on to its National Committee. It was a surprise they accepted me, to be honest, as the FSA were heavily supportive of the outstanding and credible '*Hillsborough Justice Campaign*' and here I was, a serving member of South Yorkshire Police, involved at a national level with their organisation. For the record though, I was not at Hillsborough nor did I have any dealings with any inquiry at any time. Furthermore, I was fully supportive of the campaign run by the families in their quest for justice.

Being on the National Committee of the FSA gave me the opportunity to represent the organisation on occasions in front of the Football Association at their quarterly meetings at Lancaster Gate with representatives of different fan groups. Looking back, in comparison to today, it was only tokenism from the football authorities – and while we thought we were doing some good, the reality was that the FA was only paying us lip service; something which became evident to me later in my career, as the Football Associations first ever Compliance Officer.

Within 12 months I was elected National Chairman of the FSA, mainly because no-one else wanted it – and I quickly discovered the harsh reality that the organisation was struggling financially. It was chronically under-funded and haemorrhaging members. It was a voluntary position and combining that role with my day-to-day work as a detective was extremely time-consuming. Many times, I thought to myself, 'why the fuck am I doing this?'

My first problem as Chairman was working out how to pay a £700 printing bill with nothing in the bank! And that's how it continued: bill after bill, crisis after crisis. Nevertheless, we still put on a front of bluff and bravado, claiming to speak for all supporters, when in fact we had a membership of fewer than 1,500. But in their tokenism, the FA clearly felt they had to meet with us and we used those meetings to vociferously put our points across as well as build up contacts.

For a staunch Labour Party supporter, albeit a left winger, it was manna from heaven when in the 1997 General Election the

Labour Party came to power under the leadership of Tony Blair. Whilst *New Labour* felt alien to me, it opened up a chance for me when one of the first things the Government did was set up a Football Task Force, investigating issues such as racism, disability, grass root initiatives and commercialism in football. Somewhat surprisingly they appointed former Conservative Minister and (BBC football phone-in) *606* host David Mellor to head up the group. He's probably the only Tory I've ever been civil to in my life!

Working out of the Football Foundation offices behind Euston Station in London, the Task Force went on a tour of the country, taking views and representations from supporters and all other areas of the game, with a brief to then compile reports for consideration by Government and the football authorities. The Secretariat to the Task Force Members at the time was none other than Andy Burnham, who later became Minister for Health and is currently the Mayor of Greater Manchester. He compiled some outstanding reports on the issues discussed from that tour, but sadly many of the recommendations were never acted upon by successive Governments or the football authorities.

But when I said being in the 'right place at the right time', it's also true of my time as the chair of the FSA, because those meetings on the Task Force meant that I was known to the movers and shakers of the football industry. And by sheer chance, while working on the Task Force, it transpired the FA were looking for someone with investigative experience to take up the newly formed position of 'Compliance Officer'. The role had been recommended by former Metropolitan Police Chief John Smith in his report on the infamous Premier League bung inquiry, which had been ongoing for some years. Having such a vast investigative background as a career detective and having also learnt how the game worked, (or so I thought!) I felt I was the perfect fit for the role and within weeks found myself being interviewed for the position by the FA's legal director Nic

Coward.

The first words out of his mouth at the interview were, 'this is not a job about brown envelopes being passed around in motorway service station car parks', which turned out to be ironic because just a few months later I was actually doing that very same thing - taking a brown envelope from someone in a motorway service car parks containing information in relation to wrongdoing in football - but more of that later...

In hindsight Coward's words should have triggered a warning about this being a role which was in effect an appointment to satisfy the recommendations of Smith's report. One which simply pandered to the politically correct world we were living in. In other words, the FA thought that by simply appointing me they would quell suspicions of corruption within the game. Unfortunately for them, I didn't quite see it like that. And neither did the press, because they quickly gave me the nickname *'The Sleazebuster'*, which I found quite amusing!

Having been offered the job by the FA, it was necessary to tell Mellor of my appointment and the fact I would have to stand down from the Task Force. Reading between the lines, I got the feeling some of the hierarchy at the FSA were not too happy. They felt I had jumped ship to join the enemy.

On speaking to Mellor though, he told me he had been tipped off about my appointment some days earlier. As our telephone call ended his final words have never left me, and little did I know back then but those same words were to prove prophetic. "I just hope the FA don't make you the fall guy, Graham," he said.

1 - *FERGIE TIME*

WEDNESDAY, MAY 25, 2005 is a date synonymous with arguably the greatest comeback in Champions League history. That night, in the hot and sticky heat of the Ataturk Stadium in Istanbul, Liverpool somehow overcame a 3-0 half-time deficit to beat AC Milan on penalties and win their fifth European Cup. I was fortunate to be there with Matthew, my then ten year old son to see it happen.

In the hours before Liverpool's achievement we had wandered into a back street bar to carry on the joyful festivities of being at another European final which was rammed full of loud and happy Scousers when my mobile phone rang. The screen showed it was an 'unknown number', so I assumed it was my wife calling from home checking on how the day was going. I couldn't have been more wrong. On answering I was straining to hear the voice at the other end due to the singing and chanting behind me and could barely make out who it was. I stepped outside to discover to my surprise that it was Ken Merrett, the then club secretary of Manchester United.

"Hello, is that Graham?" he said.

"Yes, who's speaking?" I replied.

"It's Ken Merrett, Secretary of Manchester United. Are you abroad? Our manager has got a disciplinary problem and wants you to represent him?"

After a slight pause I replied, "Yeah, I'm in Istanbul for the Champions League final with my son, who is a Liverpool fan." I pinned the blame on Matthew because I didn't want to do anything to jeopardise a potential role working for United. I did the right thing, too, because Merrett replied, "If we'd known that, we might not have rung you!" before laughing out loud.

I had left the Football Association in August 2003, to set up my own football disciplinary consultancy service called

'*Football Factors*', representing individuals and clubs in the game in disciplinary proceedings when they had been charged by the football authorities. I had been highly successful – my knowledge of the rules and regulations, combined with how to circumvent them lawfully or defend those charged, was appealing to the growing number of clubs receiving letters from the FA. Some weeks earlier, before the call from Merrett, I had represented Sir Alex Ferguson's son Darren, who was playing for Wrexham at the time, in disciplinary proceedings before the Football Association of Wales who alleged that he had sworn at a referee in the tunnel in a game against Hull City, but after representing him he was cleared of the charge.

In that instance I realised all my hard work had come to fruition. It looked like I'd just landed the most famous client in football. The reality was Fergie could have afforded any representation he wanted. Money was no object. And yet he came to an ex-detective from Barnsley. It spoke volumes for the reputation I was building in the game – and was one in the eye for those who doubted me at the FA.

Bryan Flynn was the Wrexham manager and we knew each other from my time at the FA when he was a member of their first ever Video Advisory Panel. Bryan pleaded poverty on behalf of his club, explaining how they were financially stricken and asked if I could do him a favour by doing the job for nothing. However, he had no need to do that because as soon as he had mentioned the name 'Ferguson', I was doing the job come hell or high water. I realised it could be an opening to bigger things, so there was no debate to be had. I was willing to take the gamble.

The payback came at the end of the case when I gently reminded Darren I'd acted for him free of charge, so I would be grateful if he could mention my services to his dad, seeing as he seemed to always be in hot water with the FA! It seemed like Darren had kept his word and my gamble had paid off. Merrett explained that Fergie had been charged by the FA for post match comments he'd made following United's 2-1 win over Newcastle a few weeks earlier and went on, "the manager wants to see you as soon as possible." So arrangements were made for him to forward the paperwork onto me to deal with as soon as I got home.

Many Liverpool supporters will no doubt recall the chaos that ensued when trying to get home from Istanbul, and my journey home was no different. Matthew and I were eventually pushed onto a plane back to Liverpool over twelve hours after the final whistle by Turkish authorities, despite the fact we'd flown out from Manchester but I couldn't care less. It felt like I had won the lottery. The last 24 hours had been a whirlwind in more ways than one.

A few days later I drove to United's training ground at Carrington to meet the great man himself. As I sat in reception, I felt like the nervous pupil being summoned to the headmaster's office for the first time. I felt anxious and my palms were sweating on what felt like such a long walk from the reception area to his office. It was practically the furthest part of the building away from the reception area, which gave me more time to feel more jittery in advance of meeting Fergie. Upon entering the inner sanctum I was surprised how big his office was. It felt like being in the footballing equivalent of the Oval Office. Fergie was the at the very centre of the national game for two decades or more, the game literally seemed to revolve around him, not the other way round. Few people get to go inside such a hallowed room but, as it turned out, I was lucky enough to do it countless times. This was the place where the greatest manager in football history plotted and planned how to make United the most successful club of the Premier League era.

As I entered Sir Alex was sat behind a desk at the bottom end with his back to floor to ceiling glass windows overlooking the pitches so he could keep a beady eye on his players. He got up and we shook hands and he ushered me to a round table which contained piles of documents and paperwork. The office was adorned with photographs of his many successes. There was an aura about him; I suppose as a Liverpool fan it should have been like meeting Darth Vader on the Death Star but Alex quickly put me at my ease.

After a few pleasantries, in which he made a joke about me being in Istanbul to support Liverpool, he said something that made me feel ten feet tall. "I've been told all about you, Graham, and I'm told you're a fighter" he said, "I want somebody that will fight for me in front of the FA and Darren tells me that's what you do?"

Fergie's words had an immediate impact on me, making me realise what it must be like for players when it came to half-time team talks on the rare occasions United were behind. You could not fail to feel up for the fight. In those few words he got me - and I was ready for it. Let's not forget that club director Maurice Watkins, was the head of a prestigious Manchester law firm that normally handled disciplinary issues for the club, but on this occasion I had been handpicked to do the job for Sir Alex. That first meeting laid the foundations for what would go on to become a long, trusting and sometimes amusing relationship. One thing Fergie made clear from the very start was that contrary to his public persona, I was the expert on the rules, so he would follow my advice. And throughout our time working together, he was true to his word. It was safe to say, my professional life would never be the same again.

During my time at the FA I'd always maintained a good relationship with the media and had a number of journalists who'd known me from the start of my career in football who were always available to help me, but once word got out that I was working for Fergie, it felt like every journalist in the country had managed to get my mobile number! Everyone wanted to become my friend, but I realised my loyalties had to be with Sir Alex, even if it was to the frustration of my many mates in the press!

My first case with Sir Alex stemmed from his criticism of referee Neale Barry. In a post match interview with MUTV, which was subsequently picked up by the *Daily Mirror*, Fergie had criticised Barry and allegedly called his decisions '*sinister*'. What he actually said was:

> *"We should have had a clear penalty - it seems to me now that we are not going to get penalties, no matter what the circumstances. It's getting ridiculous. I'm not sure if they're instructed, but it's sinister to me. The same referee gave the most frivolous decision at Portsmouth this season, which was hardly a penalty, and turned down a penalty against Chelsea in the Carling Cup."*

The headline in the *Daily Mirror* though read, **'Fergie Launches Verbal Assault on Sinister Ref'**. The FA must have been rubbing their hands with glee when they saw the report and they were straight on the case, asking the Manchester United manager for his observations in correspondence within a couple of days. In their letter to him they specifically asked him for responses to the following points:

1. Who the '*they*' refers to in your comment, "*I'm not sure if they're instructed, but it's sinister to me*'?

2. Who you are suggesting is providing these instructions – and the nature of the instructions given?

3. What are you referring to as being '*sinister*'?

4. What was your intention when referring to incidents in your games with Portsmouth FC and Chelsea FC?

The FA also wanted his '*general observations*' regarding the comments and the implication of bias against referees in general and Neale Barry in particular. It seemed that they were trying to tie him down to avoid any 'wriggle' room. As was normal, the letter contained the standard FA warning, that any response

Fergie rant: Ridiculous.. sinister..and sensational

By SIMON BIRD: Manchester Utd 2 Newcastle 1

SIR ALEX FERGUSON hailed Wayne Rooney's latest wonder goal – then turned his anger on referee Neale Barry, calling his decisions "sinister".

Rooney capped a superb day by picking up the PFA Young Player of the Year award last night and had his boss drooling over his latest rescue act.

But Ferguson was livid that Barry had denied his side a penalty when Andy O'Brien wrestled with Alan Smith and launched a furious verbal attack on the official which could land him in trouble

with the Football Association. He said: "We should have had a clear penalty – it seems to me now that we are not going to get penalties no matter what the circumstances. It's getting ridiculous. I'm not sure if they're instructed but it's sinister to me.

"The same referee gave the most frivolous decision at Portsmouth this season, which was hardly **TURN TO PAGE 51**

FERGIE LAUNCHES VERBAL ASSAULT ON 'SINISTER' REF

FROM BACK PAGE

a penalty, and turned down a penalty against Chelsea in the Carling Cup."

England striker Rooney volleyed home from 30 yards for his 16th goal of the season and 10th in the Premiership to set United on course for their first league win in three games.

Rooney was crowned the nation's top young player at last

night's award ceremony, hours after proving it with his 56th-minute opener.

Ferguson revealed Rooney scored his 30-yard wondergoal with a dead-leg – and was on the brink of being substituted when his strike turned the game.

Ferguson added: "It was a phenomenal goal, particularly since he was injured. It was maybe 30 yards out. I was getting

ready to take him off because of his injury. But while he is on the pitch he is always a danger and that is why I kept him on.

"It was very, very important to win this one.

Ferguson had some harsh words for keeper Tim Howard, whose bad clearance led to Newcastle taking the lead. "It was a bad kick from Tim – a bit of slackness," said the manager.

FERGUSON: Ref rant

would be considered part of their assessment as to if any disciplinary action should be taken against him, and if it was, the response he submitted could be used at any associated hearing.

Initially Fergie responded himself on May 4 stating his *'surprise'* that the FA had written to him, before he turned it back on the FA by asking them the question:

> *'are we in a life where no-one can say anything, when obviously Mr Barry again denied us a penalty kick? I felt it was a clear penalty. I don't know where the pressure is coming from, the press or whoever, but since the press hullabaloo at the Arsenal game, it appears to me that it could be seen that there is pressure on referees not to give penalty kicks to Manchester United.'*

It was classic Fergie. The Arsenal game to which he was referring was the infamous showdown in October 2004 that saw Wayne Rooney win a decisive penalty following a challenge from Arsenal's Sol Campbell during a tempestuous game that brought the Gunners long unbeaten record to a halt at 49 games. Fergie later admitted that he believed his side had been *'exceptionally fortunate'* to win the penalty – and *'that sometimes teams get awarded decisions in their favour that perhaps, in hindsight, they should not have'*. The footage of that incident had been given mass media coverage at the time and Fergie believed it had been used during referee training seminars for Premier League officials - and as such this had perhaps sub-consciously impacted against his team.

Fergie went on in his response to the FA:

> *'Incidentally, my comments were not a rant, as reported in* The Mirror, *but a cool analysis of a referee after the final whistle, which is how it should be. After all, these are highly paid professionals and one would expect their decision making to be of a higher standard than what we are seeing.' Even back then, like today, it felt like refereeing standards were not good enough when it came to the big decisions.*

Needless to say, the FA didn't hold back and on May 12 they issued him with a charge letter in which they alleged his conduct was 'improper', with the FA alleging that:

> *'Making public comments implying bias against Manchester United FC by match officials and/or match officials management (or some other person or authority in a position to instruct match officials), and/or Mr Neale Barry in particular, in relation to the awarding of penalty kicks, is not proper conduct for a football manager'.*

When I eventually got back from Turkey I submitted his denial of the charge and requested a personal hearing. This included a six-page witness statement, prepared by me on the basis of my conversations with him and the advice I had given to him, along with the video tape of the MUTV interview in full.

The statement was detailed and comprehensive – 'he believed that where a manager had a genuine belief that a referee had made a wrong decision during a game, or on a consistent basis, then he, or any other manager, should be allowed to express an opinion about those decisions, and given his vast experience in the game, he was able to analyse whether or not, in his opinion, a referee had made a correct decision.' Sir Alex went on to accept that referees only got one opportunity to make a decision and decide upon that decision honestly, based on the referee's judgement at the time. Additionally, he made it clear in his statement that he didn't have anything against Barry and respected him and regarded him as a generally competent match official, as well as pointing out that Barry himself had not raised a complaint about the comments. Ferguson was also very strong in his view that he didn't believe any individual involved in the management or instruction of match officials had been involved in any agenda to show bias against any individual connected to Manchester United. He argued, correctly, that it was the FA's interpretation – as opposed to anybody else. In my opinion it was a very fair, candid and open statement, given by someone who knew the game inside out.

I knew Ferguson was right about it being someone at the FA's view of his alleged wrongdoing, because the top and bottom of it was the FA Compliance Department was acting as a reactionary group. It appeared that all they had done, as per normal, was picked up on a headline from the weekend's papers. Following the allocation of the case a decision would be made as to whether or not it warranted action being taken. In reality though at that time it was down to one person to decide – and if that person thought it was wrong then they would initiate an investigation. If you were lucky and dropped on someone who was, shall we say, a little more lenient, then no action would have been taken. It was the luck of the draw, although nowadays it's fair to say that there is a little more consistency to the issuing of disciplinary charges. But at that time it was just a "free for all" with people in the department with very little experience of the game. Rather than it being the butcher, the baker and the candlestick-maker, though, it was the accountant, lawyer and the Council Standards Officer!

In his statement to the FA Fergie had made it clear he was *'sympathetic'* to the mass media coverage and the pressure that was placed on referees, especially when refereeing at places like Old Trafford. His view was that *'he'd made an honest and just comment of opinion in answer to questions regarding incidents involving his team'*. As I have outlined, the charge, in his view, had been brought as the result of *'the interpretation of my (his) comments being misconstrued.'*

Before the main hearing took place the FA, in their normal manner and which at that time was standard practice, made it clear to us that they intended to use a previous written warning from 2004 that Ferguson had received relating to allegations that he had previously made comments suggesting incidents of bias refereeing decisions against United. A pre-hearing took place, which is a hearing normally without the person present who has been charged but just the two sides' representatives to discuss and make oral or written submissions regarding certain aspects of the evidence relied upon in the case to the panel who was going to hear the full case on a date in the future. On listening to the submissions put before them, the disciplinary panel then reaches a decision specifically in relation to those points to avoid matters being raised at the main hearing. In effect, this saves a lot of time when the main hearing takes place.

I went straight on the offensive in relation to this and argued successfully that the letter should not be allowed to be used in the proceedings. I said it was unfair to Ferguson and prejudicial to his case – and put forward the argument that the FA made a judgement at the time of the 2004 incident as to whether there was sufficient evidence to bring a charge. I submitted that they had reached a conclusion that there wasn't and that instead they had issued an informal written warning. This was normal practice when you were dealing with a matter of a minor nature, or where the evidence did not reach a level where a disciplinary panel could determine that there had been a breach of the rules. In effect, it was a fall back position that had become common, which allowed the FA to flex their muscles without going through the process of having a full disciplinary hearing. It was simply them having the last word on something. These written warnings were not entered onto the disciplinary record of a participant in the game and therefore my submission was that it was not fair to Fergie to raise an issue which the FA could not prove conclusively. They were using an underhand tactic to introduce something irrelevant to support the current ongoing proceedings and it could not be ruled out that it would not interfere with the panel's considerations of the latest charge. The panel accepted that it would be prejudicial to Fergie – and rejected the FA's attempts to include the letter.

It was first blood to me.

This put the FA in a weakened position because they could no longer refer to previous incidents. The simple fact now is that this became a precedent in future cases, so it has helped others over the years. We also applied to have the *Mirror's* article dismissed on the basis that it was not a fair representation of what he said, or in the order in which he said it. This is known in the newspaper industry as *'twirling'*. We wanted the article to be replaced with the actual MUTV interview, which gave a more balanced view of the comments. However, the commission stated they would allow the FA to use the article in the hearing, but made a proviso that they would only attach *'what weight (was) deemed appropriate'*. In effect, this was another small victory, because what they were really saying was that they acknowledged the sensationalist element to the reporting, which once again weakened the FA's stance.

We were summoned to appear at the FA's headquarters in Soho Square on July 18, 2005. The image of a 'Disciplinary Hearing' held by the FA is portrayed as some sort of formal court. However, rather than being set up like a court room, people may be disappointed to learn that actually these types of hearings are normally held in small meeting rooms in hotels or corporate boxes at football clubs, where everyone is squeezed in and on many occasions sat on top of each other. Occasionally, though, you do get your own table to work at, which is something of a luxury.

Fergie, like me, was always immaculately dressed in collar and tie whenever he was summoned to appear before the governing body. Appearance is important in these types of hearings and it's vital to portray an aura of professionalism. It was also something I had learned from my career as a detective. I recall that irrespective of how long you had been working, or how hot the weather was, or how much pressure you were under, when interviewing a witness or a suspect you never, ever, undid your top button and loosened your tie. By not doing so it gave an impression of professionalism and strength as opposed to looking untidy and shabby. It's a psychological thing I suppose but it's also about pride in your appearance. I remember one day when working at the FA, World Cup winner and Arsenal midfielder, Emmanuel

Petit turned up to a disciplinary hearing wearing cowboy boots, ripped denim jeans, a brown leather pilot type flying jacket and t-shirt which privately didn't go down well at all with the panel. It gave an impression of not being overly concerned about the proceedings – it looked like he was ready for a night on the town. It wasn't a good look! Then again Petit was always a bit of a "cool dude" with his pony tail, so I suppose it was all part of his character.

Anyway, back to Fergie - after a hearing lasting two and a half hours, in which I robustly put across the solid points made by the United manager and undermined elements of the FA's case, the panel concluded that he was guilty as charged. However they stopped short of any strong or significant penalty and gave him a warning about his future conduct. This gave a very strong indication that the disciplinary panel viewed this as only a minor breach of the rules, as opposed to the major issue the FA had tried to make it. In effect it was a victory for Ferguson, who had anticipated a large fine, and we came out of the room feeling like we'd won. Fergie was ecstatic. I recall that all he kept saying was, 'Mourinho will go mad at this' and laughing loudly. Only a few weeks earlier the Chelsea boss, who had emerged as a genuine threat to Fergie's dominance, had been fined heavily by the FA for almost the same thing. It was my first introduction to how Sir Alex could manipulate issues like this to his advantage. There was no doubt in my mind that Fergie felt he had not only got one over the FA but Mourinho as well!

As if to highlight how wound up the FA were by the verdict we were asked to wait a moment – and within minutes were then told by a member of the Compliance Department that we *'may hear from them very soon'* but did not give any further details. I had an inkling that it could well be about comments Fergie had made in the previous weekend's *Sunday Times*. My immediate reaction privately was that the FA were missing a big opportunity, because they could have done an interview with him there and then with very little preparation from ourselves.

But by not doing so it bought us plenty of time, which as I will go on to explain, we used to our maximum advantage. Fergie took it in his stride and indicated that it would be another thing for me to deal with on his behalf if anything came from them (the FA). It was also another indication that he was happy with me. I knew I had done a good job for him – with him in effect rehiring me on the spot reinforcing this view. We were off and running in a working relationship that was to have a lot more twists and turns. It stuck in my mind throughout, that he thought I was a '*fighter*'. I'd proven him right, and with the possibility of another charge heading his way, I had showed just how hard I would fight for him.

Sure enough, just as night follows day, the standard FA letter arrived a few days later. It was, as I suspected, a request for Fergie's observations about comments he'd made in the *Sunday Times*. The FA wanted another explanation, this time relating to his suggestion about Arsenal FC and...

> '*The implication that they had some form of on-going control and/influence over how the Premier League fixture list is arranged*'.

Jose Mourinho, who had only been in post at Chelsea FC for 12 months, had some weeks earlier commented on the fixture list being beneficial to Arsenal, stating they had home fixtures after European away games. Fergie had supported the comments from Mourinho in the article saying:

> '*Well, he's only taken a year to find out that Arsenal run the fixture list. I'd been complaining about that for seven years – and no one has listened. Maybe they'll listen to Mourinho more. He's dead right by the way, you look at the fixtures Arsenal have after European games – it's been going on for years.*'

On discussing it in more detail with Fergie, we decided upon a strategy to frustrate the FA and provide them with as little information as possible to start with, so as not to implicate him in any wrongdoing. We responded to the FA almost immediately with a simple three-line letter of explanation, in which we said that all he was doing was:

> *'Simply passing an opinion in respect of the comments made by another individual, on an issue which can be verified by the facts to which the issue relates'*.

In conjunction with Sir Alex I'd done my homework before sending the letter. Over a period of the previous five seasons, Arsenal had benefited from more home fixtures following a European away trip than Manchester United. I decided to keep the details of that to ourselves in case we needed to use it in the future. I didn't want to give the FA any advanced notice of the lengths we had gone to in order to prove that the points made by both Ferguson and Mourinho were correct. Our response was cold, sharp and to the point.

The FA were irked. Almost immediately they replied to say they were dissatisfied with the explanation given and wanted more detail. Then they had the cheek to try to illicit information from me personally by stating in their letter they wanted *'your (mine) own assertion that it can be verified by the facts'*. This was an elementary mistake by the FA – they had absolutely no jurisdiction over me, or power to compel me to do anything. We both found this amusing and realised that even at that early stage they were floundering. In effect, they were asking me to do their job for them against my own client!

On August 3, after Fergie had returned from a pre-season tour to Asia, I finally wrote a more detailed explanation to the FA. They had sent a further letter in which they had shown their dissatisfaction at our stance and complained that they had given Sir Alex two opportunities to provide an explanation, but a satisfactory one had not been forthcoming. In the letter they went on to add that they said they would seek to exclude any subsequent arguments he wished to rely on at any further hearings because he had not given them an explanation which they regarded as sufficient. It had become a game of cat and mouse – with the Compliance Department being the mouse. They finished the letter abruptly by saying *'your client has had ample opportunity to provide his representations in this matter'*. They were clearly now well hacked off with us!

My tactics had been to slow the whole process down because I knew the longer it went on and the nearer it got to the start of the new season, the more likely it was that no action would be taken. The FA would want a clean slate to start the new season off with. It was a tactic I used time and again to dilute the impact of sensational headlines. There is no doubt in my mind that the FA found this frustrating, but the reality of it was that there were many times when I was calling the shots, despite the fact they thought it was the other way round!

We responded in more detail but played hardball with them. The first point we raised was that the FA had not spoken in detail to Fergie after the hearing on July 18, when they'd had the opportunity to do so. In my view, they had no real answer to that. They could have struck whilst the iron was hot but failed to, thereby lengthening the whole process. As I have said, it became clear the FA felt we were becoming obstructive, but we pointed out this wasn't the case because we'd answered all correspondence within the deadlines set by them. The fact that they were giving us set deadlines just played into my hands, because I normally waited until the last minute to submit the response, even though it may have been sat on my desk for a week in advance. It was all about strategy and playing your opponent. My response to them continued and I went on the attack. I pointed out to the FA that just because Ferguson was not submitting a response that they regarded as unsatisfactory was irrelevant. As a person who was subject to one of their investigations was entitled to respond in any way he considered appropriate – and I made that clear to them that in no uncertain terms. It seemed their mindset was that if the response wasn't what they wanted, then it was unsatisfactory!

'*Simply because any response is not to the liking of the Compliance Unit is not a valid reason to impose pressure on him to answer in another way. Based upon any response he gives, we would respectfully submit that the FA will, in conjunction with other evidence on which it relies, decide and evaluate how to proceed with this matter*'.

As stated, the FA had already made a veiled yet toothless attempt to exclude any future explanation Ferguson may have given. But once again we came out fighting, telling them that such a suggestion had no basis because, as we repeated, it was open to a participant to put forward *any* response they wished. We then referred to another point raised by the FA in their latest letter in which they had said '*the fact that (Ferguson) considers that he was passing an opinion is not relevant to the impropriety or otherwise of the comments*', which to me sounded very patronising and confusing. Once again we hit back and pointed out that '*it would be for a disciplinary commission to make that judgement - and not for the Compliance department to reach a conclusion*' – which it appeared to be doing. From where we sat it appeared they were acting as judge and jury, when in fact they only had one role which was to act as evidence gatherers and then put facts before a disciplinary commission to allow a panel to decide if it was a breach of the rules.

Things were getting strained and building to a crescendo with the Compliance Unit and then we decided to throw the gauntlet down to them, fighting fire with fire. We challenged them and wrote back in a very confrontational way saying, '*if you intend making (an) allegation, you should do so formally in a charge, as opposed to stating that this passage is fact. It's nothing more than an opinion of the author of the letter. Like yourselves, Sir Alex also has his opinion which, as you'll appreciate, is not in line with your thinking*'.

This was a big gamble. We were taunting them to charge him if they thought they had enough to prove the allegation, but we felt we were on strong ground and that they could not prove that the comments about the fixture programme were improper. I would have liked to have been a fly on the wall whilst they were reading the letter for the first time, because I would hazard a good guess that the air would have been filled with numerous discourteous names about me. We then upped the ante even more and lobbed a real hand grenade into the standoff with the FA when I continued in the very same letter:

> *'Sir Alex has very serious concerns at the manner in which the FA is addressing this issue, in particular with regards to the timing of it. In short, he considers himself to be the subject of a campaign of harassment by the Compliance Unit'*.

This would have been a major sports news story if it had leaked out; that the biggest name in football was complaining that he was the subject of harassment from the FA – and would most certainly not be something the FA would want in the public domain. It would cause them huge embarrassment and be headline news – and we knew that. It was shit or bust for us.

Going back to the original issue about fixture allocations… a statistical breakdown of the fixtures in question over the previous five seasons showed that 66 per cent of Arsenal's fixtures following a European away game had either been played at home or away at teams whose stadiums were within London. This was in comparison to only 47 per cent of Manchester United's fixtures being home games or within the north-west after a European away game in the same period. On that basis we proved to the FA that the comments made by Fergie were valid. I pointed this out and then ended the letter as follows:

> *'Finally, we would wish to reiterate that it's the belief of Sir Alex that he has been subjected to an unnecessary and inappropriate inquiry, to the point of harassment. He considers that undue pressure has been placed upon him by your office to give an explanation which was of a satisfactory nature in his original reply. All he was doing*

*was giving an opinion in respect of comments made by
another individual. We are hopeful that a line can now be
drawn under the affair'.*

The following day I upped the ante, increasing the pressure
on the Compliance Department by writing directly to the then
Chief Executive of the FA, Brian Barwick. I raised our serious
concerns about the way Sir Alex was being treated and pointed
out to Barwick that during the previous season two other
high profile Premier League managers had appeared before
FA Disciplinary Commission and received substantial financial
penalties for making comments to the media, whereas Sir Alex
had only received a warning in the MUTV interview case I
described earlier. I went on referring to that case by saying:

> *'The manner in which the FA Compliance Unit presented
> the case (MUTV/Newcastle United), it was clear that
> they were painting a picture of a grave and serious breach
> of the rules which, if proven, should attract a significant
> penalty. We are advised that the fact that the commission
> took another view seems to have caused some indignation
> within the Compliance Unit.'*

The truth was that I had been tipped off from within the FA
that those in the Compliance Unit office who had brought the
MUTV interview case were not happy about how Fergie had
escaped punishment. I went on to complain to Barwick about
the way in which the *Sunday Times* news article investigation had
been conducted – and that the FA could have used its Powers of
Enquiry under the rules, to conduct an interview immediately
after the last disciplinary hearing. We also complained to Barwick
about the tone of the correspondence from the Compliance
Department and considered they had acted above and beyond
their authority, with a concern that there was an ulterior motive
behind the action. We really went for it and the letter continued;

> *'Sir Alex does feel that he's been made the subject of
> harassment from the Compliance Unit in this matter and*

had this been the comments of a lesser profile individual, then the FA would not have pursued it as vigorously as they are doing at present. He is stopping short of making an official complaint into the manner in which this matter is being dealt with. However, through us, he requests that you personally take time to review the situation, so that we can all attempt to bring this matter to a swift conclusion without the need for proceedings to be initiated.'

The beauty of it was that Ferguson could get on with preparing for the new season, whilst I tackled the FA. He could just sit back and let me get on with it and watch the fallout from afar. It was a perfect scenario for both of us.

Within days Barwick responded and fudged the issue, saying it was, *'inappropriate'* for him to become involved in the matter, although he did make a point that he had *'every confidence in their (the Compliance Department's) integrity and professionalism'*. I'm sure he had much more confidence in them than Fergie and I. He passed the letter to the FA's Director of Governance, Jonathan Hall, to deal with. Barwick clearly didn't want to get involved in something that was becoming very messy and had the potential to cause major embarrassment to the FA. I like Brian and have always got on well with him but on this occasion I felt that he had bottled it and passed the buck. He should have got hold of the situation and killed it dead. It was left to Hall to respond with a comprehensive three page letter in which he made several explanations as to why he believed the Compliance Unit had dealt with the issue in a correct way. One interesting point was he wanted me to identify who had advised me of the cause of "indignation" within the Compliance Unit? He wanted me to *'out'* my source within the FA! As a former detective one of the golden rules is that you never identify your sources – in the same way as a journalist operates. I simply ignored his request and my source remained confidential.

Hall denied that Fergie had been the subject of harassment by the Compliance Unit. Of course he would say that. But we had made our point. We had muddied the waters sufficiently to cause the FA some problems.

On August 15 the Compliance Unit wrote to us again. After two pages of claim and counterclaim trying to defend their position regarding the way in which they'd conducted the investigation, they concluded the letter as follows:

> *'Having given due considering to the explanations provided, and to the above issues, the FA has decided not to pursue formal disciplinary action against Sir Alex Ferguson.'*

It was job done. The tactics had worked. I'd fought in the way Fergie had wanted me to. He was elated with the outcome, and in football terms the score was probably about 4-0 in our favour, but it was clear that we'd poked the bear in our dealings with the Compliance Unit.

More battles lay ahead...

2 - PENALTIES AND PASSION

ON THE BACK OF THE SUCCESS I had with Fergie, Manchester United offered me a twelve month contract to work for them on a consultancy basis, dealing with all their disciplinary issues. I met with David Gill, the then CEO at United, and it didn't take that long to reach an agreement. They were more than happy with the work I'd done for them, and I recognised what a good move it would be for me to be associated with a club of United's stature. I'm sure that they wouldn't have agreed to a contract without taking soundings off Sir Alex and, like he'd said to me at our first meeting, I'd fought for him every inch of the way in what was a relatively successful period in terms of the disciplinary cases I'd handled for him. However, as the relationship with the club developed, the contract was renegotiated into an additional three years and I walked out of Old Trafford with a new agreement worth in excess of £50k. I was living the dream; working for the highest profile club and manager in the world – and getting paid well for doing it.

It wasn't long before I was representing Fergie again. Following a Premier League game between United and Everton at Old Trafford on December 11, 2005, Fergie had criticised referee Rob Styles for turning down a penalty appeal in the draw. Once again it was the *Daily Mirror* who ran a back page splash with the headline **'GIVE IT A REST FERGIE'**. The article claimed that Fergie had *'pointed the finger at the official after he had waved aside the spot kick'* following a challenge in the Everton penalty area. In his post match interview Fergie said, *"I don't know if it was a penalty. I wasn't in a position to tell, but there's no way Rob Styles was ever going to give us a penalty."* The result left United 12 points behind Chelsea in the title race, and it was clear it had damaged their chances of claiming their first Premier

League title since the 2003 season.

Once again, as sure as night follows day, the now standard and expected letter arrived from the FA signed by former Council Standards Officer Jennie Pyle (now Kennedy), who was now a compliance officer at the FA, requesting Fergie's observations. However despite the letter being marked 'Strictly Private and Confidential' it didn't take long for the *Daily Mail* to run an exclusive story stating that the FA had written to Fergie asking him to explain himself. As usual we went straight on the attack, immediately raising the issue that the FA's letter had stated it was private and confidential correspondence yet details of it had appeared in a national newspaper and included an official comment from an FA spokesman about the matter!

In our reply to the FA we put forward the argument that this was tabloid sensationalism – and that Fergie did not regard the comments as a personal attack upon Styles. Some may find this incredulous on the face of it, but we had evidence that showed Fergie was perfectly within his rights to say what he had said. We argued that, as a manager of a Premier League team it was part and parcel of his role to monitor the performance of referees and in particular those who were due to officiate in games involving his team. This was something the FA had not anticipated – and the statistics in our possession backed up Fergie's comments.

Given his attention to detail, even before the game was played Fergie had done an analysis on Styles' performances and noted that he had not awarded a penalty kick in any of the 12 Premier League fixtures he'd officiated that season, up to the Everton game. We attached a schedule which showed that Styles was one of two only referees on the elite list not to have awarded a penalty up to that time (the other being Martin Atkinson). It was a statistic the FA could not counter and I'm sure it would have gone down like a lead balloon in the Compliance Office. They would have known that as soon as that statistic was pointed out that their case was all but dead in the water.

Another telling point was that Fergie had acknowledged in

the article that even he couldn't say whether or not the incident merited the awarding of a penalty, due to his position in the dug-out. We put forward that, in our view, if this was the case it followed that he was not being critical of the referee for not awarding his side a penalty kick, because he admitted that he couldn't see if it was the correct decision or not, and that the FA had misinterpreted what he'd said. How could he be critical of the non-awarding of a penalty when even he couldn't see it? It seemed the FA were looking to put their own spin on the comments, but we had other ideas.

The FA responded and spent more time on trying to give some general excuse about how the article had managed to appear in a newspaper, while the important part of the letter warranted no more than a few lines. Once again they took no action against Fergie and it was another success for both him and me. We had outfoxed them once again. It must have been galling for the FA to once again miss out on the chance to nail the main man!

A month later, in the Manchester derby, Cristiano Ronaldo was sent off following a challenge on Andy Cole. I was asked to submit an appeal against the red card on his behalf. In his statement Ronaldo said the referee had not told him why he was being sent off but claimed he had semi-control of the ball, although it was running away from him and in his enthusiasm to reach it he made a stretching lunge across the front of his opponent, as opposed to at him. In Ronaldo's view that meant he only had one intention – to try and ensure he kept possession. It seemed a reasonable argument to put forward. A photograph of the incident was submitted in which Cristiano could clearly be seen looking at the ball. However, this cut no ice with the disciplinary panel reviewing the incident and they dismissed his appeal. This meant he had to serve a three game suspension which put him out of the following week's game against Liverpool at Old Trafford, which led to me once again being called upon by United to act on behalf of Gary Neville.

I had been at the game as a Liverpool season ticket holder and was sick to the pit of my stomach when a Rio Ferdinand header in injury time secured a 1-0 win for the home team. However, the game became more famous for the reaction of United full back Neville, who was in the area of the field near to where the travelling Liverpool fans were housed when they ball went in and ran back 60 yards towards them, pumping his fists and kissing the United badge on his shirt! Most football followers will remember it. It was raw emotion and passion that can only be experienced by a professional sports person, especially in such a highly-charged game. Any last minute winner in such a high profile game would bring out such emotion, especially for someone like Neville who it's fair to say is United through and through.

But the FA didn't care less for the raw emotion and quickly charged him with improper conduct. This is what happens when you get lawyers, ex-accountants, and as I've mentioned before, former Council Standard Officers in charge of professional football. They don't see the emotion of the instance. In my day at the FA, this would have warranted a gentle letter to Neville reminding him of his responsibilities whereby actions may cause an adverse reaction from opposition supporters, particularly in such a powder keg game well known for its intensity. And that would have been the end of the matter. To me it was simple common sense. But the new breed of Compliance Officer only seemed able to see black or white, with no grey in between.

The charge alleged that *the "manner in which Neville reacted to United's goal constituted improper conduct"* and they relied on a video and letter from Greater Manchester Police. The police did Neville no favours as they described, in their report, his behaviour as being *'obscene'* and that he goaded the Liverpool supporters. However, following the game there was some disorder outside the stadium and the police acknowledged that *"a late goal in a closely contested football match is often the precursor to some disorder'*. In effect they were contradicting themselves in relation to Neville's conduct because it was as if they were trying to blame him for the trouble that occurred after the game, which given the history of this fixture was in my view nonsense. They were trying to make Neville the scapegoat. Anyone who has attended a United/Liverpool fixture, whether it be at Old Trafford or Anfield, will tell you that there is no love lost between the supporters and disorder outside the stadium has occurred on many occasions over the years.

At the original hearing, in which Neville opted to represent himself, the commission found him guilty and fined him £5,000 as well as warning him to his future conduct but Neville wanted to appeal the decision, so I was asked to conduct it on his behalf. I enjoyed working with Gary. I found him to be an honourable and passionate man who was willing to stick his head above the parapet in the defence of others, as he has shown in recent times with his barracking and criticism of the current Tory Government. He is principled, with strong views. Like me, he has a strong personality and, if I'm being honest, I don't think our views on politics are too far apart. He's as combative off the field as he was on it and I like that in a person, someone willing to go that extra mile, someone willing to fight and take on the authorities when they feel they are being wronged. So it's fair to say that my experience of working with Gary registered as one of my more enjoyable experiences in the game.

In order to prepare Gary for his original disciplinary hearing I'd given him a briefing document, and we had also submitted a video tape of Premier League players kissing their badge following the scoring of goals. It was a who's who of big name stars, with clips in high profile games, such as the Merseyside and North London derby matches involving the likes of Steven Gerrard, Thierry Henry, Cristiano Ronaldo, Wayne Rooney, Robbie Fowler, Frank Lampard and Alan Smith. At Gary's original hearing the panel dismissed the video, claiming that they showed clips of players celebrating in front of their own supporters – once again this was a typically blinkered view which was subsequently overturned.

In accordance with FA rules, we had to serve the appeal documents on the FA on or before March 3 that year, and under the Regulations for Football Association Appeals, the FA then had 21 days to respond and submit their observations to our document and outline their arguments in writing in advance of any hearing as to why the charge should be upheld. This meant that they should have responded by March 24. However the FA failed to submit their response to the appeal on time. This was an unexpected turn of events and not something you'd expect from an organisation that can afford the best legal advice and had a huge number of well-paid professionals working on legal and disciplinary issues for them.

As would be expected I waited until the expiry of the date that the appeal should have been submitted and several days later raised it with the FA. I pointed out that they had failed to comply with their own regulations – and I sought to argue that the FA should be barred from serving a written response to the Appeal Board as they were out of time. That would mean that they could not argue against the appeal.

My view was that because of the FA's failure to submit a reply to our appeal, then the appeal should be upheld by reason of the FA's failure to comply with the relevant procedural requirements. The FA eventually served a response on March 27, four days after the deadline, and then, inexplicably, tried to claim that it had been served in time! The only thing I can think of is that they were trying to change the world calendar for their own benefit!

At the appeal hearing the FA asked the Chairman of the Appeal Board to use his discretion on the issue. Unsurprisingly the Appeal Board backed the FA. To me it seemed that it was one rule for them and another for everybody else, which is a generally held view within the game. There is no doubt in my mind that had we served the appeal notice outside of the required deadline, the FA would not have allowed the appeal.

But because it was the other way round, in my opinion they got favourable treatment.

The Appeal Board ruled it was *'an administrative oversight'*, however – that's some oversight when you consider that it was relating to one of the major disciplinary stories of that season. In my opinion, the Appeal Board and the FA simply didn't want to be seen to be allowing Neville to slip through the net. And whilst it was chaired by a barrister, the two wing men were very much in the FA camp, due to their association with the organisation.

In their written reasons the original disciplinary commission had concluded that Neville's conduct was *"provocative"*. But in my submission I urged the Board to break down each physical element of Neville's celebration. The Appeal Board agreed that when the actions of Neville were broken down, such as running to the general area of the pitch and other physical aspects of the celebration, they agreed that on their own they were not provocative or improper. However the problem we had was that the whole incident had to be seen in context and they felt that the celebration could not be seen in isolation, in the way we had broken it down. They concluded that the celebration, when taken collectively, was provocative and improper, so they dismissed Neville's appeal.

There was a twist to the tale however because in relation to the video tape that we had submitted at the original disciplinary hearing, as I said earlier the commission had concluded that the majority of those celebrations appeared to have been directed at their own supporters. We submitted that this was factually incorrect and that most celebrations were in front of visiting supporters – and the video tape clearly showed that. The Board agreed with our submission and concluded that the original disciplinary commission had misinterpreted that part of the evidence. Who knows if the original disciplinary panel had taken the view that the video was supportive of Gary's case then they may have reached a different view altogether because we had shown that no action was taken against any of the players in the video. Put simply, if that was the case then how could they have justified in finding Neville guilty? It's another anomaly of the FA disciplinary system.

I was disappointed at the outcome, and so was Gary. I felt that we'd been stitched up, particularly in relation to the FA missing the date of when their response had to be submitted. I wish that I could have argued more strongly but in reality the police report had caused difficulties for us and when the Appeal Board backed the FA for breaking their own regulations, we were always fighting a losing battle.

In late 2007 the FA finally had some minor success with the United boss but in true Fergie fashion he didn't give them an inch. We decided not to attend the disciplinary hearing in question, and this was quite deliberate following our discussions about the case. He and I didn't want to give them the satisfaction of seeing him sat before them while his penalty was dished out, like a naughty schoolboy in the headmaster's office.

On November 24, 2007 United had lost a game against Bolton at the Reebok Stadium courtesy of a first half goal from Nicolas Anelka. But Fergie wasn't happy with the first half performance of referee Mark Clattenburg who reported him to the FA following an exchange in the tunnel between the pair. Any referee knows that if you report Sir Alex Ferguson, given his stature in the game, it was going to attract press attention, something that Clattenburg seemed to revel in over the years. The fact that it was in the tunnel and out of sight of the public is where it should have stayed. Over the years I've seen many incidents and heard many comments directed at match officials in the tunnel area. Referees need to have thick skins when emotions are running high at half time or full time and there is just general complaining. There is no reason to flag it up with the FA unless it's a matter of the utmost seriousness or violence.

The football authorities themselves even recognise that emotions are running high at the end of games, because a manager is not allowed to visit the referee for a set period of time after a game has ended and is not allowed in the referee's room at half time unless summoned there. Some referees just man-manage situations such as this and deal with it at the time and nothing else is heard of it, while others thrive on submitting reports to the authorities. It's just the luck of the draw as to who you get. Working in football is a rough and tumble environment where industrial language is constantly used, so unfortunately many conversations are littered with expletives which can sound damning when read out in the cold light of day in a tribunal. That's not because the individual is being nasty – it's just the way participants in the game express themselves. I'm as guilty as anyone for using such language at football matches.

Clattenburg claimed that, once they were in the privacy of the tunnel, Fergie had *"pointed directly at him"* and shouted *"you're a fucking disgrace,"* an accusation he then repeated. In response Clattenburg told Ferguson that he wouldn't be allowed to take up his position in the technical area and would be reported to the FA, to which Fergie allegedly replied, *"You can't do anything, this is in the fucking tunnel."* Ferguson was of course wrong in that assumption, because the referee can act in such circumstances, but as I've said sometimes, it's just better to leave things there and move on. As is normal in these cases, the referee was fully backed up by his assistants and fourth official, whose written reports were almost identical. Some may wonder how this happens – how can four versions of the same incident be identical? From my detective days, if you have four witnesses to an event or incident then you get four slightly different versions, which makes it more authentic because people are giving their own interpretation of what they saw or heard. It's always mystified me as to why the officials generally have identical reports; if you were cynical, you may think they have got their stories straight at the end of the game in the privacy of the referees changing room...

It took just two days for the FA letter to arrive, and Fergie was charged with using abusive language to the referee. What people don't know is that Fergie told me that he'd actually also told Clattenburg that he *"had got a fucking fat arse and couldn't run"*. Clattenburg was well known around the game for his vanity, so it's little surprise that this didn't get mentioned, assuming he actually heard it.

On this occasion, my advice to Sir Alex was that there was little chance of him escaping any penalty from the FA and I told him it was in his interests to admit the charge to try to get his punishment reduced. He did this, but not without putting a volley across the FA's bows about the standard of Clattenburg's refereeing.

As part of our preparation for his response we obtained a copy of the match assessor's report. This is a report on the performance of the referee at every game. Of course, the old boys' network went into overdrive. It was from former Premier League referee and fellow Geordie Alan Wilkie, who had been assessing Clattenburg that day. Wilkie was highly critical of the Manchester United team and claimed that both sides *"disliked each other"*. What that had got to do with the performance of the referee, I've no idea but I suppose the assessor needed to keep themselves in a job. In his report Wilkie accused Fergie of *"attempting to employ bullying tactics by offering a completely unjustified foul-mouthed volley of abuse."* So there you have it. Because Sir Alex was at his vociferous best on the touchline, it was easier to have him sat in the Directors Box in the second half. As I said earlier, some referees just deal with matters like this in the privacy of the tunnel, while others like to flex their muscles. The report also outlined a number of critical incidents in which Wilkie supported Clattenburg in respect of not awarding penalties to United - yes that old chestnut!

In his written response to the FA Fergie outlined his concerns about the performance of the match referee and that *"his players had not been protected by him in his application of the laws of the game."* Fergie also pointed out that the same referee had performed in a similar vein at the Merseyside derby some weeks earlier. His response also outlined his foresight in terms of the way the game was going because he indicated, as he always has done, his support for the implementation of full-time referees into the game. Fergie being Fergie, though, he had used his contacts to find out other information on the referee's training schedules, and discovered that the so-called 'full-time' referees were only receiving one day's training per week and at that time were allowed to continue in other employment. So in reality, in his view, they were not full-time. Things have changed since then but he was bang on the money with that comment at the time.

My letter, submitted on his behalf following his approval, ended with an apology from Fergie, "on reflection, Sir Alex regrets his emotional outburst which led to the issuing of this charge and extends his apologies for his conduct." He had to take the two-match touchline ban and £5k fine on the chin, which was still below the recommended penalty of three games. Once again Fergie had played the FA, because we'd recognised that being humble and apologising would reduce the punishment. It must have felt like some sort of moral victory, considering all the FA's previous failures to nail Ferguson. But a much more interesting case, which would have huge implications for the FA and their credibility involving Fergie, was to come along much later in our relationship which also involved comments about a referee's performance.

If ever there was a case that showed my worth to Manchester United and Fergie, it was the one which hit the headlines following United's shock 1-0 FA Cup quarter final defeat to Portsmouth at Old Trafford on March 8, 2008. It was a case which caused huge upset inside the FA, following a disciplinary hearing resulting in both Fergie and his assistant Carlos Queiroz being cleared following a lengthy disciplinary process.

Following the game Fergie was interviewed by Sky Sports and Queiroz by the BBC, during the interviews they both passed comment on the performance of the match referee, Martin Atkinson. Within days the standard letter with an accompanying transcript of the interviews from the former Council Standards Officer arrived, asking both of them to explain their comments. The correspondence suggested both of them were questioning the integrity of the officials and alleging bias. It would be fair to say, though, that the transcript of Queiroz's interview in particular was littered with mistakes and appeared to have been prepared in a rush. It was of very poor quality.

United's defeat had left Fergie and Queiroz both seething. The game had seen United spurn chance after chance and Atkinson denied them what the BBC described as a 'clear penalty' in the 6th minute when Sylvain Distin brought down Cristiano Ronaldo to leave Fergie fuming. United went out to a late penalty that also saw Tomas Kuszczak dismissed.

So, once again, and simply to delay the process and stall for time so as to frustrate the FA's enquiry, we wrote to the FA on behalf of both men and asked them to be more specific as to which of the comments had caused them concern. The interviews were quite long, so we needed to know which part had upset them so much. The reason we did this was to tie the FA down to a particular phrase or sentence so that there was no wriggle room for them should disciplinary proceedings be taken.

In respect of Fergie, the FA wanted observations about the following comment from him:

> "I think the game was decided when Ronaldo's penalty was refused. I think that decided it. I think that gave them great confidence to hang on, knowing the referee was on their side. The referee's performance (Martin Atkinson), well, Keith Hackett (Referee General Manager for the Premier League), I think is in a nice comfortable position up in his eyrie. And does nothing really. I don't think

he makes a contribution to the refereeing performances in our country and I think that has to be addressed. I think he's not doing his job properly. That guy'll go and referee a game next week, no problem. You see it time and time again, his favourites always get the games - and I think that's a disappointing factor."

The FA had also, in the interim period, uncovered a further interview with MUTV and wanted more observations on the following comments from the United Manager;

"I think Keith Hackett's got a lot to answer for in this country. I don't think he's doing his job properly. He's got his favourites, as everyone knows. Look at the referees we get away from home: Steve Bennett, Mark Clattenburg, Dowd, all these people - never get them at home, always away from home and I think that tells you everything about him. I think he's not doing his job properly and he has to be assessed - just like everyone else has to be assessed. I'm assessed as a manager, players are assessed, referees should be assessed today properly, by the right people. He (Atkinson) will referee next week, no problem. That performance today should not be accepted by our game."

In his interview, Queiroz had continued the theme saying:

"...and unfortunately the referee, it is a, it is a disgrace. This, this, this referees, they need to, someone, they call attention. It is really piteous, I feel sorry that the, the game does move to a situation that the referees, they, they also deserve red cards. This, this referee today, he deserved that somebody come inside the pitch after five minutes, give him a red card and out him out of the game. That's, at the end of the day, my opinion about the, the, this robber today. What they are expect when they elbow the player to, to the, the line and out him out, that, he becomes a saint after that? I mean, if that's an accident, that's why the Taylor's

of the game, they can survive and some of the best players,
they are out of the game. But when we cannot accept it, is
referees that they can only be able to watch the one side.
That cannot happen. This is not acceptable in the game."

We responded to the FA in writing. In Fergie's reply he
stated that he believed there had to be a degree of free speech
in respect of unacceptable performances from professionals in
all sectors of the football industry where issues of concern, in
his opinion, required highlighting. I actually agree with that
– and if experienced professionals are not allowed to do that,
then in effect it becomes a situation akin to a police state where
nobody is allowed to make any criticism towards the powers
that be. Ferguson also said that he did not question the integrity
of any individual, and that the comments should be taken in
conjunction with the manner of defeat in a prestigious cup
competition.

In relation to Queiroz, we instantly stated that there was an
inaccuracy in the translation, in particular when they claimed
Queiroz had used the quote *"this robber today"* about the referee.
We submitted that what he actually said was *"his job today"*. This
actually made more sense, even taking into account his restricted
pronunciation of the English language.

In effect the quote from Queiroz should have read, *"that's,*
at the end of the day, my opinion about the, the, his job today". This
placed an entirely different emphasis on his comments and
their meaning. We also pointed out that in relation to the player
(Taylor), he was referring to Martin Taylor of Birmingham City
(who had been involved in a challenge when the Arsenal striker,
Eduardo, had received a seriously broken leg in a tackle). The FA
had not initiated any disciplinary action against Arsenal Manager
Arsene Wenger, who had made similar comments in relation to
what Queiroz had said about Taylor.

The FA wasted no time. They obviously thought they had
got Ferguson and Queiroz bang to rights. On April 2 they issued
improper conduct charges against both of them and alleged that

they had called into question the integrity, or implied bias, on the part of match referee Martin Atkinson and General Manager of PGMOB Keith Hackett. I think the FA saw this as a real opportunity to make examples of both of them, but as it turned out, they were the ones who would end up with one hell of a bloody nose!

The hearing was held on May 28, 2008 at the FA's Soho Square headquarters in Central London, where a panel, including an independent barrister, sat in judgement on the United duo. We submitted detailed witness statements in advance of the hearing from both men and also included some supporting evidence. One item was a copy of a recent Manchester United programme in which, in his manager's column, Ferguson wrote:

> *"...the other point I would like to make on the refereeing front is that, while I've questioned the ability of some referees, I've never doubted their integrity. Yes, I've contributed to putting them under pressure, but that's for the protection of my players. Graham Poll wrote critically of me recently, but he can be assured that while there will undoubtedly continue to be criticism of officials' decision making, I don't think there is a manager in the game who would question their integrity. Our game is thankfully free of that kind of corruption."*

This couldn't have been published at a better time and was highly supportive of the defence we were putting forward that nobody's integrity was being questioned, and Ferguson had re-emphasised his views on such issues in a public column. To my mind it was exceptionally good evidence in support of Fergie and Queiroz as he had made clear his views in a separate, unsolicited environment that he would never question the integrity of referees.

The other thing that we decided to concentrate on in our defence of the charges was the specific definitions of the word *"integrity"* and *"bias"* which the FA had used in their charge against the pair. According to the dictionary, *"integrity"* was defined as *"soundness of moral character and honesty"* and *"bias"* was *"to cause partiality or favouritism"*. In my view the FA could not show that Fergie and Queiroz had acted in a manner which was in keeping with the specific definitions.

We had also submitted newspaper reports showing relatively recent quotes from participants in the game, including the then Sunderland manager Roy Keane, Middlesbrough player George Boateng, (where he had used the term *"the referee had robbed them"*), Walsall defender Anthony Gerrard, West Brom Manager Bryan Robson, Stoke City boss Tony Pulis, Huddersfield boss Andy Ritchie, Everton manager David Moyes and then West Ham manager Alan Curbishley, who had all made highly critical and damning comments about referees and their management, but the FA had failed to take any action at all against any of them.

We argued successfully that the comments made by those individuals were of the same level, or worse, than those made by Fergie and Queiroz. The theme continued that it appeared to be one rule for one and one rule for the rest. There appeared to be no balanced consistency from the FA Compliance Department. They just seemed to take action against whoever took their fancy; the bigger the name the better, and were reactive to media reports, as opposed to being pro active in disciplinary terms. It's a problem that has been consistent for a number of years.

Both Fergie and Queiroz gave oral evidence and were hugely impressive. It then came to the final submission, which I had to make to the panel before they considered their judgement on the issue. It was important that the first point the panel had to consider in my view was, had Queiroz used the word *"robber"*? Once they had decided that, they could then use their interpretation into the quote and deliberate on it from that point. And as I said earlier, depending on what they decided significantly altered the emphasis of the spoken words. We also submitted that the FA's transcript was littered with mistakes and that strengthened Queiroz's argument.

It was also my view that what the question the panel had to ask themselves and consider was:

> *"Did the comments in respect of Martin Atkinson and/ or Keith Hackett, question their integrity and/or, did the comments in respect of Atkinson imply bias in his capacity as a match referee in the fixture between United and Portsmouth specifically?"*

I had asked the FA to be specific as to the comments that caused them concern at the start of the process and they played straight into my hands. I had tied them down to a very narrow margin of what they claimed was 'inappropriate'. That was a mistake by them. They should have concentrated more on the generalisation of what was being suggested.

My next move was to put to the panel that they were not deliberating on whether the comments were improper, in that they were critical of referees generally, but as I said, the charge specifically related to integrity and bias in this particular game – and that the panel had to look at the totality of the interviews, rather than allowing the FA to use selected and cherry-picked pieces. And that by reading and watching the full interviews, then it all came into perspective. As I pointed out, we played strongly on the definition of the word "*integrity*" and in layman terms it's meaning was quite simply, "honesty". As I put it, by definition, the FA were alleging that Ferguson and Queiroz had questioned the honesty of Martin Atkinson in the game and the evidence was overwhelming that they had not. They may have been critical of his performance generally, but they never questioned his honesty. The FA could not – and did not – produce any evidence to back up that allegation. It was pretty poor from them in such a high profile case.

Interestingly there was a clue to the FA's desperation about proving guilt against the two of them about a week before the hearing. The FA had, at a late stage, referred to various newspaper columns to try to reinforce their case, including one from the *Sunday Telegraph*, regarding the use of the term *"robber"* by Queiroz. To negate this, I approached journalist Patrick Barclay, who was the author of one of the articles and worked for the *Sunday Telegraph*, and he was very happy to submit a letter in support of Queiroz and the interpretation of his comments. This was only possible because of long standing relationships with journalists and showed the benefit of developing such types of relationships with the media, so that, in times of necessity, favours could be called upon.

I also made a big play of the media reports and that, in any regulatory system, there had to be a fair and equitable one adopted. We had highlighted issues of a more serious nature, where no action had been taken by the FA. Quite simply, we put forward that if the comments in those articles were not deemed to be improper, then how could the comments of my clients be dealt with differently?

After what seemed like an age, the panel gave their verdict – the charges against both men were not proved, and the case was dismissed. The written reasons produced later by the Appeal Board were dynamite and stated that they were:

> *"...not persuaded that the relevant comments were sensibly capable of being said to call into question the honesty of the officials and that the real issue, on the totality of the evidence heard, was whether the words used by either by Fergie or Queiroz, had implied bias".*

And they unanimously concluded that "they were not satisfied that the standard of proof had been reached". The Commission also concluded that when seen in both isolation and collectively, the comments made by Fergie were not of a kind that could be said to improperly question the integrity of officials or apply bias. The same followed in respect of his comments about Keith Hackett. Importantly, in respect of Queiroz, as we had said from the start, he'd not used the word *"robber"* and the Commission agreed with us.

In reality this was a stunning victory against the FA, and in the days that followed I was contacted by a number of internal FA sources who told me that it was as if a "nuclear bomb" had gone off inside Soho Square, where there were inquests into how the FA had failed to prove the charge. I was told that the then Chairman of the FA, Lord Triesman, was particularly unimpressed – which made the victory all the sweeter.

The fact that the Compliance Department had gone into meltdown over the outcome didn't bother me one bit. I revelled in their misfortune. In all honesty, I made hay while the sun shone and quickly published and distributed a newsletter from *Football Factors* with all the media headlines, and sent it to every club in an effort to promote my business. We wanted to publicise our fantastic victory over the FA as far and wide as we possibly could. The newspaper headlines were advertising that money couldn't buy.

Ferguson and Queiroz had left the hearing early, before the final submissions were made, as they had a flight back to Manchester to catch. When I came out of the hearing I phoned Fergie. He was obviously up in the air, so I left him a message saying he had been cleared. He rang me back as soon as he'd landed and he was laughing, his first words to me were "Well I didn't expect that". I have to say, neither did I. He thanked me and said he would be in touch the next time he was in trouble. I felt that come what may, despite the strong defence they had, the FA would make sure that they eventually got Fergie, but sometimes you get the rub of the green – and we got it that day. In all the time I have been involved in football disciplinary representation, this was one of my finest hours.

Such was the concern within Soho Square that on 13 June, 2008, the FA issued their own press release outlining the reasons why they did not intend to appeal against the decisions in the case. They had even gone to the extreme of taking external legal advice on the issue, but still found they had no credible grounds to appeal. They ended the press release with the words:

> *"In light of the Commission's decision we will review the process by which we address inappropriate media comments made about match officials by participants in the game".*

That was one hell of an admission in my view. They recognised that they'd been well and truly beaten, but it was obvious that the battle-lines had been redrawn and that the FA would continue to pursue Fergie. They had been chasing him for a number of years now while I'd been representing him, but they had still not really laid a glove on him, never mind delivered a knock out blow. However the law of averages suggested that there would come a time when he would have to one on the chin.

3 - "I'M SORRY..."

RIO FERDINAND WAS ONE of the greatest players of his generation following a stellar career with both England and United, but he will also be forever synonymous with a missed drugs test that led to an eight month ban from football in 2003. After this return to the game Ferdinand went on to become one of those most regularly targeted by the control body that governs doping control in sport, United Kingdom Anti-Doping (UKAD), not only at games but also in his personal life as part of the penalty imposed against him. He was always fully compliant in respect of these random tests and never gave any further cause for concern.

However in August 2008, following a game between United and Newcastle United at Old Trafford, an incident occurred which has been kept under wraps... until now. If it had become public knowledge at the time, it would have caused sensational headlines and left Ferdinand in danger of becoming infamous for all the wrong reasons. It may even have ended his career.

The "In Competition Testing Programme" is a very simple process. This is how it works. Shortly after half time Doping Control Officers (DCOs) will turn up at a stadium where a game is being played. This happens several times a season at each professional club. An official from both clubs is summoned to the tunnel and changing room area where the independent and random drawing of two players' names from each team takes place from those players on the team sheet for drug testing immediately after the final whistle. As soon as the match is finished the DCO's wait in the tunnel and, as the selected players leave the pitch, they immediately isolate them and inform them of their selection and escort them straight to the doping control room. The players would be unaware that they had been selected until they'd left the pitch.

Those chosen wouldn't be allowed to go anywhere but the control room for fear of potential contamination. They wouldn't even be allowed in the dressing room for a post match team talk from the manager. These things normally go very smoothly, but most players find them very frustrating for a number of reasons, not least being unable to join up with their team mates in the dressing room to celebrate a victory or have an inquest into a defeat, then there is the common problem of struggling to pass urine due to dehydration. Sometimes it can be a very long process!

On this occasion Ferdinand had been randomly picked out to be tested, but he was angry because United had been held to a 1-1 draw and the team had not performed well. What happened next was the subject of an FA investigation.

The DCO reported that Ferdinand had come off the pitch and, when told to report to the doping control room, he had instead gone to the home dressing room where he sat down and got a drink. Almost immediately the team doctor went into the dressing room and took him back out to the doping control room. That in itself was a minor breach of the rules, but the DCO also claimed that, as he came down the tunnel he'd told Ferdinand to report for the test immediately and the defender had replied, *"Oh fucking hell, not another fucking drug test,"* He observed that Ferdinand wasn't in a good mood which was *"apparent from his body language and facial expressions"*, and one would assume that was because of the team's performance and subsequent result.

Furthermore, the DCO also claimed that en-route to the testing room, which was beyond the United changing room, as they reached the dressing room door, Ferdinand had said, *"I'm going in here first, you can fucking well wait here"*, before going in. Although Rio subsequently countered this by later saying he'd told the DCO to join him in the dressing room while he got a drink, the DCO refused to do so in accordance with procedures.

On the other side of the coin however the DCO in his

report conceded that Ferdinand was *"perfectly compliant"* with the testing procedure and had *"apologised for his earlier behaviour"* when he re-joined him. But the upshot was that the FA were quickly informed and once again they immediately wrote to Ferdinand stating that they wanted to interview him about it.

United got in touch and asked me to help. The first thing I did was to write to the FA to ask for advanced disclosure of the drug testing team's report so that we could see the specific account of the DCO before the interview, meaning Rio was in a position to give a full and open explanation. However the FA wrote back and refused to give this because, in their words, *"they wished to give Mr Ferdinand the opportunity to provide his recollection of the incident, without reference to the doping controlling officer's version of events."* In my view this was the FA being obstructive and awkward, as there was no valid reason as to why they would wish to withhold those reports other than attempting to ambush Ferdinand with their line of questioning in an interview. They were very "cloak and dagger" about it, when all Rio wanted to do was to draw a line under the matter and be as open and honest as he could with them. There was never any chance that he was going to deny what had occurred. It seemed a very bizarre stance for the FA to take. The silly thing is that if Rio had decided not to make any comment in any interview, the FA would have had to disclose what was being alleged and he could then have put across his version of events. It seemed a pretty petty decision by the FA in my opinion.

A date was set for the meeting and the interview took place at United's Carrington training ground. In the room were myself, Rio, the then Club Secretary Ken Ramsden and two employees from the FA's Compliance Department. My immediate opinion of this incident – and it never changed – was that all that had happened was Ferdinand had come off the pitch in an emotional and frustrated state and those emotions had got the better of him. There was nothing sinister in the incident, other than the fact he'd not gone straight to the doping control room. I understand the DCO had to do his job, but nobody seemed to consider the player's state of mind. Although you can imagine the furore in the press if this had come out at the time!

Fortunately, after an anxious wait, the FA accepted Rio's explanation and wrote to him advising that while they considered his conduct to be in breach of regulations, they decided not to bring formal disciplinary proceedings against him. In my opinion this was the correct course of action and, for once, the FA used common sense, as opposed to trying to flex their muscles.

At the time United kept the story within a very close circle of people at the club, but even now I'm still amazed it never leaked out. In fairness to Rio he dealt with this in a very mature way and was fully cooperative throughout the investigation process. After all, he had absolutely nothing to hide and once again, as in the Gary Neville case, this highlights the emotional highs and lows that players have to go through during and after games, where their actions are more adrenalin-filled than would normally be expected.

In September 2006 Fergie reignited his complaints about Keith Hackett, the Premier League's Head of Referees. In a series of newspaper articles he accused Hackett of showing favouritism to Chelsea, after John Terry was let off from receiving a three match ban following his dismissal by Mark Halsey during a game against Manchester City. The Chelsea captain had been sent off for deliberately blocking another players run towards goal, but he appealed the red card to the FA. The appeal was successful, which meant that he didn't have to serve a ban at all. Referee Halsey, meanwhile, got demoted and was made to referee a game in League Two between Chester City and Shrewsbury Town the following week.

What upset Fergie was the fact that, had Terry been made to serve a suspension, he would have missed an important game against United at Stamford Bridge in the race to see who would win the title that season but because the FA overturned Halsey's decision, it meant Terry was free to play.

Fergie had said in the days following the FA decision:

> *"My information is that Hackett told Mark Halsey to rescind the red card, but he would not do it. Now I understand that Halsey is being made to referee in the Second Division this weekend. I just don't understand how this could have happened? If it had been a Manchester United player, Hackett would never have done this for us."*

The FA pounced and wrote to Fergie asking for his observations, launching yet another investigation against him for his post-match comments, and in particular his comments about Keith Hackett. Sir Alex and I discussed how best to approach this case and we decided we should tackle the FA head on with it, because there was generally a strong view that the FA appeal panel had messed up in overturning Terry's red card. We didn't mess about. I replied in a straightforward way, following Fergie's instructions, with a short but sharp response which simply said:

> *"In respect of your request for his (Ferguson's) observations in this matter, our client wishes to confirm that he did make the comments referred to in your correspondence, but does not consider that they were in breach of any FA rule or regulation."*

What we were doing was throwing the gauntlet down to them by saying that if the FA believed that Fergie had breached the rules, then they should charge him. Fergie was up for this fight, and so was I. We started planning our defence, part of which would highlight what we saw as a perverse decision by the FA's appeal panel to reverse the red card. It would have been embarrassing for the FA.

In the meantime Fergie and Hackett had agreed to meet to discuss 'matters of concern'. On October 23, 2008, though, a letter arrived from the FA advising the United boss that no further action was to be taken, I think this was because Fergie had been pro-active in setting up the meeting with Keith Hackett and was trying to address the issues that concerned him. In effect, this had weakened any FA case, but I also think that they knew it had the potential to become embarrassing. It was another let-off for Fergie.

However he was never far from trouble and less than a month later he was back in the FA dock, where they finally had some success against him. On November 1, 2008 United had won 4-3 against Hull City at Old Trafford, in a game refereed by Mike Dean. Dean reported to the FA that Fergie had, at full time, stormed 30 yards towards the centre circle, pointing his finger at him and shouting, *"Today you failed in your duty as a referee. You're a fucking disgrace."* It appeared the United boss was upset at a number of challenges on his players which he viewed as being dangerous, and that Dean had failed to caution some Hull City players. Dean received the hairdryer treatment in full view of the Old Trafford crowd - and the home team had won! God knows what would have happened if they had lost!

The inevitable charge of improper conduct came from the FA on November 4. *"Here we go again"*, I thought to myself. As well as the referee's report, the FA relied on a number of still graphic photographs which showed Fergie giving Dean the full hairdryer treatment as his captain Gary Neville looked on.

A few days later I went to see him at his office and he was still raging about the performance of Mike Dean and the lack of protection afforded his players. As soon as I walked into his office and before I'd even sat down he said to me that he wasn't prepared to admit the charge and wouldn't go to the hearing. He was still fuming about it. I can understand where he was coming from. The multi-million pound superstars at a club like United are big assets both on and off the field and if they are not protected then the stakes become very high, both in terms of commercial activities, value and the availability of the player for selection, not to mention the ability of the team to win trophies.

However, I realised that to get a decent outcome he had no

option but to admit the charge. It would have also been in his interests to appear at the hearing in person. The photographs were damning and it was also on film and Dean was fully supported by all of his fellow officials. There was no way out for Fergie and to deny the charge would just make him look ridiculous and attract a more severe penalty. I had to take the emotion out of it and get him to see sense. That's one of the strengths of being an independent advisor and consultant. You can remove yourself from the emotion of an issue and deal with it in a level-headed way, to get the best outcome for your client.

I just knew that if I could get him into that room he could get his points and frustrations across, and would have the Disciplinary Commission eating out of the palm of his hand. I knew I had to get him there to get the best possible outcome. Telling someone like Fergie to go against his wishes can be quite intimidating, but this was what I was getting paid for, so I had to bite the bullet and get him to agree to go to the hearing. But in true Fergie style he put a condition on it, he wasn't prepared to travel to London for it.

That worked for me. I knew I had another hearing in relation to a different case at Manchester City's stadium the following week. It was a perfect scenario, so I made an agreement with him that if we could get him in at that hearing as well, would he attend and he agreed. He also accepted, having gone through the case in detail, that he had no option but to accept the charge. As he left, he joked about my influence, in that when I entered the room he was doing the exact opposite of what we eventually agreed he would do!

We submitted a detailed witness statement on his behalf, along with another from Gary Neville. As you would expect, Neville was highly supportive of Sir Alex. The following week we ended up at the Etihad in front of the Disciplinary Panel, where Fergie was true to his word and admitted the charge of improper conduct. My gut feeling was correct, because the panel were in total awe of him and allowed him to get across all the points and frustrations he wanted to. In normal circumstances people are just cut off when they go down the road of criticising officials, but on this occasion Fergie was given a free rein. The panel asked him a lot of questions, in what turned out to be more of a chat about football than him being dealt with formally. It was one of the easier disciplinary hearings that I've done, that's for sure.

I recall that at one stage Fergie even said that he was only sitting before them because the referee was Mike Dean and had it been the more grounded Mark Halsey, he wouldn't have even reported him, because he'd have just have given as good as he got and that would have been the end of it. I think we can all see where Ferguson was coming from in relation to what I regularly refer to as "The Mike Dean Show" whenever he referees – let's just say he's not one of my favourite referees.

We left the room while the panel were deciding on the penalty and on our return they delivered the verdict. Fergie was given a two game touchline ban and fined £10,000. Given the fact he'd received a similar penalty for the Clattenburg incident only a few months earlier, we both felt it was a fair result. But one thing that really sticks in my mind from that hearing is that when the panel announced their decision they actually apologised to him for having to suspend him. From memory their words were, 'We're sorry but we do have to impose a touchline ban . It was as if they were actually in agreement with some of the points he had made so well about the standard of refereeing, not only at that particular game but also in general. I found that really amusing and it's something that has stuck with me.

In October, 2009 I had to deal with one of the most controversial outbursts of the Fergie era following United's 2-2 home draw with Sunderland in the Premier League, when Sir Alex made a highly critical assessment of the fitness of the match referee Alan Wiley. To say that the referee's union went into meltdown about his post-match comments are an understatement.

Fergie was obviously not in the best of moods following the drawn game in which United rescued a point courtesy of an Anton Ferdinand own goal. He ranted about Wiley and during his post match interview he said:

> *"I was disappointed with the referee. He didn't add on any time for the goal. He played four minutes and two seconds. He was also walking up the pitch for the second goal needing a rest. He was not fit enough for a game of that standard. The pace of the game demanded a referee who was fit. He was not fit. It is an indictment of our game. You see referees abroad who are as fit as butcher's dogs. We have some who are fit. He wasn't fit. He was taking 30 seconds to book a player. He was needing a rest. It was ridiculous."*

Almost immediately there was a massive media backlash and the comments were all over the newspapers. People from a union called 'Prospect' who identified themselves as *"the referees union"* jumped on the bandwagon, even though in all my time in football I (and I think I can include everybody else in the game on this) had never heard of them before. It seemed a perfect opportunity for their secretary, a man called Alan Leighton, to have his own fifteen minutes of fame and he made himself available for the sound-bites the papers required. It was also said that *"friends"* of Wiley claimed in a *Daily Mail* article that he was *"distressed"* and had *"considered quitting the game"* Even former referee Jeff Winter got in on the act with the rent-a-quote accusing Fergie of being a coward:

> *"It was a cowardly attack – Sir Alex wouldn't have said it to Alan Wiley's face. Every game Alan Wiley takes charge of now where he makes a decision which upsets some fans is going to result in chants of 'You're not fit to referee', he's going to be known as the 'unfit ref'. Sir Alex won't care though. He's a knight of the realm and he thinks he's*

He has goaded referees for years but now they've had enough and are insisting...

SHUT FERGIE UP FOR GOOD

REFS UNITED v FERGIE

They want FA action

By PAUL JIGGINS

REFEREES urged the FA to throw the book at Alex Ferguson for his attack on Alan Wiley.

The FA launched a probe as the Manchester United manager said ref Wiley was not fit enough after his side's 2-2 draw with Sunderland.

Premier League assessor Dermot Gallagher said: "Alex's comments are laughable. Alan is **Turn to P51**

The tabloids went nuts when a self-appointed referee's union called 'Prospect' went for Fergie following his criticism of the fitness of Alan Wiley to referee at the top level.

untouchable, bullet proof."

Winter's blast didn't hold water, because as far as I'm aware, what he said would happen to Wiley never did. It was a free-for-all and felt like an open season to vent anger towards Sir Alex. Both mine and Fergie's views were that these were just concerted efforts to put pressure on the FA to deal strongly with Fergie. In effect, they were trying to influence the proceedings before they had started. The FA didn't waste any time in requesting Fergie's observations on the issue. We responded, but not before I advised Sir Alex to make an apology about the comments, which he did several days later via the club's website saying,

> *"I apologise to Mr Wiley for any personal embarrassment that my remarks may have caused, and to the FA for going public with my views. In retrospect, I accept that this could be deemed as expressing those views in an inappropriate forum. It was never my intention to bring the focus of intense media attention on Mr Wiley. I intend to contact him personally after I return from a trip overseas during this international break. I would wish it to be noted that I have always respected Mr Wiley's integrity and that I did not state or imply that Mr Wiley is a bad referee, that he was in any way biased, that decision-making generally during the game was poor, or that he missed any key incident during the game My only intention in speaking publicly was to highlight what I believe to be a serious and important issue in the game, namely that the fitness levels of referees must match the ever increasing demands of the modern game, which I hope will now be properly addressed through the appropriate formal channels."*

However, following our response to the FA, it did not deter them from issuing a charge of improper conduct against Fergie, which arrived on the 19th October. The FA relied on an interview with ESPN, but had also obtained a witness statement from both Wiley and a man called Simon Breivik, who was the Head of

Sports Science for the PGMOL and whose job it was to assess the fitness of Premier League referees. He fully backed Wiley in his report. Wiley, on the other hand, cited that Fergie had made him feel embarrassed by his comments. He also explained that since the 2006 World Cup he had *"purposely took time when cautioning a player to ensure it had been recorded correctly"*, citing the infamous incident involving Graham Poll, when he booked the same player three times. In my view, Wiley was making the most of it and laying it on thick.

Fergie and I both knew that the reality of the situation was that there was no way out of this charge. He was going to have to take his medicine. The best we could hope for was damage limitation. Having said that, it didn't deter us from seeking evidence to support the fitness levels of Wiley, which included one Sunday morning me taking a phone call from Sir Alex asking me to visit him the next morning. He had uncovered something on Wiley. Eagerly, I went across to Carrington and on sitting down I was surprised when he produced a photograph of Alan Wiley at a fancy dress party dressed as a spaceman! It was believed that it had been taken the night before the game, so it had potential to support the comments put forward by Fergie that Wiley was unfit during the Sunderland game. However following further enquiries it transpired that the photograph had been taken some weeks earlier. Alex never disclosed how the photograph had come into his possession and I never pushed him for an answer on it but it showed just what could be got if you knew the right people!

The disciplinary hearing was held at the Royal Lancaster Hotel in Central London on 12 November, 2009. Things didn't get off to a great start as efforts had been made to keep the date and venue of the hearing secret to avoid press scrutiny, but as usual these things leak out and when Fergie arrived at the front doors of the hotel the TV cameras were waiting for him. My feeling was the tip off had come from within the FA because this was one of the biggest disciplinary cases of the season which had generated huge headlines and given that Fergie was admitting the charge, it was the FA's chance to highlight a rare victory over their nemesis.

The hearing was pretty straight forward and chaired by Peter Griffiths, QC. In advance of the hearing, we had submitted a fully detailed witness statement from Fergie, in which he explained the reasoning behind his comments:

> *"I accept that there is a perception within the football industry and the media that I am critical of match officials. From the outset I would wish to make it clear that I am not. I am supportive of officials and try to give constructive feedback regarding their performances and status in the game. Football is a passionate game and sometimes emotions cause an individual to act inappropriately, or vent their frustrations at match officials. However, talking generally, I do have a good relationship with match officials and try to enter into cordial discussions with them whenever I meet them, whether that is on a match day or at an environment away from football.*
>
> *I do have issues surrounding the fitness of referees generally. This is not a new issue I have raised in recent weeks. I have been outlining my concerns for a long time to the Chief Executive of Manchester United FC, David Gill, who is also a member of the Board of Directors of the FA, with a view to him raising it at the appropriate forum.*
>
> *I am contractually obliged to attend television interviews after every game. This game was no different. The result was a 2-2 draw and in all honesty, my team did not play particularly well. At the end of the game I conducted a number of TV interviews. During the course of those interviews, I passed comment relating to my opinion about Mr Wiley's fitness. I considered that he did not appear to be sufficiently physically fit for the game and made my views known about this. I recognise that this was an inappropriate forum to make those views known. I fully*

accept that Mr Wiley has passed the required fitness tests conducted by the Premier League and therefore is eligible to officiate at their games.

"When I made these comments, it was not my intention to embarrass or offend Mr Wiley. I understand though, in hindsight, that the comments may have been interpreted in a manner which caused his embarrassment and may have offended him. I can honestly reiterate that was never my intention and consequently I recognised that by making a public apology to him and writing to him personally offering my apologies. I would reiterate that I make an unreserved apology to him and the FA."

We produced copies of the public website apology and letter to Alan Wiley in support of Fergie. It seemed that the panel recognised that there was some genuine remorse from him, because they only issued him with a two game immediate suspension with a further two games suspended, as well as a fine of £20,000. In their written reasons, they made it clear that had Sir Alex not admitted the charge or made the apologies that he had done, then he would have received a four game touchline ban and a fine of £30,000. All in all we felt it was a decent result and could have been much worse. It rankled with 'the referees' union' and Mr Leighton saw his chance for another fifteen minutes of fame with the papers, by criticising the FA for being soft on Sir Alex. We, on the other hand, slipped out of a rear door and jumped into a waiting taxi to avoid the waiting TV cameras, before heading to the *Les Ambassadeurs* private club in Mayfair for a spot of lunch.

There was another episode of the 'Mike Dean Show' again in January 2011 when he reported United full back Rafael Da Silva for his behaviour during a Premier League game against Tottenham at White Hart Lane. Da Silva had been booked in the first half of the game and then received his second caution in the 74th minute, when Dean reported the player had tripped an opponent, giving him no option but to send him off. In his report to the FA Dean went on to say *"After I used the red card, Mr Da Silva refused to leave the field of play and reacted in a very aggressive manner towards me."*

The FA charged Da Silva the following day with improper conduct, under the then newly introduced fast-track disciplinary system. On review of the incident I concluded that Da Silva had no option but to admit the charge and advised him that in order to get the best outcome, he would have to do this. Our main aim was to avoid any additional suspension – and admitting the charge was our best chance of succeeding in that quest. There were strong mitigating circumstances and through me he requested a personal hearing.

In their wisdom the FA set it for 1pm the following Friday at Wembley Stadium, which was the day before the weekend's fixtures. Even though Da Silva was ruled out of the weekend's game due to his double yellow card which meant he had to serve a one-game suspension, there still had to be full team preparation by the manager, who also wanted to attend the hearing to support his player.

Because Da Silva required the attendance of a translator and also the fact that Fergie wanted to be there, we requested that the FA give consideration to moving the hearing to Manchester, or allow it to take place via video link. It seemed ridiculous that a player would have to attend a hearing in London on a Friday afternoon. The FA agreed to the video link request and I believe it may have been the first hearing of its kind held in that way.

In his statement to the disciplinary panel Da Silva said he believed referee Dean had made a mistake in awarding a foul, but understood that he had to make an immediate decision. The player went on to say in his statement;

> *"My recollection of the incident is that the Tottenham player was moving forward and I was chasing him at speed*

from slightly behind, but at an angle to his body. In effect, I was attempting to get alongside him, with no significant contact between us. As I did so, we seemed to make contact with our feet as I attempted to get out of the way. This caused him to fall to the floor. As I was in the process of this movement, I made a conscious effort to keep out of my opponent's way and this is supported by the video, which shows me raising my arms to avoid making contact with the player, but unfortunately slight contact was made and this caused him to fall over. The contact between us was completely accidental.

"On viewing the video of the incident, it can be seen that there was no deliberate attempt to foul the player, this was just an unfortunate yet unavoidable incident.

"Almost immediately the referee showed a yellow card to me and then a red card to send me off the field. As I saw the yellow card being shown, I said out of frustration, 'Fuck Off', or words to that effect. This was not directed at the referee, although I accept that I was facing him at the time I said the words, but it was said in frustration and bewilderment at being cautioned for what was essentially an accidental contact between me and the Tottenham player.

"I immediately began to walk towards the touchline, as I did so I had to pass the referee and so I took two paces back towards him to ask him why he had cautioned me, as I knew the contact was accidental. I recall I said to him, 'Hey, I didn't do anything. Why?' As I spoke to the referee, I held my arms out in a pleading position. The referee indicated me to be quiet. This lasted no more than a few seconds and he pointed in the direction of the tunnel, so I immediately walked off the pitch, making a gesture with my arm in total frustration. I have seen the referee's report. He says I refused to leave the pitch, but this is not correct. I never refused to leave and the video shows that I was actually walking straight off, but then spoke to the referee

momentarily and after I said the few words I've described,
I immediately walked off."

In support of the player, both Fergie and Harry Redknapp,
the Tottenham manager, submitted reports on his behalf. Fergie
said in his report:

> *"I believe the boy has suffered enough and to add any*
> *further punishment would be a complete travesty of justice.*
> *The decision could have cost Manchester United the game*
> *and, who knows, the league. I don't think the club should*
> *be punished in this way. Rafael is an honest, enthusiastic*
> *player and plays with a free spirit as an attacking full back*
> *and I think this should be recognised."*

It's unusual for an opposition manager to submit a letter of
support on behalf of a rival player, but Redknapp did this and
didn't hold back. He said:

> *"The second yellow card received by Rafael, which led*
> *to his sending off, was in my opinion unwarranted and*
> *completely out of context of the game. Rafael was running*
> *at speed and clipped Benoit Assou-Ekotto's heels from*
> *behind as he was trying to get out of the way. Rafael did*
> *not break stride and did not trip Benoit. This was my*
> *immediate opinion at the time of the incident from my*
> *view in the dugout and I believe the TV replays confirmed*
> *this.*
>
> *"Given the situation that brought about the second*
> *yellow card and subsequent sending off, I can sympathise*
> *with Rafael. The view of the majority of pundits who*
> *witnessed the match was that it was a harsh decision and*
> *not a dirty game. To therefore punish the player would, in*
> *my opinion, be wrong, bearing in mind the circumstances*
> *that led to the incident."*

It was clear that Redknapp was doing his best to help us out
and this didn't go unnoticed by all involved. In addition to this

Da Silva also made a public apology via the media.

The hearing was held in a side room at the club's Carrington training ground with Fergie in attendance, as well as the player and his translator. In our submissions, we highlighted the player's outstanding disciplinary record and his public apology, but also raised concerns about phrases used by the referee in his report, as well as submitting a short video which showed a number of other sendings off where a player had shown some reluctance to leave the field and had contested the decision, where the FA had not taken any action, including at least one incident involving Mike Dean. This is where the FA falls down in its application of the issuing of disciplinary charges. There are always video clips available of similar incidents where the FA have not taken any action - and it comes back to bite them on the backside. You would have thought they would have learned their lesson by now.

The panel considered everything we had said, including the supporting correspondence, and fined the player £8,000. But more importantly, they did not issue any further suspension. As I said earlier, this was our only aim in this case, for the player not to get a further ban, which we all viewed as a success. The thing about players I have found is that you can fine them as much money as you want and it doesn't really bother them, but suspend them for a game and they are crestfallen, such is their desire to play. By this stage I had developed a strong relationship with Fergie. He trusted me, but I never realised just how much until an incident with amusing connotations took place almost on my own doorstep that I'll never forget

United were due to play Barnsley in the League Cup and it coincided with one of the many disciplinary cases I was dealing with on Fergie's behalf. We agreed to meet at the team's hotel, the Tankersley Manor, on the outskirts of Barnsley on the afternoon before the game.

"I'm Sorry…"

It's rare when the opposing manager supports a player dismissed against his team but Harry Redknapp did just that for Rafael da Silva following his red card against Tottenham.

TO DARE IS TO DO

I am writing in support of the appeal against the charge imposed on Manchester United player Rafael following his sending off in the match at White Hart Lane on Sunday 16 January.

The match was played at a fast tempo and was highly competitive but played in a good spirit by both teams. The second yellow card received by Rafael which lead to his sending off was in my opinion unwarranted and completely out of context of the game. Rafael was running at speed and clipped Benoit Assou-Ekotto's heels from behind as he was trying to get out of the way. Rafael did not break stride and did not trip Benoit. This was my immediate opinion at the time of the incident from my view in the dug out and I believe the television replays confirm this.

Given the situation that brought about the second yellow card and subsequent sending off I can sympathise with Rafael. The view of the majority of pundits who witnessed the match was that it was a harsh decision; it was not a dirty game. To therefore further punish the player would in my opinion be wrong bearing in mind the circumstances that led to the incident.

Harry Redknapp
Manager - Tottenham Hotspur

Tottenham Hotspur
Football & Athletic Co Ltd
Spurs Lodge, Luxborough Lane,
Chigwell, Essex IG7 5AB

Telephone: +44 (0)20 8506 9818
Facsimile: +44 (0)20 8506 9815
tottenhamhotspur.com

Registered Number: 51195 England

PUMA

However earlier that morning my phone rang and Sir Alex was on the line telling me he was "in a bit of trouble" - I feared the worst. This wasn't the type of "trouble" you would normally associate with him - he asked me to go to Marks & Spencer's in Barnsley and buy him a white, long sleeved shirt, 16-inch collar, and bring it to the hotel. He had left home that morning without his shirt to wear at the game that night. So off I went! I thought it would be a simple task but was horrified to discover that M&S didn't have any of the required shirts in stock, so I tried Burtons and Next but with the same outcome… no white, long sleeved shirts with a 16-inch collar. I couldn't believe it. I'm like, "For fuck's sake, all I want is a white shirt." By this time I was scraping the barrel and tried TK Maxx where to my frustration, they also didn't have what I wanted!

By now I was becoming desperate, to the point of panic and in a final throw of the dice went into Primark, where they had the shirt in stock at the grand price of £4.99. I snapped it up and then nipped to my mother-in-law's to give her the job of ironing the shirt of a true VIP, telling her she was part of a major operation to dress the most famous football manager in the world! Fergie was impressed when I told him about the personal touch.

That afternoon I delivered the shirt and Fergie took out a wad of £20 notes to pay me for it. Rather sheepishly I made the excuse of not wanting to be paid for it and just mentioned that I'd had to get it from '*elsewhere*' as M&S didn't have what he wanted. I daren't tell him it had only cost a fiver from Primark! We agreed on 2 tickets for that night's game instead. Following the game, whilst he was being interview on Sky, I couldn't resist texting him with the cheeky message, *"Nice shirt, who's your fashion stylist?"*. I got a curt and tongue-in-cheek response, which I'll leave to your imagination!

The following week United were due to play a Champions League game at Old Trafford and I had another meeting with him that afternoon. So for a bit of fun, en-route to the Carrington training ground I called in at M&S and this time bought him a size 16, long sleeved, blue pin striped shirt.

As I went into the office I handed him the carrier bag and he asked what it was. I told him, whilst trying to keep a straight face, that seeing as it was match-day and being as he'd forgotten his shirt the previous week, I thought the safest thing to do had been to bring him one just in case. He thought it was hilarious and we were both laughing. This then became a bit of a standing joke between us and I recall on his birthday, which is New Year's Eve, sending him another shirt to wear for a New Year's Day game. Upon receipt I got a text back from him saying *"Thanks for the shirt Graham, I must be your best dressed client?"*. It was a sign of just how much our relationship had developed.

4 - A RIGHT SPECTACLE

WHETHER YOU SUPPORT THEM or not, Liverpool FC are one of the great clubs in world football. They have given their supporters so much joy over the years, particularly in Europe. They are a true 'working class club' whose values resonate with those of my own.

In 2004, as a result of my friendship with the late Bryce Morrison, who was then Liverpool's club secretary, I was offered the opportunity to secure two season tickets at Anfield. Given the fact that I have a wife who had followed Liverpool with a passion all her life and as a youngster and who was a regular visitor to Anfield, coupled with the fact that her passion for the club had been handed down to my youngest son, it was an opportunity I couldn't turn down. If I hadn't done, I don't think I'd have been allowed back in the house. My belongings would have been in a pile on the front garden!

We hold those season tickets to this day and have travelled across the UK and Europe following Liverpool and witnessed all the highs and lows. Bryce was a great bloke, but I have to say he had the untidiest office I have ever seen in my life. There were files piled up all over the place, how he ever located anything he urgently needed only he knew.

When the chance to secure a contract working for Liverpool arose in 2006, I was pretty pleased with myself. In football terms, like most people who work in the industry, I don't find myself 'star struck' by the people you meet. To me it's just a job and I just get on with it. Friends of mine wonder how that can be, working in such a perceived 'glamorous' environment, but it is what it is. I find myself quite cynical about the game because it can be very ruthless behind the scenes but working for Liverpool was different. It was a great experience. I was accessing places like the Melwood training ground, where supporters can usually only wait outside to catch a glimpse of their heroes – and here I was with a practically free rein to get in and out of the place.

The securing of the contract came about as a result of my friendship with the then new club secretary, Ian Silvester, who I had worked closely with when he was at Leeds United. He is one of the good guys of the game, whose work and attention to detail is of the highest quality. I regard him as a good friend and wherever he has worked he's always used my services, as he does in his current role with Blackburn Rovers.

"That referee needs glasses" is a well worn phrase uttered by supporters up and down the country for almost as long as the game has been played but Rafa Benitez took the phrase to a whole new level following the opening game of the 2009/10 season. After Liverpool's 2-1 defeat away at Tottenham, Benitez criticised referee Phil Dowd in his post match interview for failing to award his side a second penalty after Steven Gerrard had converted the first one early in the second half of the game. During the interview, when questioned about the second penalty claim, Rafa had said:

> *"I think everyone could see there was a penalty, especially to (Andriy) Voronin, it was so clear. (The penalty appeal) was so clear, it was unbelievable. Can you get two penalties at an away ground? No. With this referee (Dowd), I knew that this was impossible."*

Once again the FA sprang into action, resulting in the them issuing three charges against the Liverpool manager. The third charge related to a non-verbal response when Benitez was asked another question about the penalty incident involving Voronin – when he simply took off his glasses theatrically, as if presenting them for inspection. In effect, this was his way of saying the referee needed some glasses. Most people there thought it was amusing, but the sense of humour at the FA was certainly non existent.

There's no doubt in mine and most other people's minds that

this was an example of Rafa's sense of humour and there was no malice in what he did. But the deadpan party poopers at the FA thought it was a clear case of improper conduct! Liverpool got in touch and asked me to help. In all my years doing what I do, I'd never known a manager get charged three times from one press conference. It was a unique situation as far as I can recall. It was on the back of the FA's new *'Respect'* campaign, but we soon put a big hole in the side of that. We responded by denying the charges and asked for a personal hearing, which was held in Manchester in October, 2009.

In the period between the charges being issued and the hearing date I'd visited Rafa on a number of occasions at Melwood and discussed the case in detail, but sometimes our conversations went onto other Liverpool issues, to the point where one day Rafa gave me a lesson in zonal marking, using chairs as players in the canteen! I was mesmerised at his attention to detail, even using the office furniture to demonstrate tactics. One thing about Rafa is that he's very focused and intense, but it soon became a pleasure to work with him. In fact, on the day of the actual hearing, I even gave him preferential treatment by picking him up from Melwood and taking him to and from the hearing in Manchester. Not many Liverpool supporters get to chauffeur the club's manager around. It felt like having royalty in the car. For once in my career I was star struck. However as we drove into Manchester city centre we got spotted by a fan of one of the Manchester clubs because they aimed a two fingered salute at the car, to which Rafa just smiled and waved back!

In order to be successful in the defence of the charges I knew that I had to show that the comments made by Rafa were factually correct and then submit that if this was the case, how could he be guilty of improper conduct? Taking a leaf out of the *"Fergie manual of analysing referees performances"* I did a full analysis on Dowd and his record for awarding penalties to an away side. This analysis proved that Rafa was correct in his view – that Dowd had never awarded two penalties to the away team in the

The Liverpool Football Club
& Athletic Grounds Limited
Dreystrook Lane, Liverpool, L12 8SY
Tel: 0151 282 6888 Fax: 0151 252 2206
www.liverpoolfc.tv

Melwood Training Ground

Rafa's letter to Keith Hackett at the height of his feud with Fergie following the Spaniard's infamous 'facts' press conference

RB:CT

Keith Hackett
Mr Keith Hackett
PGMOL
Referees Dept
The FA Premier League
30 Gloucester Place
London
W1U 8PL

01 September 2009

Dear Mr Hackett

One year ago we had a Managers Meeting regarding the Referees, and you agreed with me in this meeting that Sir Alex Ferguson's criticising of the Referees was destroying the "Respect campaign"

This year we have seen Sir Alex, after the Charity Shield game, complaining on the pitch, and both Neil Warnock and Arsene Wenger doing the same. The other day you publicly apologised to Arsene Wenger, which I have no issue with and credit to you for doing that.

However, both Sammy Lee and myself are facing charges by the FA for bringing the game into disrepute because we complained of two penalties which we though should have been given and were not. We also thought the fourth official managing the technical area was inconsistent, and showed a lack of respect.

My question to you is do you consider our behaviour towards referees any worse than that of the other Managers as mentioned earlier? If the answer is yes, please let me know why.

Do you have any record of Phil Dowd giving two penalties to an "Away Team" in the same game within the last five years?

Please explain to me if you consider your referees were submitted to offence more from us at this particular game, than from the others at the games mentioned earlier..

Sammy Lee has his hearing tomorrow 2 September, and I am waiting to confirm a date for my hearing.

Do you consider it fair that both Sammy and I find ourselves in this situation, if you compare it with the others?.

I am not asking for a public apology, just your thoughts and recommendations for the future.

I would appreciate your thoughts on the content of this letter and hope to hear from you in due course.

Yours sincerely

Rafa Benitez
MANAGER, L.F.C.

By Fax : 02078649228

Premier League up to that time. Some may say that's a rather subjective argument to put forward because Dowd, or any other referee come to that, may not have had cause to award a second penalty to an away team but we played heavily on the factually correct statistics – and the FA disciplinary panel swallowed it yet again.

We also submitted to the panel that on the very same weekend the then Crystal Palace boss Neil Warnock had done exactly the same thing [proffered his spectacles] to an Assistant Referee during a game against Bristol City, but the FA had not even charged him. It was a typical example of the FA's inconsistent approach. Why would you charge one manager and not the other for doing similar things on the same weekend? It made no sense. One of the arguments Rafa put forward was that this was done in a non malicious and humour filled manner, relieving the tedium of the standard post match quotes.

As far as I can recall the FA never did explain why they had decided that Benitez's had actions warranted a charge, even though they were done in the privacy of a press conference, but yet Warnock had made his gesture in public during the game with the crowd watching and his actions hadn't. Benitez had also fired a letter off to Keith Hackett complaining of double standards using comments made by Fergie and Arsene Wenger as comparisons to his own to raise his concerns.

In respect of the display of humour with the spectacles, we put forward that this was exactly what it was – a joke – and that everyone could see that. In my view it was ridiculous, petty and trivial point scoring from the FA. Following the hearing the Commission accepted Rafa's explanation about Dowd and his statistics and cleared him of the first two charges relating to his post-match comments (which were the more serious element of the allegations against him) but bizarrely found the case proved in relation to him taking his glasses off, deeming it *"offensive"* and warned him as to his future conduct. In their summing up of the case, the panel made it clear though that they were non-too impressed with the fact that the charges were made in the first place.

It seemed to me that, not only was it a complete waste of time, but the penalty imposed reflected exactly what the panel thought about it. I still can't believe they found that part of the case proven. It was as if they knew they had to find something just to support the 'Respect' campaign and if this was the best they could do, then it was only a matter of time before the much ridiculed campaign collapsed.

Following the hearing Andy Hunter of the *Guardian* reported that the Benitez case:

> *"Represented the first test of the FA's new hard line stance, (the Respect Campaign), but that the governing body was left with a bloody nose over a petty charge."*

I was also quoted about the Benitez case, saying,

> *"This has exposed the Respect campaign for the PR exercise that it is. The Commission clearly indicated that the charges should never have been brought. It would have been easier for the FA to write to him to remind him of his responsibilities, but instead it has been left with a bloody nose over a petty charge."*

At the same game Assistant Manager Sammy Lee had been charged with misconduct following his removal from the technical area. His case highlighted the poor quality of some match officials' reports, when fourth official Stuart Attwell reported that in the 89th minute of the game "*Sammy Lee had approached him in an aggressive and confrontational manner in relation to a decision against Liverpool.*" As a consequence he informed the referee Phil Dowd, who instructed him to leave the technical area.

It was crystal clear though that the FA were not happy with the referee's vague report, because they emailed him asking him to outline exactly what Lee had done during the incident referred to. Attwell replied,

"There were no specific words that I can recall, however his general attitude and manner of communication was both aggressive and confrontational."

I found this amateurish at best from Attwell, because he was alleging inappropriate conduct from a senior professional on the touchline, yet he couldn't remember what had been said? The FA must have felt like it was pulling teeth with Attwell trying to get him to give a stronger and more detailed report to back up a charge. They went back to him and specifically asked him if Lee had used any particular words during the incident? Attwell responded again without committing himself, stating:

"As stated previously, his aggressive and confrontational behaviour was manifesting itself through shouting at me and the aggressive nature of his body language towards me. This was, in my opinion, irresponsible behaviour in accordance with the guidelines we are given and was ultimately the reason for his removal from the technical area".

I have never known a referee unable to recall at least some of the words or phrases used by someone in such circumstances, but Attwell was adamant that he couldn't remember. I think Attwell just overreacted to the incident and soon found himself in too deep when the FA wanted more specific details.

Still the FA weren't satisfied and asked him again to provide more details, but Attwell still couldn't provide them with any words that Lee had allegedly said and simply claimed it was his body language towards him that had been the issue. If I had been dealing with this case inside the FA by now I would have simply written it off as a lost cause and sent Lee a written advisory letter, whilst referring the poor report to Attwell's supervisors for them to give him advice on writing reports in a more detailed and structured way. Having passed my referee's course many years ago I can remember that it was drilled into you that you should always put into any report exactly what was said, but it seemed

Attwell had completely chosen to ignore that advice. It seems to me ridiculous and unprofessional that a referee officiating at Premier League level, despite several requests, could not give any details as to what has been said to him by a coach who was arguing with him. I will leave it to the reader to make their own mind up why that was?

Nevertheless the FA, which had to be seen to be supporting referees following the big PR 'Respect' campaign, issued a charge of improper conduct against Lee. He admitted it, on the basis that he'd vented his frustration at Attwell over a decision late in the game. Lee also said in his witness statement that:

> *"I feel that the fourth official actually built up the situation and that a more passive and open attitude to reactions in the heat of the moment would have eased the tensions, particularly considering it was so late in the game. I put this down to his inexperience, as opposed to anything else, but do consider that given the lateness of the incident, a more experienced official may have dealt with this matter differently."*

I think Sammy was right, a more experienced official would have either dealt with the incident differently or at the very least would have made a more detailed report. Lee was also supported by a statement from Rafa Benitez. Interestingly, we obtained the match delegate's report, which had been compiled by former football manager Peter Shreeves, who stated:

> *"Sammy Lee, for Liverpool, made his feelings clear to the fourth official and when he protested at a second, less worthy shout a minute later, he was sent to the stands. I have had this lad as a player and in all of his time both as a manager and a coach he has conducted himself extremely well and this action was completely out of character."*

We attended the hearing with Sammy in Birmingham and, having listened to our submissions, the disciplinary panel simply warned him as to his future conduct. Once again it was another case where, in my view, it had been a complete waste of time and could have been dealt with by a more common-sense approach, by way of a warning or advisory letter. What is the point in going through the full disciplinary process and case preparation from both the FA and the person who has been charged, to simply be warned about their conduct at the end of the process? My belief in this case what that the panel had looked at the problems the FA had in extracting information from Attwell, which had influenced their decision to only warn Lee.

★

The 2006 FA Cup final between Liverpool and West Ham became known as the 'Gerrard Final' because of his last minute equaliser, but it was a stunning goal from Luis Garcia in the semi final versus Chelsea that had got Liverpool there in the first place. Unfortunately Garcia didn't make the team for the Final in Cardiff due to suspension. Two weeks earlier Liverpool had played West Ham in a league game at Upton Park, where referee Howard Webb had sent Garcia off. Webb reported;

> *"In the 86th minute of the game, after conceding a free kick near to the halfway line, Luis Garcia of Liverpool deliberately threw an elbow into the back of his opponent. He was then sent off for violent conduct. After the game Garcia visited the referee's dressing room, where he apologised to me for his actions. In my presence, he also apologised to the opponent who had been involved in the incident. Garcia showed a great deal of remorse for his actions, which he stated where not intended and occurred in the heat of the moment."*

I think Webb realised Garcia was going to miss the Cup Final and so was trying his best to soften his report in case there was an opportunity to appeal the ban that he knew was coming the player's way. Webb also sent off Hayden Mullins for pushing Garcia in reaction to the incident. Garcia's sending off resulted in a three-game ban, which meant he would miss the forthcoming Cup Final. The only way we could try to ensure he was available to play would be to make an appeal against his dismissal. Having watched the video I knew this was a nigh on impossible task, but the opportunity to play in an FA Cup Final doesn't come along very often, so making an appeal to get the decision overturned felt like a no-brainer.

In Garcia's statement to the panel requesting a review of the sending off, he stated that both himself and Mullins were attempting to win control of the ball, both being physically strong and holding onto each other's shirt. Garcia conceded Mullins was physically stronger than him and managed to gain *"exclusive possession of the ball by using his body strength"*. Garcia went on to explain further that he had been knocked off the ball and

> *"My own bodily movement caused me to swing around backwards, leaving my trailing elbow, which assisted me in my balance, exposed and making contact with Hayden's back. My movement was not intentional and I didn't intend to harm the player."*

Mullins made a witness statement supporting Garcia, in which he stated:

> *"I would reiterate that as far as I'm aware, there was no deliberate for intentional contact. I was not injured and the contact between us was minimal."*

West Ham were also appealed the sending-off of Mullins and in support of him Garcia returned the favour by providing a witness statement in support of his opponent. In effect it was an attempt by both clubs to help each other try and overturn the red cards, so both players would be available for the final.

During our written submissions I referred to the case of Tal Ben Haim of Bolton, who I'd also represented in 2005, in which the FA set a precedent in respective of issues between players and the analysis of evidence relating to contact between players. I will go into more detail about this case later as it was a landmark ruling. However the basis of the argument was that the only individual who could give evidence about the effect of any contact would be the recipient of that contact, and that in this case, the only person who could say whether Garcia's actions were intentional or not, other than Garcia himself, was Mullins. And he had backed Garcia.

It was going to be a hard case to win and, as expected, Garcia and Mullins lost their appeals and had to miss the FA Cup Final. But this indicated the lengths clubs were prepared to go to in order to try to overturn a decision. As a thank you for helping him, Garcia sent my son Matthew a signed photograph of him holding the Champions League trophy in Istanbul. Matthew is 26 now, but it still has pride of place, along with a signed photo of both Steven Gerrard and Fernando Torres, on his bedroom wall, even though he left home a few years ago!

Sometimes the most interesting cases go 'below the radar' and don't get the publicity they warrant. One of the more interesting cases I dealt with involving Liverpool concerned a reserve game against Everton in October 2006 when, as is often the case amid the intensity of a derby, a large number of players from both teams got involved in a brawl. Both clubs received a fine, but that was only half the story, because the main incident arising from the game involved the dismissal of Liverpool goalkeeper Jerzey Dudek.

The referee in this game was a young up and coming Michael Oliver and in the 56th minute he reported that he'd sent Dudek off for aggressively pushing an opponent in the face twice. The referee assessor also submitted a report, asking that a video be sent to the FA to review the incident of the confrontation between the players, to see if any further acts of misconduct had occurred. The FA did this and decided that Dudek should be charged with improper conduct because:

> *"He failed to leave the field of play promptly following*

A typical referee's report, this one by Howard Webb on Luis Garcia's red card that would see huim miss the Fa Cup final

the red card he received and instead, made physical contact with the match referee."

I found this astounding because Oliver had not made any mention of it in his own report – and neither had anyone else!

The video of the incident the FA relied upon was also not consistent with the charge, and I didn't hang around in challenging the FA over this. After all, this was my club and Dudek had hero status after his 2005 Champions League exploits!

On November 2, 2006 I wrote to the FA pointing out that there was no basis for the charge of failing to leave the pitch promptly, because the video proved that from being shown the red card to beginning his walk from the field was timed at only

18 seconds. I raised the point that in a Premier League game the very same week, Jon Obi Mikel had been sent off for Chelsea in a game against Reading, where he had not left the field for 34 seconds, but the FA had not taken any action. We asked them to explain the difference in reaching the decisions they had in respect of Dudek while not charging others. We also relied on four other cases of failing to leave the field promptly involving players at Reading, Newcastle, Wycombe and Blackburn. We obtained videos of those four sendings off, which proved beyond any doubt that the players involved had all taken longer to leave the field, but had not been charged by the FA. The FA's response to my query was that Dudek had pulled the referee back and that they still intended to proceed with the case. As you can see, there is a real picture of inconsistency in the charging process emerging in with the FA.

In light of the FA's decision to continue with the case against Dudek, I decided to make an application for a member of the Compliance Department to attend the hearing to give evidence. I wanted to use that opportunity to cross-examine them as to why the charge had been issued, when there was a clear lack of consistency when compared to other cases. I felt it was only fair that if the FA were going to show such inconsistency in their charging policy, then they should be made to explain why that was. My very robust submission touched a few nerves inside Soho Square. The FA really didn't like the tone of our application and sent a stinging response, arguing why a member of that department should not be made to attend to give evidence. It was obvious to me they were running scared and I felt that when placed under pressure by way of cross-examination, their case would fall apart. Realistically, though, I never expected to be successful because the FA didn't like their staff being exposed to critical cross-examination. Unsurprisingly, my prediction was correct and members of the Compliance Department who had brought the charge, were supported by the disciplinary panel and protected from giving evidence.

In his witness statement Dudek accepted that he had reacted to a challenge by lunging at an Everton player and as a consequence, the confrontation between both teams occurred. Dudek then said:

> "*I approached the (Everton) player and held out my hand to shake his hand, to show there was no hard feelings. He refused my gesture, telling me to 'Fuck Off'. The referee then showed him a yellow card and I then said to the referee, words to the effect of, 'have you seen that, he doesn't want to shake my hand. Will you be putting that in your report?' The referee then beckoned me close to him and began taking my details. I assumed he was also going to show me a yellow card and was shocked when he produced a red card and immediately in the same movement, began to walk away without saying anything. As he began his movement to walk away, I momentarily took hold of his elbow and said to him, words to the effect of, 'Why have you made this decision?' As I took hold of his elbow the referee turned into me to answer my question. I can say I did not hold him forcefully or aggressively and it was a similar type of contact that occurs between players and referees on many occasions. I simply wanted to know why I was being sent off, when the Everton player had only been cautioned. I believe it was a reasonable request to make in the circumstances. The referee did not object to me holding his elbow and was amicable and willing to explain his decision, which I listened to. He said to me, 'Jerzey, you have to go because you raised your hands' - and indicated for me to leave the pitch. A number of other Liverpool players were also querying the referee's decision. Once the referee had given his explanation and indicated for me to leave, I listened to his explanations and then did so.*"

The hearing was held at the Piccadilly Hotel in Manchester four months later and took a very unusual turn. In fact, it was a scenario I've never known happen before or since, involving cases I've dealt with. As I said earlier, we were refused an application to have a member of the Compliance Department attend to give evidence about the case. On reaching the venue I was very surprised when Tarik Shamel of the Compliance Department and the person responsible for investigating the case, turned up. There was absolutely no reason for him to be there and in my view they were just rubbing our noses in it. In effect they were saying, "we can do what we want and there's fuck all you can do about it". However, myself and Dudek had the last laugh in what turned out to be a very embarrassing situation for the FA. In fact, it was a delightful moment and left me with a grin akin to a Cheshire cat.

Prior to being invited into the room to start the case, we were all asked to wait outside. I wondered what on earth was going on and really didn't have a clue, as there had been no indication as to what was happening behind the closed doors. A few minutes later we were all summoned into the room and took our places ready to do battle, only to be told that the case was being dismissed without any evidence being heard! This came not only as a shock to me, because when I looked across the table, the FA Compliance Department members were sat there open-mouthed. Even they couldn't believe what was being said. The Panel Chairman, and FA Councillor, Peter Clayton advised that written reasons would be circulated for their decision in due course and when they arrived a few days later they were an absolute embarrassment to the Compliance Department:

> *"The members, having studied the written statement from Mr Dudek and having reviewed the video evidence prior to any evidence being presented from the FA Compliance department, unanimously decided that the video clip on which the charge was based did not show, in their opinion, any breach of FA Rule E3 and therefore there was no case for Mr Dudek to answer.*
>
> *"Firstly, from the match official's report before them, the*

Commission were aware that the referee had not reported Mr Dudek for either failing to leave the field promptly, nor for any physical contact made on him by the player and were therefor justified in thinking that the referee did not consider either action sufficiently serious to warrant report.

"Secondly, from the video evidence supplied by the Compliance Unit, whilst accepting that Mr Dudek did attract the referee by taking hold of his arm, it was the commission's view that this was not done in a confrontational manner, but in order to attract his attention. The referee had shown the red card to dismiss him from the field and the Commission accepted that Mr Dudek was seeking clarification from the referee, who had turned to walk away. The referee acted passively to Mr Dudek taking hold of his arm and appeared on the video to be comfortable in speaking to him to provide an explanation.

"Lastly, the Commission could not see justification for the charge of failing to leave the pitch promptly. As stated, Mr Dudek could be seen talking to the referee on being shown the red card, but that conversation was interrupted due to the intervention of other Liverpool players. Once those players had dispersed that conversation was quickly concluded and Mr Dudek immediately left the pitch."

This was absolutely damning on the FA and Compliance Department and reinforced the points I'd been making since the charge was issued four months earlier. It made the Compliance Department look idiotic and was a huge embarrassment for them. For what it's worth, it's my belief that the very experienced FA Disciplinary Manager at the time, the late Alan Wilkes, who also acted as secretary to the Commission, had whispered in the Commission's ear and told them what a *"load of bollocks"* the charge was. And on that basis, they had then followed his advice. "Wilko" used a lot of common sense in his role and had the FA Disciplinary Committee's confidence. I can't say this for definite, because Alan passed away some years ago, but I genuinely do believe that's what happened.

Because of the ridiculous stance that the FA had taken and the fact Shamel had turned up at the hearing, I wrote to the FA in the strongest possible terms, complaining about it. The response from the FA's director of governance, Jonathan Hall, saw him attempt to defend the FA's position. But it didn't matter what he said, because the written reasons were unequivocal in being damning of his department. This was one episode which once again highlighted the total incompetence and inconsistency of the FA's charging procedures, but because it was a reserve game, did not get the attention it deserved in the media, apart from the local paper. Dudek proved to be a top bloke. He gave me a signed shirt after the hearing. Not only that, but I also once went to Barcelona to watch Liverpool in the Champions League and he clocked me in the arrivals hall at the airport and went out of his way to beckon me over for a chat. There I was sat amongst the whole squad talking to Jerzy as if we were old mates, and yet my wife who was standing with us was going weak at the knees and star struck acting like a lovesick teenager. She couldn't believe it.

On May 23, 2007, Liverpool lost 2-1 to AC Milan at the Olympic Stadium in Athens, in what was a repeat of the Champions League Final of two years earlier. I went to the game with my son and can only describe the pre-match scenes outside the ground as chaotic, with crushes taking place when supporters attempted to get into the stadium. There was no organisation and the stadium entry points were totally inadequate. It was a very scary experience and I recall my son and I ended up standing in a part of the ground that our tickets were not for. We passed through three ticket verification points and at no stage were our tickets checked. We were just let through and the tickets remained intact, with no stubs torn from them. It was chaos and for my son, who was then a 13 year old boy, it must have been terrifying.

What people don't realise, though, is that in June 2007, a

month after the game, UEFA issued Liverpool with a disciplinary charge for lack of order and discipline in and around the stadium and improper conduct of its supporters. This incensed the club and its supporters and, together with a legal team, they put together a robust defence of the allegations. Liverpool fans have been castigated on many occasions over the years for issues in and around stadiums, but this was one case for which they were most definitely not at fault. It was the incompetency of the organisers and local authorities that caused these issues. I assisted the legal team and submitted a witness statement based on my own experiences of being in Athens that night. I recall that, as well as myself and others, one of the other witnesses was the former MP, Leader of the Conservative Party, and now Peer, Michael Howard. All the witnesses were saying similar things about the lack of organisation and bottlenecks being caused by the lack of stewards and police. The response from Liverpool consisted of a detailed 50 page document and, on receipt of it, UEFA quietly brushed the matter under the carpet and discontinued proceedings. It was obvious they had recognised that their own organisation of the event was not up to standard. This was yet another example of football bureaucracy looking after itself, while looking to blame others for its own failings.

In yet another infamous Manchester United versus Liverpool clash on March 23, 2008, which resulted in Liverpool and Argentina midfielder Javier Mascherano being sent off when referee Steve Bennett dismissed him for his second booking just before half time.

In his report, Bennett stated:

> *"Having shown the red card, he (Mascherano) failed to leave the field of play and then became very aggressive, before players from his own side restrained him."*

Liverpool were well beaten on the day, losing 3-0 to United and it didn't take long for the FA to rub salt into the wounds after such a resounding defeat. Three days later the expected charge arrived, with an allegation of improper conduct *'in that he (Mascherano) remonstrated with the referee, thereby delaying the restart of the game'*.

We went through the video of the incident, analysing timings and actions and following my advice, Mascherano accepted the charge and submitted his own witness statement, as well as a stellar line up of witnesses who were supporting him. These were manager Rafa Benitez, together with Xavi Alonso, Ryan Babel and Steven Gerrard. I also advised Mascherano that it would be in his interests to prepare a written apology to be sent to Bennett – and he did this immediately. It was all about damage limitation. Even as only a mere supporter, I knew how valuable Mascherano was to the team.

In his statement, Mascherano outlined how he had complained to the referee about Fernando Torres being issued with a caution, saying:

> *"I cannot explain why I suddenly began to run towards the referee, but as I reached him I was smiling and held my arms outwards, asking him 'What happened, why?' I repeated this and at that point the referee showed me my second yellow card and then a red card. I could not understand why he had done this, because I had not used any bad language to him. I had only asked him to explain why he had given the yellow card to Fernando, but he had not replied to me. I continued to ask him, but he began to walk away. By this time I had moved from the field of play beyond the touchline and had been approached by a number of my team-mates, who were attempting to calm me down. I continued to shout to the referee, asking him why, but at no time during the whole incident did I swear at him. I recall Xavi Alonso saying to me, 'Stop, there's no point doing anything, it's going to make it worse'. I also recall Alex Miller of the coaching staff and Steven Gerrard speaking to me, and at that point the manager Rafael Benitez took hold of me with both hands cupped*

around my face and looked straight at me, almost nose to nose and said, 'Listen, it's finished. You're sent off. Be calm. It's finished. Go.' His influence was very calming and I immediately listened to what he had to say and made my way to the dressing room."

A hearing was convened within days of the game, but Mascherano couldn't attend, so myself and Liverpool CEO Rick Parry represented him. Despite admitting the charge, the disciplinary panel extended the suspension from one game to three games, as well as fining him £15,000, which we both felt was very harsh. This is what I mean when I talk about the FA and its inconsistency. Mascherano received this harsh penalty, yet other players would only get a fine for the same thing. There needs to be a set tariff for such a rule breach, so that each and every player knows they are being treated on a consistent and equal basis.

We submitted an appeal to the FA against what we considered to be the excessive penalty and this time Mascherano attended the hearing at Soho Square in London with me. We also needed a translator, but despite putting forward a robust case the FA were going hard on the 'Respect' campaign and the appeal failed. Mascherano had to sit out the three games. But this case also highlighted the difficulties of working with players who didn't have a good command of the English language and needed to use translators, which made life so much more difficult when trying to get points across.

Whilst working for Liverpool, I had the pleasure of also working with an absolute gentleman, in the shape of the late Gary Ablett. Gary was a total professional and very passionate about the game. Whilst reserve team manager at Liverpool, in 2008 he completely lost the plot with a referee in a reserve team game against Bolton Wanderers, when the referee claimed he'd walked onto the pitch, shook his hand and then, with a deadpan face, said, *"You're a fucking disgrace, you don't know how fucking bad you are."*

Despite his outburst, he was an absolute gentleman and admitted the charge, presenting himself very well at the hearing, where, on the basis of the mitigation I put forward for him, received a suspended £500 fine.

I found it a privilege to work for Liverpool and throughout my whole professional career, and regard it as one of my favourite periods of time in the game. It opened many doors for me at the club, including being invited by Rafa to watch training with my son at Melwood. However, once Ian Silvester and Rick Parry, my two biggest allies at Anfield, had left the club to move onto pastures new, sadly my contract wasn't renewed. Of course I was disappointed by this, but a new regime had taken over at the top of the club's administrative management and they had their own ideas on how they wanted to do things. In football you have to accept things change and just move on to your next project. One thing that can't be taken away from me, though, are my memories of dealing with, what in my opinion, is the greatest club in the world.

5 - THE MAD HOUSE

IT WAS ONLY WHEN I WORKED inside Leeds United that I appreciated the size of the club, with a passionate and global fan base. After Liverpool and Manchester United (in that order!) it's my view that Leeds United are the next biggest club in the country. The likes of Arsenal, Chelsea and Manchester City may have won many more trophies in the last twenty years or so, but in terms of their stature they get nowhere near Leeds United. They are the original "Sleeping Giants".

My pathway to working at Elland Road came about because in 2014 I'd been working as a consultant for the prestigious London law firm *Mischcon De Reya*, helping them in their sports law department. Around that time they had been handling the takeover of Leeds by the controversial Italian businessman Massimo Cellino. The Italian's reputation preceded him. He was known as the *"Manager Eater"* in Italy after going through more bosses in his 22 years at Cagliari than he'd had pepperoni pizzas, and it felt like he revelled in the notoriety. The media took an instant interest in him – and little did I know that, in just a few months time, I'd be working for him.

Following a recommendation from Mischcon's, I found myself parachuted into the eye of the storm inside Elland Road. Cellino had no experience of how the English game worked, not to mention the fact that he'd already sacked the CEO and Head of Football Administration within weeks of seizing control of the club. In effect, the club was rudderless in terms of its adherence and understanding of the rules and regulations that govern the game. So I found myself taking a phone call from Cellino out of the blue whilst I was in New York attending a football conference, in which he made it clear to me he'd heard good things about me and was keen to get me involved at the club to help him out.

When I returned from the States I went to Elland Road to meet up with a finance expert working for Cellino called Andrew Umbers. We had a very short meeting and there and then, on the spot he told me to come on board and start work immediately by reviewing all the player and agent contracts to work out if there were any areas of concern. I even got my own office. Andrew and I got on straight away. It transpired that his family were the former owners of the Barnsley Brewery so there was some connection to my home town. But in my view, while his expertise was in financial restructuring and he was obviously very competent in that area, I quickly realised he had little understanding of the real operational practicalities of the day-to-day running of a football club.

It was clear that he'd been instructed by Cellino to cut costs throughout the club, irrespective of the serious impact it was having on the running of the place. For example, the cleaners at the Thorpe Arch training ground, along with the chef, had been made redundant. The ladies who did the laundry for the playing kit were also deemed surplus to requirements, together with many others. Cellino's twisted logic was, why use three people to do three jobs when you can use just one person to do all three. The much lauded Head of Welfare at the Academy, Lucy Ward, who is now one of the leading pundits and co-commentators in football, found herself being ordered to cook all the players' meals, including those in the first team. However, in my view, as I've told her on many occasions, she's not really up there with Delia Smith! Her standard of cooking includes putting baked beans in pasta! It has become a standing joke between us and many the time I've said to her *'Who the fuck puts baked beans in pasta?'.* God knows what happens in her household when it comes to meal times! It's a reasonable assumption to say her partner Neil Redfearn, the former Head of the Leeds Academy, doesn't ask for anything pasta based!

As a result of this cost-cutting a heavy strain was placed upon the operational side of the club and in my view it couldn't function in the manner expected of a club of United's size.

Talking of Lucy, the work she did at Leeds United cannot be underestimated and many of her young protégés are now fully-grown high profile professional footballers such as James Milner, Fabian Delph, Kalvin Phillips, and Lewis Cook which is testament to the outstanding work she did with them. They all speak highly of her, as does everyone she nurtured through the Academy in good times and bad and she was a major loss to Leeds United when Cellino's vindictive nature forced her from her role at Elland Road. Lucy had the last laugh though, absolutely smashing Cellino into oblivion with a successful sexual discrimination claim following her departure. It was as big a victory for all women in the game as it was for Lucy personally.

To give an example of how Cellino operated; staff morale was the lowest I'd ever seen at any place I'd worked during my entire career. Generally speaking, the staff didn't like Cellino – and certainly didn't trust him. They feared him, or should I say the consequences of getting on the wrong side of him. This troubled me, and at one point I felt I needed to talk to him about it, but he struggled to understand the issues I was raising. However, he suddenly did grasp it when I told him that, in my view, if he were to invest the relatively small sum of £50,000 into the staff wages budget to give them all a pay rise, seeing as they hadn't had one in a number of years, it would have given them a lift and made them more productive and receptive to what he was doing in the club. I pointed out that many of them were doing the work of several people, but not receiving any extra pay. By investing that amount it would have meant each member of staff would have got an extra thousand pound in their wage packet over the year.

Cellino shot me down straight away in his usual tantrum manner, questioning why he should give them extra money and claiming the previous owners should have been responsible for this. He bluntly refused my request, or to even consider it, but as I was leaving his office he then raised another issue with me, about sourcing an Audi R8 sports car for his son Eduardo's birthday. He knew I had a contact within the game who supplied cars to players and I had already secured delivery of a Mini for the same son some weeks earlier. I asked him what his budget was, so I could relay this to my contact, and he told me he was willing to pay up to £80,000. Quite simply put, he wouldn't share £50,000 between all those who worked so hard for him at the club, but would blow £80k on a vanity project for his spoiled and indulged son. It summed him up perfectly.

My first meeting with Cellino had been an eye-opener. I saw him on the first day I spent at Elland Road and the first thing he did was take the piss out of my weight, with a string of insulting comments. This went down like a lead balloon. When I sat there listening to him carrying on, it was clear to me that he was a very charismatic man with a brazen sense of humour, but as the weeks and months went by it became blindingly obvious he was prone to serious mood swings and would frequently lose his temper, sometimes over the most trivial of matters. Then, almost immediately, he could turn the charm on again. It was like flicking a switch, so me and the other members of staff became very wary of his irrational side. Don't get me wrong, at times there were some very humorous moments and Cellino could be very funny with some of the things he would say or how he would put them across in his passionate Italian way but ultimately working at Leeds would prove to be one of the most bizarre experiences of my professional career. At times it genuinely felt like I was working inside a mad house. My time at Leeds inevitably ended in acrimony and we faced each other in a tribunal which resulted in Cellino being hit with a big fine and a lengthy suspension from football. The club itself was also fined, but more of all this later.

There were times when I seriously questioned myself over the following months about continuing to work for him, due to his nasty temper tantrums, which were akin to dealing with a spoiled child. It was draining and stressful. However, I quickly learned that the only way to deal with him was to stand up to him and give as good as you got. Due to his volatile temper, at first it was difficult to separate when he was simply expressing himself with his passionate Italian personality and mannerisms and when he was actually losing his temper. But as time went on it became much easier to distinguish between the two. I was the only person prepared to stand up to him, because everyone else at the club lived in fear of him. His temper was such that he would become completely irrational at times, raising his voice to the point of not being able to decipher what he was saying, building himself up into such a frenzy he would literally start frothing at the mouth. He would be rude to many people without realising it, using offensive language in English, with his most common phrases being *"motherfucker"* and *"dickhead."* Whenever I raised issues with him regarding the FA, his standard response was *"Fuck the Federation"*, a sentiment I tended to agree with most of the time!

Having said all this, there were times when his logic in addressing certain issues was reasonable. For example, one thing he did which I thought was sensible, and I'd never heard of it being done before in the English game, was to eliminate the use of a bonus sheet for any new signings. The bonus sheet is an agreed document between the club and the players regarding bonuses to be paid on top of their normal wages and is usually associated with appearances. Normally, before the start of the season, a meeting would be held between a group of senior players and the club executive management and a payment structure would be agreed. Cellino would have none of it for the players who came into the club that summer. Instead, he had it written into the contracts that in the event of the team getting promoted to the Premier League and a player making a certain number of appearances that season, he would pay them a bonus of a full year's salary instead. For example, if a player was earning £1m-a-year and Leeds went back into the top flight, the player would receive the same amount again as a bonus at the end of the promotion-winning season. However, the odds were always in Cellino's favour because only three teams out of 24 could go up and, in any event, getting into the Premier League would have been worth around £200m to him. Not only that but given the hold he liked to have on any team manager, he always had the option of influencing team selection to ensure a player didn't reach the required number of appearances or is that me being just a little bit too cynical? This was one of his brighter ideas, but sadly, these turned out to be few and far between.

One of the biggest problems working for him was that Cellino didn't seem to do mornings. He rarely turned up at Elland Road before lunchtime. This meant you were restricted in what you could actually get done, because his micromanagement was so intense that no-one at the club dare do anything which might have caused an outburst from him. He also had some weird and wonderful superstitions, like eliminating the number "17" from the club and not using the colour purple. One day he even told me to make sure I got high-earning goalkeeper Paddy Kenny out of the club because he was born on the 17th and that he just couldn't risk him being at Leeds United. You will also recall I mentioned that he had bought his son a Mini, but when we sought to arrange the delivery of it Cellino refused to allow it to be delivered on a Friday, because *"Friday was a bad luck day for delivering cars"* Like I said, it was like working in a mad house at times.

At the time I met Andrew Umbers we discussed the terms of my contract and I felt that, in order to guarantee Cellino had the best guidance and the role he wanted me to perform, it needed to cover a full season – and should be 12 months long. That way it would cover two transfer windows and a first full season for Cellino in the English game to help him and the staff adjust to the cost cuttings that were being made and the operational workings of the club. Umbers agreed with me. But on speaking to Cellino, he wanted to give me a shorter deal, which would only take me up to the end of September, meaning the summer's transfer window would be covered along with the first few weeks of the 2014/15 season. However, Cellino eventually relented and a 12 month contract was agreed and signed, but as I was to learn later, the duration of the deal wasn't worth the paper it was written on because coincidentally, he terminated the contract at the end of September anyway. This showed that his intention all along was that once I'd got him through the summer transfer window and early part of that season, I'd be out the door.

Football is not a nine to five job, but to give some indication of the time I spent at the club between June and August, I worked over 700 hours such was the intensity of the role. When it came to managers, one of Cellino's theories was that he wanted a coach instead of a manager. His thinking was the club, or should I say him or his Sporting Director between them, could select the players he wanted to sign and a coach should just coach them. Theoretically that meant that when a coach left the club, a new coach could just pick up where the old one left off, with the same players but having little or no influence on transfer thus eliminating any conflicts with players. In effect, he was playing a real life game of *Football Manager*. When you consider how many managers he went through in his time in football, you could argue that it made sense. The problem with his system however was that if the players were not of the required standard for that level of football, even the best coach in the world would struggle to make a silk purse out of a sow's ear.

As the weeks went on, Cellino relied more and more on me and would confide in me about members of staff he believed were leaking information to the media, along with staff members he wanted to sack. I was caught between the devil and the deep blue sea, because by this time I had become a senior reference point for the staff who viewed me as the person to go to in order to air any concerns. So it was difficult at times. Maybe it's the trade unionist background of my parents that influenced me, because I have always been a supporter of the workforce against the hierarchy wherever I have worked. I have always looked out for them, but my time at Leeds was one of my more difficult briefs in this regard.

At one point, during a pre-season training camp in Italy, an aptly named guy who was a former drummer called Stix Crossland, who had served the club for many years, was ordered home by Cellino mid-tour, despite already having agreed for him to travel with the team. I clearly recall Cellino ranting about Stix when he discovered he was in Italy even though this had been approved by him, saying his job was not to travel with the team, but to *"drive his car for him and clean his fucking shoes"*. He made it clear that he wanted to end Crossland's employment and Stix discussed his concerns about losing his job on many occasions. He was Leeds through and through, and I went to see Cellino on behalf of him to insist he kept his job, because at that time I thought that he was an asset to the club. Nobody knew the workings of the club and people associated with it like Crossland so it was common sense that he should remain on the staff with his intimate knowledge that would be helpful to anyone joining the club. But this act of kindness and support was brutally repaid some months later by Crossland who was happy to side with Cellino when it came to the termination of my contract, as were a number of other employees who I had very good working relationships with. It just showed that when the chips were down, some people would do anything to keep their jobs, undermine former workmates and were generally prepared to do anything to keep in Cellino's good books. I viewed it as a betrayal by people I had supported and helped.

A month after I joined Leeds Cellino stunned club supporters by appointing the relatively unknown Dave Hockaday as the new First Team Coach. Hockaday's managerial experience amounted to being a youth coach at Watford and Southampton, then four years of being manager of Forest Green Rovers when they were in the National League. I've absolutely no idea why Hockaday was appointed and had no part in his recruitment, but from his first day in the post it was obvious to me it would all end in tears. I got on well with Dave and he was a really nice bloke, as was his assistant Junior Lewis, but the reality was, they were both out of their depth at Leeds United, although you can't blame Dave for taking the opportunity. One thing I will say about Dave is that in discussions about incoming players in meetings with Cellino, myself and agents, identify two outstanding players that would have transformed the club. One was a certain Virgil Van Dijk, then at Celtic. Unfortunately Cellino decided to ignore this advice and signed Guiseppe Bellusci on-loan from Italian Serie B side Catania. Known as "*The Warrior*" in his native Italy because of the way he played, Bellusci thrived on an undeserved hard man reputation, but I can think of another word starting with "W" that is more appropriate for him. He made his debut in a 4-1 defeat to Watford and things didn't improve much from there – he wasn't liked by many of his teammates or the club staff

The other target Dave suggested was Andre Gray, who was then at Luton but went on to play for both Watford and Burnley in the Premier League. Instead of signing Gray, Cellino sanctioned the signing of a guy called Mirco Antonnucci from Ternana, who lasted just two seasons, scoring 19 goals. In effect, Hockaday had identified two players that, had Cellino chosen to sign, would have seen Leeds make a huge profit in due course and may even have resulted in promotion but as I say, it was like Cellino was playing his own real life game of *Football Manager*. The only thing he didn't do was sit in the dug out on a Saturday afternoon.

Hockaday didn't have any real input into signings, as this was mainly done by Cellino and his sporting director, Nicola Salerno, who had been an associate of Cellino's for many years and was said to know the Italian game very well. All in all, I knew Hockaday wouldn't last very long – and I was correct. After just 70 days, on August 28, 2014, he and Lewis were sacked. In his time at the club, he won just one league game, against Middlesbrough, along with a League Cup game against Accrington Stanley. Four players were also sent off in his six games in charge.

The manner of Dave Hockaday's dismissal is a good illustration of the inner-workings of Cellino's mind. On August 23, 2014 Leeds crashed to a 4-1 defeat at Watford and the performance was very poor. Leeds also had two players given red cards. You could see that the team was just not functioning as they should have, and I'm sure all the off-field issues associated with the club were having an effect on the players, including the way Cellino was involving himself in things. Midway through the second half Cellino completely lost the plot in the directors' box in an embarrassing tantrum episode after he learned that some of the players were not travelling back with the team but had planned to be at a function in London. A guy called Steve Holmes, who had been working in the Academy but had been promoted to become more involved in assisting the first team in travel arrangements and other matters, got the full force of Cellino's outburst. I felt so sorry for him. It wasn't the first time that this had happened and it was one of those embarrassing moments when you just want to slide down in your seat before disappearing underground. Fortunately Steve saw the funny side of it a few days later saying "I hope Sky's third eye camera wasn't on us at the time!"

The upshot of his outburst was that Cellino gave the order that all players must return to the club's Thorpe Arch training complex that night, and that message was relayed to the dressing room after the game, which caused real antagonism among the squad. It was the last thing they wanted to hear. Hockaday was in an impossible situation having to deal with the aftermath. In fairness to the players, they stood their ground and I know of at least one player who phoned the PFA from the dressing room to complain and find out where he stood under the terms of his contract. In any event, I think many of the British players by this time had had enough of Cellino and his antics. There were good seasoned pro's like the very sensible and friendly Steven Warnock, Steve Morrison, and Billy Sharpe, so it wasn't as if Cellino was trying to impose himself on some young kids. The players just ignored his edict to return to the training ground and this highlighted just how chaotic things were becoming at the club. On the journey home Cellino phoned me on several occasions saying he wanted to sack Hockaday. I advised him that if that was what he wanted to do, then he should wait until the following day so that appropriate arrangements could be made. Social media was going into meltdown and it was obvious Dave was on borrowed time, but I think he knew that.

However by the time I got to my local pub that evening, the 'Commercial Inn' in Barnsley and sat down with my first pint, Cellino had called me again and told me he'd decided he wasn't going to sack him. It seemed Dave had dodged a bullet after all! But his mercy didn't last long, because four days later Leeds were knocked out of the League Cup at local rivals Bradford City. The team were drawing at half time following another poor performance and were down to 10 men after the sending-off of Luke Murphy. Once again, we had a huge tantrum from Cellino, who left the ground at half time and stormed off into the night with his family. The following day the mood at the club was very sombre and as usual Cellino didn't surface until after lunch after most of the staff had gone home. I was sat in the office when Cellino rang me. All he said to me was, *"Sack Hockaday"*. Straight away, I responded by telling him that, as the owner and person who appointed him, he should do the decent thing and speak to Dave himself but Cellino responded by saying he couldn't do it, because he *"didn't like confrontation"*, which sounded like the understatement of the decade to me! He also told me to sack Junior Lewis as well. I rang them both to give them the news – and it was clear they had both been expecting it.

Most normal club owners would have done the sensible thing and lined up a replacement manager before sacking their current one but Cellino was far from normal. That same evening, and within a couple of hours, I was summoned to his office, where he asked me who I thought we should appoint as the next manager. I was shocked, and made it clear I was having no input, because I didn't want it coming back on me further down the line. With that, Cellino decided there and then that he wanted Steve Clarke as the next boss. He was out of work at the time, so I got his number for him. Cellino rang him straight away and it was obvious Clarke wasn't interested in the job. So immediately, Cellino resorted to Plan B and, on a whim, decided he wanted Paul Clement, who was assistant to Carlo Ancelotti at Real Madrid at the time. Cellino made the call to Ancelotti on speaker phone from his office and, talking half Italian and half English between the two, told Ancelotti he was interested in taking Clement and wanted to know what his salary was. Bearing in mind Hockaday had only been on £130,000-a-year, when Ancelotti told him it was over 1m Euros a year, the conversation ended very quickly!

As this farce unfolded, I just sat there thinking how surreal it all was and how fans wouldn't believe what was really happening inside their club. Cellino then reverted to Plan C, which was to put Academy Manager Neil Redfearn in temporary charge while he sourced a permanent boss. Redders had done a sterling job at the Academy over a number of years and in my view is one of the best coaches in the country when it comes to developing young players. His success rate at Leeds was phenomenal, nurturing Academy graduates such as Lewis Cook, Charlie Taylor, Sam Byram, Bailey Peacock-Farrell, Alex Mowatt and Kalvin Phillips. Many of these players went on to play in the Premier League and others were sold by Leeds for huge profit. Redfearn was responsible for that, and as I have said previously the club should have been eternally grateful to him and his partner Lucy Ward for the way they had developed those young men, as good people as well as outstanding players who made the club millions of pounds in transfer fees. Instead

Cellino, some months later, brutally sacked both Redfearn and Ward.

Remarkably, given the talent brought through at Leeds, Cellino had initially been intent on closing the Academy down and it was only the sterling efforts of Redfearn, Ward, Steve Holmes and a lady called Mary Lally, who produced the documentation and reports to prove to him that it was a viable concern, that changed the Italian's mind. One interesting point, though, is that Cellino actually told Redfearn during one of his spells in charge of the first team, to get rid of future England international Kalvin Phillips because he *"wasn't good enough"* yet Redfearn stood his ground and refused. Considering Phillips has gone on to become a cult figure at Elland Road and starred for the national team at Euro 2020, it shows just how poor Cellino's judgement was when it came to players. It was the same with Steven Warnock who was a great pro and good to have around the club but was a played Cellino was desperate to get rid of and used his age as a factor to try to sell him. Steven really took the piss out of Cellino though when he scored the only goal in a one nil win against Bolton Wanderers at Elland Road when his goal celebration included him pretending to walk like an old man with a stick. We all knew what he meant apart from Cellino who was ignorant to the fact that the piss was being well and truly taken out of him whilst everyone else was laughing at him. I had a number of supportive conversations with Steven about his future and I constantly argued with Cellino that he should be kept at the club for his ability and experience. One day Cellino was once again on his high horse about Warnock saying he was a certain age and I was telling him he was wrong so I challenged him to tell me the year he was born and of course he got it wrong, but in true Cellino fashion he then told me he only said that to see if I knew my stuff. Anything to save face from being proved wrong! This is what I was up against on a daily basis!

Anyway, back to the hunt for a new manager. With Redfearn in temporary charge Cellino reverted to Plan D and asked me if

I knew Gary Megson. Cellino was concerned about the number of players who had been sent off in the first few games of that season and wanted someone with a reputation as a disciplinarian. He'd been told by someone that Megson fitted the bill. I knew Gary quite well and set up a meeting at Cellino's apartment next-door to the swish Malmaison Hotel in Leeds city centre the following day. However, about an hour before the meeting, Cellino rang me to say he'd changed his mind and didn't want Gary after all, so it was all cancelled. It was another example of how farcical things were becoming. Things then went very quiet and Cellino and Salerno kept their own counsel about their next target in the apparently never-ending quest to find Leeds' next manager. Then suddenly and without warning, a little known Serbian appeared on the scene called Darko Milanic. I'd never heard of him, and neither had most of the Leeds fans. After listening to his first press conference, I just knew he wasn't going to last long. The only surprise was that he lasted a month, leaving on October 25, 2014, by which time I had also left the club.

During my time as CEO at Leeds, Lewis Cook was the biggest talent at the club and one of the hottest properties in English football. Premier League scouts were watching him week in, week out and he was obviously destined for bigger things. He was also in the final year of a contract worth just £600-a-week and didn't even have an agent. I continually told Cellino he needed to get him tied into a new deal and in my view, the best way to do it would be to up his wages to £1,000-a-week on a long-term deal before any agent got involved with Cook and his family. Cellino ignored my advice and kept saying he'd deal with it when his contract expired, which I knew would be far too late. He just wasn't interested in doing what I advised, I assume because it would mean paying out extra money. After I left the club and Lewis's deal got closer to ending, it must have dawned on Cellino that he needed to do something by which time it was too late because Lewis had been snapped up by leading football agency Stellar, which meant that any discussions on contracts and financial arrangements were even more difficult and costly to the club. Once again, it was an example of Cellino just not listening and thinking he knew best.

The signing of Liam Cooper from Chesterfield was arguably the most successful signing during the Cellino era but true to form that transfer was not as it was portrayed by Cellino. In July 2014 Chesterfield hosted Leeds in a pre-season friendly and centre half Cooper was one of the star players for the Spireites. I had been tipped off about his ability and that Chesterfield were open to offers on the player. In conversations with the then Chesterfield CEO and ex-player Chris Turner, he let it be known that for the right money, the club would consider selling Cooper.

Before the game I spoke to Salerno and told him to watch Cooper. Within fifteen minutes of the match kicking off, Salerno turned to me and said he was going to speak to Cellino about Cooper, because he wanted to sign him. Several days later I confirmed with Salerno whether he had discussed going for Cooper with Cellino and he confirmed he had, but still nothing progressed. I knew that if Leeds didn't get him then somebody else would and so over the next few weeks I mentioned signing Cooper to Cellino on many occasions, badgering him to do a deal with Chesterfield. I knew Cooper's quality and ability far outweighed any of the sub-standard players Cellino had been bringing in and everyone I talked to about the player spoke highly of him. But Cellino wouldn't commit himself to the transfer and kept putting it off. In the end I think he got that fed up of me badgering him about it that one day, out of the blue, he agreed to make an offer of £600,000 with add-ons, which took the fee up to about £1m. I personally negotiated the terms of the transfer with Chesterfield and, taking into account that I later became their CEO, I think that we got Cooper cheap, because we would have been prepared to go much higher for him given that he has gone on to captain Leeds in the Premier League and is a Scottish international. Terms were quickly agreed and the deal was finalised within 24 hours. However, some months later, when Cooper was receiving rave reviews for his performances, I was amazed to hear Cellino claim that he'd seen the player playing in the game against Leeds and realised he just had to have him at Elland Road! He portrayed himself as the one who'd identified him. But what was even more astonishing was that he wasn't even at the game to see Cooper play that afternoon!

During my time at Leeds I was involved in over 40 contract transactions, which included 15 incoming transfers, several loan contracts, seven outgoing transfers and six lengthy negotiations which didn't end up proceeding. Included in these incoming transfers were 11 from overseas including two from South America. To be honest, the vast majority of the players selected by Cellino and Salerno were sub-standard and nowhere near good enough to play in the Championship for a club the size of Leeds United.

If one incident proves just what an absolute madhouse Leeds had become under Cellino, it was the deal involving Italian goalkeeper Marco Silverstri. It was the pre-season of 2014 and Marco was making his home debut in a friendly against Dundee Utd at Elland Road. He made quite an impression on me, too, for all the wrong reasons. At half time the teams went to the dressing rooms, but while I was walking to the LUTV studio I went along a private corridor that led to the car park and noticed Silvestri stood outside in the car park in full kit. I went over to see what the hell was going on and discovered he was having a cigarette, while the rest of the players were having a team talk inside the home dressing room. I asked him what he was doing and he said '*I have smoke*'. In response I told him to get his arse into the dressing room. I spoke to the manager and

Cellino about it but no action was taken. Most players have a suck on an orange at half time, but Silverstri obviously preferred to suck on a ciggie! Unbelievable really.

Another thing that Cellino targeted in his cost-cutting was the expenses associated with full medicals for incoming players, he usually signed them following a brief check by the club's physiotherapist and doctor. These were very limited and the pair did the best they could in difficult circumstances. The bottom line was that if Cellino wanted the player it just didn't matter about the state of his fitness; the player was coming to Leeds United. It was as simple as that. I recall that in one case the physio and doctor both came to see me and reported that a player who was being examined had got the *"worst knees they had ever seen on a young player of his age"* and recommended the transfer should not progress. I rang Cellino to give him the news, only to receive the expected abusive response with Cellino saying, *"Fuck what they say. I say sign the player. Just fucking sign him"*. The trouble was that most of the players who were being signed were shit, to put it bluntly. Cellino also didn't want to pay the medical insurance premiums that clubs have to pay, saying he preferred to have his players treated by top Italian surgeons. This was impractical, so we let him go on about it whilst still ensuring the premiums were paid so the players could receive the treatment they needed.

I don't know how the Leeds supporters put up with it for so long. Eventually an organised campaign was started to try to force Cellino out but the fans had been very patient for a long time. But I'm really surprised that by the end of his tenure he had not actually been accosted by some fans, such was the damage he had done to the club and the bad headlines he had generated The supporters should have upped the ante earlier in terms of their campaign to get him out. Leeds fans can be intimidating at the best of times, and it was as if Cellino thrived on the fight against them.

Agents would just turn up unannounced from around the world and on a number of occasions, it would turn out some of them were not even internationally registered through the FA, so before we could even start discussions, we would have to ensure that they were registered correctly. Great. Just what I needed. This took time and delayed things, but it was the way the club was being run and it drove me mad that things were being dealt with so amateurishly. Furthermore, because of the influx of foreign players, they insisted on all contracts being calculated in Euros at net, as opposed to British players, where the calculations were in Sterling and at gross levels. This caused all sorts of complications because of the potential fluctuation of the Euro, which would mean the contract payments could change from time to time.

I recall how, during a pre-season training camp in Italy in 2014, Cellino and Salerno had negotiated a loan deal for Souleyman Doukara from Catania, with a view to a permanent transfer when the loan expired. But they had made a basic and potentially costly mistake because they didn't agree on what the wages would be for the player if the deal became permanent. This meant that if the player was highly successful then clearly he would expect higher wages. A few days before the transfer window of the 2014/15 season closed a decision had been taken to accommodate another loan player being brought into the club. To facilitate it, we had to make the Doukara deal permanent. So, when it came to negotiating terms, the agent involved started to up the ante in terms of wages. I went to discuss this with Cellino because they had not agreed the terms at the time of the initial loan and he needed to explain to me what had been agreed at the original discussions in Italy. He blew a fuse about it and started to rant and rave, blaming me for it, He was shouting at me across the desk. I'd not had any involvement in it or even been in Italy at the training camp. The truth was that he had realised a big mistake had been made. This was just one rant too many from him and I snapped, launching myself out of my chair and across the desk at him with my finger pointing close to his face, shouting as loudly as he was, *"Don't you ever fucking blame me for something that's nothing to do with me. You fucked this up, and nobody else"*. Cellino's face suddenly changed. He shit himself and I genuinely think he thought I was going to get hold of him. He quickly backed down and retracted what he'd said, then went on, in true Cellino style, to blame Salerno for the fuck up!

In all my time working as a police officer and in football, I've never experienced pressure like I did on the transfer deadline day of September 1, 2014. It was intense, with the club involved in several deals throughout the day. It's certainly not as it is portrayed on Sky Sports – it's much more intense than that. The first problem was that Cellino had decided to fly back to Miami a couple of days before the window closed with a number of deals still ongoing. Because of the time difference this created its own problems. But just to add to the complications, Cellino had lost his mobile phone! Contacting him was even more difficult. I was in the office by 8am that day – 3am Miami time.

At one point I had three sets of agents for three different players in three different areas of Elland Road moving between one group to the next finalising transfers. I recall at one stage, once we'd discovered a new phone number for Cellino and offers were being made on some players to transfer away from Leeds United, I was in the intolerable and ridiculous position of having to discuss things with him by text. It was farcical. I was pushing him for a decision on a player called Dominic Poleon, whom Oldham Athletic were trying to sign. I couldn't believe it when he replied to me with a text that said, *"it is night in Miami"*, meaning he was more interested in sleeping than assisting in finalising the transfers. It was a ridiculous situation and indicative of the way he was running the club. It was only when he finally got his backside out of bed after lunchtime in the USA that we could start making some progress. Then about 45 minutes before the transfer window closed, I took a call from Cellino in Miami saying we were now going to sign yet another

Italian "non superstar" player. We waited and waited for the information to come through so we could prepare the contract, even though we knew it would be difficult. This all led to an infamous message posted from press officer Matt Diamond on the club's official *Twitter* site saying, *"don't go to bed just yet"*. Matt was reacting to what Cellino had just informed us, that another player was coming in, but the transfer fell through and by bad coincidence and timing it was also announced around that time the club had sold striker Matt Smith to Fulham. Sadly young Matt was crucified by the Leeds fans because they thought that tweet related to the sale of Smith, as opposed to the potential incoming of a new player. I felt really sorry for Diamond because it affected him quite badly. The Leeds fans didn't hold back in their thoughts and opinions, when in fact their anger should have been directed towards Cellino. The Matt Smith transfer was really weird, though, because only a week or so before he transferred to Fulham Cellino had sanctioned a new improved contract for him – so it just didn't make sense.

Then again nothing made much sense at Leeds under Cellino, to be honest, and my time at Leeds came to an abrupt end a few weeks after the transfer window closed on September 25, 2014 in dramatic fashion! In the days leading up to it I'd noticed that for some reason Cellino had gone "cold" on me. It was one of those feelings when you just know something is in the air. The day before the sacking he had held a meeting of senior club staff and I was omitted from the meeting. I asked him why this was and he gave some bland excuse about it not being relevant to me, so I just knew something was going on. It was unusual for me not to be in those meetings. On 25th September I'd attended a Football League meeting at Walsall on behalf of the club and as I drove home I received a call from Fay Greer, the club's financial controller. I had worked closest with Greer in my time there and she went on to tell me that Cellino had discovered that a fixture between Leeds and Reading had been changed, without his consent. I had agreed to it, because at the time I believe Cellino was away from the club.

The simple fact was that Reading's match prior to the Leeds game had been changed from the Saturday to the Sunday for TV coverage, so under league rules the game, which had been scheduled to be played on Tuesday, September 30, had to be moved to Wednesday, October 1st in accordance with EFL Rules. Dave Hockaday had been consulted and agreed to it at the time. I also pointed out that if we had not agreed to it then the EFL would have just imposed the change in any event. By agreeing to the switch it just removed a lot of red tape. In any event this would not normally be something you would consult a club owner on. It would be dealt with between the administrative staff at both clubs with the input of the team managers so there was no reason to refer it to Cellino. Fay told me the Italian was *"apoplectic"* and *"going bat shit crazy"* and that she'd *"never ever seen anyone so mad"*. She said he was actually foaming at the mouth and demanding an explanation. I took it all in my stride, because as far as I was concerned this was yet another infantile tantrum. I told Fay the circumstances to relay back to him and said I'd speak to Cellino the following day when I was back in the office. A few minutes later she called me back saying he was still kicking off and that because of my conduct she was having to be the bearer of bad news and told me my contract had been terminated with immediate effect. A letter was being sent out to me by email. I was shocked by this and quite annoyed considering all the hard work and effort I'd put in over the months.

It was all over something so trivial. But in all honesty, it still came as a bit of a relief, as not only had I been tiring of Cellino's attitude and behaviour, but I was suspicious of some of the practices he was starting to engage in with agents. I had raised this with my own lawyers and was in any event considering my position because I wasn't happy with the way Cellino was going about things. But by doing what he did, I realised he would have to pay up my contract. Getting the money out of him, well, that was much easier said than done. The letter arrived by email and stated as follows;

Dear Mr Bean,

<u>TERMINATION OF CONTRACT DATED 28th MAY, 2014</u>

It has come to my attention that the Reading fixture, originally scheduled for Tuesday 30 September 2014 was moved to Wednesday 1 October 2014 upon consent given to Reading FC by you.

I believe that from the outset of your contract I have made it clear that all business decisions must be authorised by myself as President of Leeds United FC. At no point did you seek or obtain my permission, or even notify me as a matter of courtesy, to move the Reading fixture and as such I consider that you have committed a serious breach of your contract.

I feel that I am left with no alternative to terminate your contract under clause 9.1 with immediate effect."

Yours sincerely,

Massimo Cellino
President
Leeds United Football Club Limited.

I still smile when I see the state of his signature on the letter because he must have been raging, it takes up about a third of the page. I telephoned Cellino and he ignored the first couple of calls. He eventually answered. I said I was coming through to see him and made it clear, in no uncertain terms, that I would be giving him a piece of my mind and wanted to sort out my termination payment. Cellino very rarely left the club until after 10pm so I fully expected him to be in the office when I arrived at Elland Road at about 7pm that evening. But guess what... *"Elvis had left the building"*! Not only that, he'd cancelled my staff pass so I couldn't even get into the stadium to collect my things. It was pure cowardice by Cellino, something which I was to call him to his face some time later. To me it was obvious that this was just an excuse to get me out of the club on the terms he originally wanted when discussing my contract with Umbers some months earlier. I had done what he needed over the summer and was of no further use to him, so like many other staff members, I was just discarded without a second thought.

It was a decision that would come back to haunt him.

The size of Cellino's signature says it all - he must have been raging!

6 – FACE TO FACE...

HAD MASSIMO CELLINO USED his common sense, rather than allowing his narcissistic personality to rule him and paid up my contract without a fuss, his life would have been so much easier. But he didn't – and instead he proved to be the master of his own downfall.

Just a month after I'd left Leeds Cellino did an interview in *The Sun* newspaper, in which he said, "*I am not a normal person. I'm a trouble maker, I admit that.*" I couldn't have phrased it better myself. The problem he had was that he'd chosen the wrong man to pick an argument with. I'm sure he thought that things would blow over, but he couldn't have been more wrong. It's little wonder that after I had left the club, and in conversation with my good friend Neil Redfearn, he was still very prickly about me and told him "*I want Bean in the ground*". We had a good laugh at that. It was a typical example of Cellino hot air.

After being told I had lost my job at Leeds I returned to Elland Road the next morning to collect my belongings. On arrival I was met by one of Cellino's disciples, Mark Broadley, who had been ordered to 'shadow' me while I did what I had to do. I was in the stadium no longer than twenty minutes. I collected my things and then told Broadley that I needed to go to Cellino's office to make sure the invoice I'd prepared for what was owed to me was put on his desk. One thing I have learned over the years is that once you leave a football club's employment you have to go into a certain state of mind where emotional feelings are put to one side. You just have to be hard nosed. The club is the enemy and your previous workmates are no longer as close to you as they once were. As such I didn't trust those at the club to make sure he got it.

Broadley told me he had been instructed that I couldn't go in but I ignored him and jumped into the lift. He promptly followed me up to the fourth floor where Cellino's office was situated. All I wanted to do was place the envelope on his desk and leave. On leaving the lift the security door was locked so I couldn't gain access to the corridor leading to Cellino's office. I asked Broadley to open the door, which he did without any problem. From there I walked down the corridor and through Cellino's secretary's room and into his connecting office. It was before lunch time, so it was no surprise that Cellino had not arrived, so I placed the envelope on his desk, made a comment to his secretary about making sure he got the invoice and immediately left the building.

About a week later a letter arrived from Leeds United. After giving a more detailed explanation about the termination of my contract, I was then accused of "*Breach of Confidence and Harassment*" and that the club had even discussed the matter with local police. Amongst a number of allegations were those that I had sent Cellino inappropriate text messages, had written the words "Cellino is a Cunt" on a wipe board at the training ground and also told staff that he was planning to sack them. The letter also claimed that when making my way to Cellino's office in the company of Broadley, on reaching the security doors I had said to him, "*If you don't let me through the doors I will fucking break them down*" and then went on to "*force my way into Cellino's office shouting expletives*", (Cellino's office door was wide open by the way!). It all sounded very dramatic. The account in the letter was a total lie and fabrication. I don't know whether or not Broadley gave that explanation to Cellino or another senior person within the club to cause them to write in that fashion but however it came about, it was completely false. I've never seen Broadley to this day so I have never had the chance to challenge him about it but as the saying goes, "every dog has its day" and I am sure one day our paths will cross and I will be able to front him up about it. More importantly it was a sign of things to come and an foreshadowing of the dirty tricks that Cellino would resort to as I sought my compensation. Then again, he was not the only one who could fight dirty – as he was about to find out. The letter ended with a demand that I should give an undertaking not to go within 500 yards of either the Elland Road stadium or the Thorp Arch training ground for a period of 12 months. I just ignored it – but it was clear that Cellino was rattled.

Now I'll admit there had been text exchanges, and if I'm being perfectly honest, looking back, it all got a little out of hand from both sides, to the point of being juvenile at times. It wasn't my finest hour, but I was annoyed at the manner in which I had been treated after all the work I had done for him and saw his behaviour towards me as unacceptable. As I have said, if he had done things the right way then it would have avoided a lot of pain and discomfort for everyone involved. Once Cellino and Leeds had refused to pay me what I was owed, it was only then that the efforts began to recover my outstanding fees. However, a few days later I got a call from West Yorkshire Police asking me to call into the station to see them. It was laughable. Cellino had gone through with his claim that I'd been harassing him. These were classic Cellino tactics – he was cowardly and would usually get someone else to do his dirty work. As if the police hadn't got better things to do than massage the ego of an egotistical club owner? It was pathetic by both him and those officers who allowed themselves to be taken in by him.

By now I was suspicious of every move he made. Several days later I called in at the police station taking my lawyer with me for advice and protection against an ambush by the officers who'd been charmed by Cellino. When I got there the police advised that they had to record the fact a complaint had been made but were taking no action. It seemed a complete waste of time. They gave me a notice to that effect which I refused to sign and I recall telling them that if I ever ran out of toilet paper, I'd "wipe my backside with it because that's all it was worth". But what Cellino had done, nevertheless, was make an already delicate situation even worse and now I was really gunning for him – I decided I'd fight tooth and nail to bring about his downfall if the opportunity arose.

I was left with no option, under the FA rules, to commence arbitration proceedings against the club to recover what was owed. I lodged the appropriate documentation to enable the process to start. I had made it clear throughout that I was willing to sit down and discuss it amicably, like any normal person in a similar dispute would, to reach an agreed settlement. But Cellino had no interest in doing this at that time. It was yet another mistake by him, but he always wanted to be in control. I knew that whatever he did the contract between me and Leeds United was watertight and, irrespective of when it happened, he would have to pay me, yet by delaying the inevitable he just racked up more legal fees.

As expected the club rejected my claim and then, in their response, made the most ludicrous, unsubstantiated and distasteful allegation that they suspected I'd received a *"personal benefit"* from a scouting agreement the club had entered into with James Grant Sports Management, which I had signed on Cellino's instructions on 7 August 2014. It was farcical, but not only that, the agent involved, Peter Morrison, had done more work for Leeds United that summer than any other agent. The club claimed though that I'd committed Leeds United to paying £40,000 to an agent in fees who had not done any work for the club and were seeking to make a counterclaim to recover the fee back. Cellino was trying to bully and scare me, but in all honesty it was like water off a duck's back. Once again, just as the alleged incident involving Mark Broadley had been false, this was another downright lie and the slur incensed me to the point that I subsequently made a formal complaint to the Football Association. I complained that Cellino and Leeds had made a serious allegation of fraud without any evidence whatsoever and therefore this was improper conduct and should be investigated. He was using dirty tricks again and it gives some indication of just what an odious individual he is.

Then again if Leeds believed that I had actually received a

personal benefit, they had actually broken the FA rules themselves because they had failed to report a suspicion of misconduct taking place, which they were obliged to under FA Regulations. The rules are very clear in that respect, and it showed me that the club had no grasp on the rules by which they were governed.

By now battle lines had been well and truly drawn. Over the next few months the arbitration proceedings went back and forth between myself, my lawyer, and Leeds, but the eventual outcome was that Cellino caved in and a settlement was agreed without the need to resort to a full hearing. The reality of the situation was that Cellino had caused himself all that hassle, plus what was still to come, when in fact what he could have paid me up months earlier and never have heard from me again.

For several weeks prior to me leaving Elland Road, and unbeknown to Cellino, I had been having off-the-record conversations with the FA about my concerns over the Italian's running of the football club. I was getting very uncomfortable about the way things were being done without my knowledge, in respect of arrangements with agents in the incoming international transfers. Agents were turning up unannounced from abroad and it just didn't sit well with me. It was around this time that I was starting to contemplate my future at the club and began taking advice about walking out and where I stood legally.

One deal in particular stood out - the signing of Adryan, who had joined Leeds from Cellino's former club Cagliari in the summer of 2014. He'd joined on loan, with an option for Leeds to make the move permanent. For weeks Cellino had been raving about him being George Best, Pelé, Lionel Messi and Cristiano Ronaldo all rolled into one, when in fact he was nothing special at all. Since leaving Leeds Adryan has made fewer than 70 appearances for five different clubs which tells you how good he is! He was Brazilian in name only. There was also a strong rumour circulating that Cellino's daughter was close to him.

At the time of the deal being done I kept out of all discussions but something didn't seem right. It was just a gut feeling that I had. It just didn't feel right. It was all very "cloak and dagger". My main worry was that the player might have been the subject of a third party agreement where he is part "owned" by an agency, in addition to the club he plays for. This is outlawed in football and is viewed very seriously by the authorities. I had spent some time making my own enquiries about whether there was any third party ownership of the player without any success, and I even took advice on the matter from the Football League. In the middle of my dispute with Leeds I restarted my investigations and began to do some more digging, especially after one of the agents involved handed me an additional document relating to the transfer after it had been completed which confirmed, following a lengthy translation, that there *was* third party involvement in the player. I had no option but to hand this document to the FA to allow them to make their own enquiries and I understand that, despite following various paper trails, they were unable to reach a satisfactory conclusion and were in no position to proceed with it. But they were certainly not happy with it. The whole thing certainly wasn't right, that's for sure.

The Adryan deal was very complicated because of the number of agents involved – and the fact that the player was actually contracted to Flamenco in Brazil but had been loaned to Cagliari. This meant that Leeds had to reach an agreement with two different clubs because it was the loaning of a loan player. In effect, you'd got a Brazilian club, Italian club, several agents and then Cellino all involved! It was just very messy. It was made even worse by the fact that when it came to finalising the signing of the player Cellino had disappeared to Miami just before the transfer deadline. But the FA's investigation into the Adryan inquiry was only one part of the enquiry which ultimately led to Cellino's downfall in English football.

The FA struck gold when they looked into the transfer of Ross McCormack from Leeds to Fulham, which had taken place in the summer of 2014. In fairness to Cellino, this was one of the surprise deals of the close season after he secured a fee of almost £11m for the striker. Cellino personally handled this transfer and the negotiations himself and I was kept well away from it. As it happens, I'm glad about that, considering what was to follow. It took everyone by surprise at the club, because we only got to know about its completion the morning after it had been agreed when the news broke on *Sky Sports*.

McCormack had made it known that he wanted to leave the club in the period leading up to the transfer being finalised. There had been a lot of antagonism inside the club, caused predominantly between the player and Cellino who was, in my view, messing him around. Cellino was making ridiculous demands that McCormack should do things like pay for his own flight to join the summer training camp in Italy when in fact, according to McCormack, Cellino had given him permission to speak to other clubs. It was just another madcap period at Elland Road in keeping with the rest of that summer.

Following the finalisation of the transfer the relevant documentation was submitted to the governing body including the agent declaration form required by the FA, which every club has to sign in a transfer deal. It indicated that an agent had not represented the Leeds United side of the things and Cellino signed the form to confirm that. The agent fees had all been paid by Fulham to a company called "Arena Sports Management" in a correct and proper way.

The events I'm about to describe are well-documented in papers prepared by the FA following a disciplinary hearing that took place a couple of years later in London, involving Cellino and Leeds United surrounding the McCormack transfer, in which I was called as a witness for the FA.

In mid-September of 2014, about a week before I left the club, I was called to Cellino's office. I met him in his office along with another man I'd never met before and didn't recognise who was introduced to me as Barry Hughes. Cellino immediately told me that he had to pay Hughes £250,000. I asked him what the payment was in connection with, and he said it was money he'd promised Hughes for the work he'd done on the McCormack deal. This issue had been raised previously by some lawyers representing Mr Hughes in a letter to the club some weeks earlier so it was absolutely clear that there was a genuine belief from Hughes that he was entitled to the payment. I had written back to the lawyers on behalf of the club on Cellino's instructions advising them that the monies would not be paid, so I knew he had previously refused to pay it.

I don't have any issue with Barry Hughes. If he made an arrangement with Cellino for a payment in connection with the transfer of McCormack then that was a payment that should have been honoured right from the start and he would have been entitled to it but to do so Cellino should have ensured it was recorded in the form of a legal agreement. That way it would have been legitimately recorded by the club and in all probability would not have led to the problems that it subsequently occurred.

I immediately explained to Cellino that this payment to Mr Hughes was not part of the agreement and therefore could not be paid for what was being described to me as 'agency fees'. I suggested we contact the FA in an attempt to be transparent and explain the oversight. But this suggestion was declined by both men. Hughes was not a registered agent but appeared to work closely with various players and Cellino just said, "I have to pay the guy".

The discussion continued about the outstanding money when I realised that Ross McCormack still had a balance of around £65,000 outstanding on a club loan. I suggested to Hughes that he should recover this from his client, reducing the so-called debt of Cellino and Leeds to £185,000. All Cellino kept on saying, whenever I resisted arranging the payment, was that we had to pay Hughes. I tried to explain to him that as far as I was aware, there were no documents that existed relating to this agreement – but it didn't seem to make any difference to him.

By this time I was thinking, how the hell do we get out of this? I wanted to get out of the room and give myself time to think of a possible solution, if there was one, when reference was made (not by me I should add) to making the payment through a scouting agreement. The suggestion was that the money could be paid to another agent called Derek Day and his company Shadow Brands, by way of a scouting agreement. A scouting agreement is a contract between a club and a football agent or agency which allows payments to be made by the club to the agent in exchange for the identification and sourcing of players on behalf of the club. They are commonly used in football. Leeds United had done some work with Derek Day during the close season regarding another player and I found him to be a really decent agent to deal with. He was very professional and, like Barry Hughes, he was based in Glasgow. It was apparent from the conversation that the paired worked together closely and had a common interest in working in the football industry. I decided to buy myself some time to think through the situation and told both Cellino and Hughes I would be in touch, before leaving the meeting. I just needed to think it all through.

Because I'd not been involved in the transfer of McCormack, I wanted to check with Fulham that an agent fee had been agreed and paid by them. I recall when speaking to them asking if the payment had been in the region of £250,000, but was told it was '*north of that figure*". It later transpired from the FA documents that the eventual figure was more than £800,000

Once my conversation with Fulham ended I went back to see Cellino by which time Mr Hughes had left. I told Cellino that an agent representing Arena Sports Management, with whom Hughes was associated, had been paid by Fulham. Cellino already knew this and replied:

> "*Yes I know they've been paid, I know they earned money at the end of the deal, but I promised the guy (Mr Hughes)*

I'd pay him and I have to keep my word. So just pay him."

I pointed out again to him that this was not within the rules but Cellino had made it clear that the payment had to be made. This caused me real concern and I was struggling with it but my concerns increased the following day when I was contacted by Derek Day, who seemed to be aware of the discussions that had taken place. I was nervous around the agreement and didn't want to be part of it. I don't think Derek did either, but Cellino had ordered me to facilitate the payment.

A payment schedule was initially discussed with Derek, drawn up and a pro-forma scouting contract created, which was later taken to Cellino for him to approve to ensure he was happy. Cellino's preferred method of payment for most things relating to agency payments was to pay by instalments – and he very rarely paid them on time. Indeed, he was already at that time in dispute with a number of agents over payments including the Arena Sports Management company.

FA Regulations state that a club has five days to lodge any such contracts with the FA and so, rather than send it immediately I delayed as I was still working out how we could avoid going through with it. One of the thoughts I had was a misconstrued view that if I left it beyond the five day deadline it would invalidate the contract and I could then stall any payments. In the meantime I was confiding in my lawyer regarding all my concerns and continuing to mull whether it was time to leave. If truth be known, my head was all over the place about it. Despite the trials and tribulations the job brought, part of me enjoyed working inside such a big club but the rest of me was exhausted by the strain of working with Cellino. I was just tired of his attitude and his *modus operandi* was alien to how I worked.

In the meantime there were emails passing between myself and Derek relating to the payment, whereby it was clear pressure was being applied on me to sort the issue out. I continued to stall on things but it transpired that, despite our conversations, there were other conversations taking place between Cellino and Hughes about the agreement, of which I was unaware. A revised contract had been sent to Cellino, via his personal secretary, for the full £250,000 to be paid as opposed to the £185,000 that had been discussed in my presence. I had been kept out of the loop on this and was unaware of the new arrangement. Based on the new arrangement agreed between Cellino and Hughes by Monday, September 22, the final contract had been drawn up and I took it to Cellino for him to sign, which he did in my presence. In effect, I had managed to stall the whole thing by almost a week since the meeting between Cellino and Hughes, but time had run out and I had no other excuses to delay it.

At that point I knew I had until Friday 26th September to lodge it with the FA, so I decided to hold onto it and do nothing with it. However Cellino terminated my contract on Thursday, September 25, so the paperwork for this contract was left on my desk and no-one was dealing with it.

Coincidentally, on the afternoon of September 25, the day my contract was terminated, I was copied into an email from the club's finance department which indicated a number of payments had been made to various agents. Included in that list was the first scheduled payment to Derek's company, *Shadow Brands*, which was obviously in relation to the scouting agreement based around the McCormack transfer for which Cellino insisted on paying Hughes. Normally the payments that were due to be made to agents were run past me for me to check before being authorised by Cellino, but I had not been notified in advance about the payment to Shadow Brands being made. It was highly unusual for Cellino to make an agent's payment so quickly - and took me by surprise.

The big problem however was that the payment had been made without the contract having been lodged with the FA. When payments are made to agents the FA acts as a "Clearing House". The payments are made to an FA Account and they are then cross-checked against whatever contract is registered with them before the payment is forwarded to the agent by the FA. Because the club were making the payment quickly, this would have raised issues with those at the FA because there would be no contract to marry the payment up with as it had not been lodged at that time because I was holding onto it for reasons outlined earlier. Quite simply, by making the payment in haste, Leeds had run the risk of had drawn attention to themselves. There must have been a conversation between the Leeds United finance department and Cellino to approve the payment being made which I was not privy to because I was out of the office. When I returned to collect my belongings at the club on Friday 26 September the contract was still sitting on my desk untouched! This meant that it must have been submitted to the FA sometime later by another employee of the club. One thing is for sure, it certainly wasn't submitted by me. In reality, my sacking gave me reason to breathe a huge sigh of relief because I'd escaped being in the position of not going through with the deal. I have absolutely no idea which club employee sent that contract to the FA.

At all times before this point I'd done as I was instructed, although allowing myself to be manipulated into such a position is still something I'm not proud of. It shouldn't have happened. However this wasn't the last time I'd hear about this issue, because following the FA's investigation into Cellino it resulted in him, the club and Derek Day being charged with various serious rule breaches relating to this whole tawdry episode. I suddenly became the star witness for the prosecution. I was interviewed by Ian Ryder, the Anti Corruption Manager at the FA and, as a result of that interview a witness statement was prepared on my behalf by him. I've always been against wrongdoing in the game, and in this particular case I felt obliged to cooperate. I also knew it was highly likely it would bring me face-to-face with Cellino across the table in a Disciplinary Hearing. I had no gripe with either Leeds United as a football entity, Derek Day or indeed Hughes for that matter, but my feelings towards Cellino were different.

Having said all that, given the experience that was to follow at the hearing and issues relating to reimbursement of my loss of earnings, knowing what I know now, I would never assist the FA again unless it benefited someone that I was involved in representing. My advice to anybody would be that unless you are compelled to assist them because you are under their jurisdiction, give it a very wide berth and think very carefully before agreeing to help them. Put bluntly my advice is very simple; just don't do it, it's not worth the hassle. Afterwards I felt like the FA had hung me out to dry and misled me in relation to reimbursement of my loss of earnings. I was told that I would be fully reimbursed for expenditure such as travel and other out of pocket expenses. I lost two day's work because of the requirement for me to attend the hearing, so I issued them with an invoice to cover loss of earnings as well as my general expenses. However, in my opinion the FA moved the goalposts and only agreed to pay my travel and hotel expenses, meaning I was out of pocket.

I was summoned to a disciplinary hearing on September 15, 2016 where I finally came face-to-face with Cellino for only the second time since leaving Leeds. On the first occasion I had been at a game at Ewood Park watching Blackburn Rovers play United. As I came up the stairs towards the directors box, Cellino coincidentally happened to be emerging from the boardroom. We laid eyes on each other and my cold stare must have intimidated him. He looked like he shit himself on the spot, spun on a sixpence and ran for cover back into the sanctuary of the Ewood Park boardroom. Anyway, back to the disciplinary hearing – remembering his dislike of the colour purple due to it being unlucky, I made a point of wearing a tie of that colour! There was an army of lawyers for all sides, but I was dismayed in advance when I learned that the Commission Chairman was an individual called Nicholas Stewart, QC, who regularly chaired FA disciplinary hearings. I'd never got on with Stewart. I don't like him and I got the impression he was none too keen on me. On a personal basis I have found him to be one of the most pompous individuals I have ever met in my life, and I've met a lot! I'm sure he's a very nice man away from the disciplinary forum but he was someone I wouldn't want to engage with away from it. From my own experience in representing clients in disciplinary hearings I found that he had a habit of continually interrupting when you were making submissions on behalf of a client and I found this very irritating about him. As an esteemed lawyer it may be that he just wanted to progress the case more quickly and was trying to help the swiftness of the proceedings, but I found it so annoying.

Stewart didn't disappoint at the hearing and was very attentive to everything that was being said and whilst he made detailed notes I never felt comfortable in his presence. It was probably due to my dislike of him. I gave evidence for over four hours about what had occurred and on a number of occasions made it clear that Cellino was, in my view, a coward because of the way he went about his business. The cross examination was intense but having given evidence in Crown Court many times as a detective, felt that I had handled it competently.

One of the things I thought was wrong at the hearing was that Fay Greer, Leeds United's financial controller, had attended the hearing as a witness for the defence, but was allowed to sit in the hearing throughout. This meant that she got to hear my evidence, rather than it being between just myself and those being defended. She should not have been allowed in. Normally witnesses must wait outside the room in such hearings until they are required to give evidence. I felt she was given special treatment by being allowed to be present in the room whilst I gave my evidence. I also recall, when being cross-examined by the defence counsel of Derek Day, I used the phrase "*You're knocking on an open door*", as I knew that Derek was a victim in all of this and wanted to try to help his case, as he had been caught in the crossfire of Cellino's dispute. I wanted to get that message across.

Following the FA's refusal to pay my full expense claim I was very annoyed. I felt that they had gone back on their word. I'm sure they would disagree with my conclusion, but I suppose we will just have to agree to disagree. However at that point in retaliation I made an ill-judged decision informing them that I intended to withdraw my evidence and assistance, because I felt they were not being true to their word.

This, quite correctly, drew severe criticism from the Disciplinary Panel in their written reasons when they stated it was a "petulant reaction". They were right in that analysis. The reality of the situation was that I'd given the evidence and it stood as part of the proceedings, irrespective of my overreaction. I regret acting in this way and accept I should have just dealt with the matter in an altogether more reasoned manner, dealing directly with the FA instead of shooting from the hip. It gave the defence some ammunition to claim that this was some sort of pay-off for giving evidence in the hearing, which it most certainly was not, but I can understand why they would have thought that. I later learned that the defence lawyers had made an application to recall me to give further evidence about the issue, but the application was refused by the panel hearing the case. It's a good job it was, really, because there would have been no way on earth that I would have attended. I suspect the panel realised that.

Following the hearing the charges against those involved were all found proven. The club and Cellino were fined £250,000 each, although Cellino's fine was reduced on appeal to £100,000. In addition Cellino was suspended from all football for a period of 18 months, reduced to 12 months on appeal. Derek was fined £75,000 and suspended from acting as an agent for seven months. All three were also ordered to pay the costs of the hearing, however the written reasons were also critical of my part in the issue, even though I had been a witness, although the panel said they viewed my evidence as crucial to the proving of the charges.

I felt that the disciplinary panel had used an opportunity to stick the boot into me when in fact I was helping the FA as opposed to hindering them. Had it not been for my evidence then the panel would not have had a case to listen to. The panel continually referred to the scouting agreement as a *"sham contract"* and said that I'd played an *"unedifying part"* which I thought was a little over the top, as I was openly hostile to the arrangement and only did it on the orders of Cellino to ensure the payment was made. Furthermore, I felt that the written reasons didn't really cover the concerns I'd had. They seemed very one sided. But what really fucked me off was that the panel said that, *"despite his (mine) long involvement in football, he does not always fully know what he's talking about."* This was disingenuous by them, and they did not expand on the statement they made so I have no idea to what they were referring. It was bad practice to make such a sweeping statement without substantiating it or explaining further. I viewed it as the panel having another dig. The thing is I've probably forgotten more about the practicalities and difficulties of running a football club than some people who sit on disciplinary panels have ever known. The FA utilises many lawyers nowadays to oversee its disciplinary panels and they always seem to look at it from a legal perspective but the truth is that the practicalities of how a football club operates is far more complicated than that.

I'm a blunt Yorkshireman who tends to say what he thinks, without heirs or graces. If I don't like somebody I don't hide the fact. As a police officer I have seen too much of the good, bad, and ugly facets of day to day existence for some people so I'm quite hardened to the rough and tumble of life itself. It makes no difference to me what somebody thinks about me and like I've said I don't like Nicholas Stewart and I don't think he cares all that much for me but I won't lose sleep over that. Would I share a couple of pints with him in a bar? No, thanks, I think I'd rather wear an Everton shirt for a month.

Looking back, Cellino and Hughes could have resolved this issue between themselves without it going as far as it did and without Cellino involving anyone else. It was Cellino's pigheadedness in not acting in a proper way towards me at the end of my tenure at Leeds that influenced the whole scenario. He could have just paid Hughes out of his own pocket and no one would have been any the wiser. But that would have involved him spending some of his own money, even though at some stage he would have been able to reclaim it back through the club, particularly when he sold it.

I genuinely regret becoming mired in this whole issue. In hindsight I should have resisted from compiling what was a standard pro-forma contract and should have walked out of the club there and then. I regret that I didn't. It put a black mark on my reputation. I can't turn back the clock and, as it turned out, I left the club before the contract was lodged, so we will never know what would have happened had I remained in situ. One thing I do know is that, despite what the panel considered, I would not have lodged the contract and any difficulties it would have caused in terms of finance payments would have had to have been sorted out directly by Cellino. In any event, by taking that stance it would probably have led to Cellino terminating my contract, so I would still have been in the same situation.

This hearing was a bitter ending to a difficult relationship with Cellino, but as it happened, he left the club and as a consequence Leeds seemed to grow and progress in his absence and they are now in the Premier League. Ultimately had it not been for me then it could be that be that Cellino would still be in charge at Leeds to this day – and who knows where the club might be?

All in all this episode was a disaster for me. It wasn't my greatest moment in football, but if I am going to write about my good experiences in the game, it's equally important I write about my bad ones as well, where I fell short of the standards expected. But I learned from it. It made me a more rounded and professional football administrator. It's a part of my career that I have put behind me and I try not to think about. It's water under the bridge now. I do wonder what would happen if mine and Cellino's paths crossed again, but to be honest I have moved on from it all, so the reality is I would no longer be bothered by it.

Those were mad days at Leeds; a basket case club at the time when you felt you were on a roller coaster ride that was out of control but thankfully the club have recovered from it and their fanatical fans are now getting the club they deserve.

7 - NOT SO SWEET FA...

BACK IN THE SUMMER OF 2003, during my final few months at the Football Association, myself and my boss, Nic Coward, were barely on speaking terms. Our relationship had deteriorated to the point where we hardly acknowledged each other. He was the Legal Director at the FA and a highly competent lawyer who had also stood in as Acting Joint CEO of the organisation together with Executive Director David Davies following the demise of the former "advertising guru" Adam Crozier, who had abruptly left the governing body and later became Chief Executive of Royal Mail. Coward's role as Acting CEO ultimately led to me leaving the FA after almost five years, following a meeting of all the staff in which I challenged him. Coward had also been heavily criticised in the book *Broken Dreams* by Tom Bower, which examined wrongdoing in football. I always thought Coward suspected I had been responsible for all the criticism levelled at him in the book, but he was wrong.

I never bought into Crozier's vision. It felt it was all about PR and vanity and to be honest I thought he was an over-promoted, short-arsed pipsqueak. He appeared more interested in branding, marketing and appearance than the real issues in the game. Many good people were culled at the FA who had forgotten more about the game than he knew. Money was thrown around like confetti in the commercial and marketing departments to the detriment of other areas of the organisation, and it caused serious resentment between the staff and departments. He turned the FA into an "Us and Them" organisation which made it a very unhappy place to work. The marketing department thought they were the *"dogs bollocks"* and everything revolved around them. Crozier, as CEO, was ultimately the cause of that culture.

A typical example of one of Crozier's vanity projects was replacing the lovely and very experienced ladies on the reception desk who had done their job professionally for years with young attractive women who didn't have a clue who was where. The old guard were sacked on the Friday and the new intake were in their seats the following Monday morning... and the FA Board just let him run amok. It all came crashing down a few years later when, after his exit, the organisation faced up having to make good people redundant because of the financial carnage that had been left behind. It seemed that the then FA Chairman Geoff Thompson's media comments at the time of Crozier's departure were somewhat premature when he said:

"He leaves the FA in a very strong position financially"

I had arrived to a fanfare following my appointment in late 1998 when I was presented at a press conference and immediately tagged 'The Sleazebuster' by the media. I walked into the then headquarters of the FA at 16 Lancaster Gate as their first ever Compliance Officer on the morning of Monday, January 4, 1999, which just happened to be in the middle of a governing body crisis. During the late part of 1998 it had emerged that the then Chief Executive, Graham Kelly, and FA Chairman, Keith Wiseman, had become involved in a "cash for votes scandal" involving the Welsh FA when it was alleged that a £3m loan from the FA to the Welsh governing body was intended to buy the FAW's support for the election of Wiseman as a Vice President on FIFA, which in turn could help the FA's 2006 World Cup bid. This had caused serious questions to be asked about the turn of events and led to Kelly resigning his position even before I had started working at the FA.

That first morning I was dispatched to the Centre Point complex in central London to attend a hastily-arranged meeting of the FA council where I watched the political in-fighting following the resignation of Wiseman in stunned silence. Sheffield and Hallamshire County FA man Geoff Thompson was appointed as the new Chairman but what struck me most was the way in which the FA councillors displayed parasitic traits when it came to filling in expense forms. I watched as, despite a lavish buffet having been put before them, one by one they were completing their subsistence forms claiming for meals allowances! It was an eye opener for a new kid on the block and told me just what being a FA councillor was all about – getting on the gravy train. A month later more scandal erupted at Lancaster Gate when the then England manager Glenn Hoddle's tenure came to an unceremonious end following his comments in an interview with *The Times* sports journalist Matt Dickinson, in which he said he believed that disabled people and others were being punished for sins in a former life. It caused uproar and his contract was quickly terminated. I felt like the grim reaper: since being announced as 'The Sleazebuster' I'd seen off the FA's CEO, the FA's Chairman and England's manager in a matter of weeks! It was a standing joke within Lancaster Gate that I had made a great start in my new role!

Nevertheless they were generally good days at Lancaster Gate – it was like a happy family where everyone bumped into everyone else. The place was like a rabbit warren with corridors and quirky little offices. It was quite plush with lots of character and working there was a delight before Crozier arrived and moved us to an anonymous concrete building in Soho Square with open plan offices which in my view never really worked after the intimacy of the Lancaster Gate building.

I have never told the story of what exactly happened in relation to my exit from the FA, although at the time there was lots of speculation about it in the media. Nobody ever got it right. If I'm being totally honest, I had been considering leaving the FA for some time. I was fed up with the lack of support from the organisation, being away from home and to top it all, Coward had brought a guy called Steve Barrow in above me, so I'd just about had enough. When Coward appointed Barrow I think the FA thought I would disappear in a huff and leave in protest there and then. By the time I eventually decided to leave

I became a regular face on the tabloid back pages following my appointment as the FA's first Compliance Officer and I arrived at Lancaster Gate with the FA in total chaos.

I plotted an exit on my terms. Barrow was an okay type of bloke, but in my view he was no leader, more of a yes man and more suited to the FA stereotype employee – ie. totally the opposite to me. Perhaps his obedience was the reason they brought him in? Maybe I was becoming too troublesome for their liking?

I had conducted highly successful investigations into serious wrongdoing at both Chesterfield FC and Boston United FC, but the Disciplinary Panels had shown excessive weakness in the penalties handed out to both clubs and it had made me question whether it was worth the effort. Both clubs were successful in gaining promotion in the season they were dealt with by the Disciplinary Panels, who then allowed them to be promoted. The reality of the situation should have been a punishment denying them that success. In effect they were being rewarded for being cheats. It was a complete joke. It was weak and spineless. It was little wonder that Chesterfield were nicknamed 'The Crooked Spireites' in a pun on their nickname that related to the twisted spire that adorns the town's main church. Boston United players even had brown envelopes waved at them as they played. I knew that I needed to engineer a way out for my own benefit in terms of timing and a financial package. Some people had mocked the FA following the success of the Chesterfield and Boston enquiries saying we only went after the little clubs, but what people seem to forget is as a direct result of my investigations into these clubs it came about that club officials appeared before the courts charged with criminal offences. Some even went to prison. I can't recall the FA Compliance Department having that type of outcome since I left.

A couple of months before the decision was made for me to leave the FA, Guardian journalist Danny Taylor had written that I was *"disillusioned with my employers and thinking of resigning"* and that I had twice come close to doing so. He was correct and it was only from being talked out of it by people close to me that I remained there. Taylor continued:

> *"Well placed sources at Soho Square have confirmed that his relationship with his employers has deteriorated to the point where there are potentially irreconcilable differences".*

Taylor stated that in my time at the FA I had *"done a commendable job in trying circumstances"* but reported that *"Bean is far from flavour of the month and senior figures at the FA would readily accept his departure"*. Looking back, I think he was spot on with his analysis.

Whilst at the FA I had conducted detailed investigations into the transfer of Nicholas Anelka from Arsenal to Real Madrid which fizzled into nothing once I submitted the file of evidence never to be seen again. I also gave the football agent Dennis Roach a real run for his money with his various practices, where in my view there was ample evidence to commence proceedings, but as per usual the various governing bodies were reluctant to pursue things. In Roach's case, the legal advisors should have noticed that at the time only FIFA had the jurisdiction to bring charges against him, when they wrongly brought charges under the FA's own disciplinary system. There was certainly enough evidence against him for his alleged conduct in the transfer of Paulo Wanchope from West Ham to Manchester City, when he acted for both the player and the buying club in the same transfer when it was illegal to do so at that time, as well as the protracted transfer of Duncan Ferguson from Newcastle United to Everton. Tottenham also raised concerns about his behaviour and a lengthy investigation into his conduct at Spurs was made. I recall that at one point in the Roach investigation, during a highly charged interview between us, he jumped up and stormed out of the room screaming at me, *"I'm writing a book and you're going to be in it"* before slamming the door as he walked out. I don't know if he ever did write that book, or whether I made a cameo appearance in it!

On another occasion I was visited at the FA Headquarters in Soho Square by another agent who wanted to meet me personally, because he *"had something to tell me"*. When we met he was under the misapprehension that I was investigating him; which I wasn't, but he thought he could try it on and tried to warn me off, telling me I would regret crossing him. My response to him was to ask him to choose between fucking off out of the room straight away, or choosing which window he wanted me to throw him through. He soon changed his tune and the non-investigation of his activities very soon turned to a live investigation...

There were a number of other investigations that I conducted where I felt that the FA had failed me in their lack of action. These included the transfer of George Boateng from Coventry City to Aston Villa in 1999, when we had signed statements from the Chairman and CEO of Coventry City as well as manager Gordon Strachan. I think Doug Ellis, the Villa chairman, was on the FA council at that time, and I interviewed him about his involvement in an unauthorised approach to sign the player, but it seemed that 'Deadly Doug' had already given his version to Nic Coward before I even got to him. This was how the FA worked!

One case in particular, which in my view was overwhelming in its evidence of wrongdoing involving agents and which I dealt with during 2003, was the transfer of Titi Camara from Liverpool to West Ham in the year 2000. Football agent Willy McKay was paid £100,000 by Liverpool and a further £250,000 by West Ham for his work on the transfer – once again this was a case in which an agent was representing both clubs at a time when that practice was not allowed. I had obtained signed statements from the CEOs of both clubs, as well as supporting documentation, so it was all there in black and white. I submitted the file for the issuing of charges just before I left the FA, but once again no action was taken.

Investigating agents could be quite an exacting experience and led to trips around the world on enquiries about them. My travels included trips to Milan, Copenhagen, Marseille, Rome, Malaga and Los Angeles. The trip to Los Angeles was something of a mini holiday; I flew out on the Monday, drove a couple of hours north on the Tuesday, met the agent for two hours on the Wednesday and took a short witness statement, drove back to Los Angeles on the Thursday (using the scenic Pacific Coast Road via Malibu) and flew back on the Friday! Five days for two hours work! One day I was told I had to go to Perth, so imagine my disappointment when I realised it was Perth in Scotland to visit St Johnstone FC and not the city in Australia!

By this stage I'd had the idea of setting up a disciplinary consultancy "one stop service" for clubs to deal with all the disciplinary charges that the FA or EFL may issue against them or their employees. Early on in my time at the FA, the idea had been planted in my mind when I saw how there was a lack or representation being used for players, managers and clubs that had been charged and were summoned to appear before a Disciplinary Hearing. They were getting hit with big fines and suspensions because either they had no representation, or their mitigation had not been put over in a structured or strong way.

I saw it as a niche opportunity and from that idea eventually my company, *"Football Factors"* was born thanks to my departure from the FA.

Going back to my exit from the FA; the staff had been summoned to a meeting with Coward and Davies to discuss the way forward and update everyone with what was happening inside the organisation. The room was packed and Nic and David were stood at the front. The remainder of the FA Management Team sat on the front row, akin to a political party conference when the leader is making his conference speech. Coward and Davies gave an update to us all about the situation the organisation found itself in. I was sat there listening, but then they said something that really irked me when they raised the issue of staff redundancies. I'm sure that when they said that they never wanted to make anyone redundant they really meant it, and I believed it when they said it had caused them a lot of upset to have to do it but something was eating away at me and I saw this as a chance to set into motion the wheels for my departure.

I had been tipped off from a very reliable source within the media, whose information was always credible, that it was alleged that Coward had inferred to the FA Board that he would leave the organisation if he didn't receive a "bonus" for his acting CEO role. If true, this would have left the FA in a very awkward and difficult position because the FA Board were reliant upon Coward's legal advice and outstanding legal ability. There was absolutely no doubting his ability when it came to his grasp on legal issues, but in terms of the operational practicalities of overseeing investigations, I found him wanting. In over twenty years of investigative experience, he was no match for me in that respect. Going back to the issue of him allegedly threatening to leave his role, for him to have walked out would have left the FA floundering. But what had upset me was the thought that some very good people who were on relatively small salaries had been made redundant, yet here was this allegation that whilst this cost-cutting was going on a bonus was being demanded by one of those at the top of the tree.

Having listened to what was said I decided to bite the bullet, so I put a question about the bonus demand and whether it was correct to Coward and Davies. There was a stunned silence in the room. Coward just looked down at the floor and didn't respond, while Davies made some sort of spluttering response which glossed over my question. To be fair to Davies, several days later a message was passed onto me from him confirming that he had not asked for a bonus, I think he just wanted to clarify his position. I always got on well with David Davies. I liked him and found him to be a very charming man who was always open to having a direct conversation with you. He could take a joke and a bit of banter if you took the mickey out of him about something he had said or done. The meeting ended soon after my bombshell question and together with a few others, I went across to the Carlisle Arms pub in Soho just around the corner from FA Headquarters. The topic of conversation was all about my query and the reaction to it. I knew then that my days were numbered, so it was a win–win for me.

The following day I was driving to Plymouth on an investigation I was working on when I took a call from the FA's Head of HR, Paul Nolan who had been present at the previous days meeting. In his broad Scouse accent he asked me about the comments I had made and told me he thought I was out of order in asking the question. My response was as you would expect. I didn't think I was and the response, or lack of it, suggested I had hit a nerve. I wasn't due in the office for another week, so Paul told me to call in and see him when I was next around. I read between the lines and knew exactly what that meant. On my return to the office a week later I called in to see Nolan. We had always got on well and I liked him. We had a similar sense of humour. His only problem was that he was an Evertonian, but I suppose we all have a cross to bear. We sat down and he repeated his opening line from the previous week that he thought I was wrong to raise the issue of the bonus payment and my reply was exactly the same. I knew what was coming next but didn't expect it in such blunt terms as he uttered those immortal words...

"Do you want a cheque to fuck off?"

Fair play to him, it was straight and to the point. I had no complaints about how it was put. Perhaps in this day and age more of that "in your face and straight to the point" attitude is needed in the workplace. No messing around – just how I like things to be. I had expected it and it meant that I could put my disciplinary consultancy idea into practice. It was obvious that the hierarchy at the FA just wanted me out of the door (which Nolan later confirmed in an off the record conversation). I didn't fit their mould and knew I was better off out of the place. I was completely open to the suggestion he had made, but I wanted to play for a bit of time and so we agreed I would take some legal advice on it, which he agreed the FA would pay for, and then we would look to move it forward. I was due to go on holiday the following week, so things were left until after that. However on my return things stepped up a gear and weeks of negotiations took place to get an acceptable agreement that we were all happy with. I had to work my three-month notice period but used that time to further my idea of the disciplinary consultancy with people in the game. Once again it was a win-win situation for me. I was still getting paid, had negotiated a decent settlement, and was able to seek clients for my new business. But in that three month period my relationship with Coward was almost non-existent. It seemed to me that the bombshell question in the staff meeting had been the straw that broke the camel's back and I walked out of the FA building as an employee for the last time on 29th August, 2003 before my contract formally ended two days later. To celebrate I went to the pub with, of all people, Paul Nolan!

However, during the three months' notice period that I worked, what annoyed me was that it seemed every time we had a round of discussions about my leaving arrangements, it seemed to appear in the newspapers. I had my suspicions as to who was leaking the information and made it known. On one particular morning something appeared which could only have come from within the meeting I'd had some days earlier. A few days later I was back in the office and still annoyed at what I had read, so I bounced into Nolan's office and let it be known in no uncertain terms what I thought about it. I came out of his office and who did I bump into in the corridor, none other than the well-spoken yet diminutive FA Chairman Geoff Thompson, who greeted me with *"Hello Graham, Are you OK?".* It was the wrong question at the wrong time. *"No! I'm fucking not!"* I exclaimed, *"And if people in this place keep leaking stuff every time I have a meeting about my leaving, I'm going to get very annoyed".* At that Geoff was speechless and scuttled out of the way. By now I was on a roll and bounded up to David Davies's office and went in. As usual David was his courteous, charming self, but I was having none of it, telling him vociferously:

> *"You lot need to listen carefully. If this leaking continues, I'm just going to fuck off and take you lot to an employment tribunal where I will stand and give evidence against you. And remember, I've done that dozens of times in court so that won't bother me one bit, but you lot haven't, and I will make you, Nic and Nolan have to sit there and answer questions from my lawyer so you've been told. It stops now"*

At that I left David open-mouthed and went about the rest of my day before returning home to Barnsley. The following morning though, which was a Saturday, I took a call from Paul Nolan – it was unusual to be contacted by HR on a weekend. Davies had been onto him *"choking on his breakfast"* about my outburst, saying the last thing he wanted to do was to have to go and give evidence. Nolan asked me to call and see him next time I was in the office again so it could be sorted out once and for all. It seems that I had got the message across…

But even once the settlement and terms of my leaving were

agreed, there was still a hurdle to get over. In their haste to get rid of me, the FA had agreed to pay my legal fees, which had accumulated as I took various lines of advice. The bill came to £8,000. The problem was that they had not put a cap on the amount, so it was an open cheque book for me. I retained the services of an employment barrister, as well as a solicitor. When it came to settling the bill, and after I had left, they only forwarded three thousand pounds, so that caused another disagreement. When I challenged Nolan on this, he said this was because when others had left the FA their legal fees were only that amount, so he couldn't see why mine was so high. I didn't mess around and told him straight what would happen if the FA didn't cough up. He was left in no doubt that if the issue hadn't been addressed by close of business that day, I would be issuing legal proceedings to recoup the outstanding money through the courts. That would mean that the statement I would make would be made public, where I would give a full and frank account of how the FA had been with me. I then told him that I would then let him choose which Sunday newspaper he wanted it to go in where the FA's conduct would be exposed – and would even arrange the publication of it for him. At 4.45pm that day he rang back to confirm that the legal fees would be paid in full. When you are in a situation such as that you can't fuck about. You must be hard and sometimes brutal. It's not personal. It's just looking after one's interests.

During my time at the FA I conducted a lengthy investigation into suspicions of financial irregularities at Hull City, which had been taken over by a group of Sheffield businessmen including the flamboyant former Sheffield United director Stephen Hinchcliffe. He had been investigated by the police and subsequently convicted of bribery and fraud offences. The investigation was a bitter battle of wits with complaint after complaint going in from the group to the FA about my enquiry.

I had the backing of many Hull City fans who were not happy about what was happening at their club and wished me to carry on putting pressure on the owners. One of the problems I was encountering though was the over the top "love in" reporting by the local paper's Hull City correspondent, John Fieldhouse, who I felt was being leant on by the club owners. I had been told he had been threatened by members of the group, and it seemed that word had got back to them that I had been asking him questions about it. Fieldhouse was cautious, as you would expect and didn't really want to get involved, but sometimes as a journalist you have to put your head above the parapet to help expose wrongdoing. I didn't feel that Fieldhouse was prepared to do that, and confirmation came when the FA received a letter from the club complaining that I had been speaking to Fieldhouse about certain issues. It could only have come from him, which suggested that they had some form of influence over his reporting.

My enquiries were revealing to say the least. There were all sorts of unusual transactions taking place in the running of the club including the purchase of a team bus from Hinchcliffe's company at what appeared to be an over-inflated price, along with the hiring of private aeroplanes for directors to travel to away games. Expenses were through the roof. It seemed to me that the club was being used as a cash cow by a chairman who didn't understand the game. This was a team at the lower end of League Two who were spending like a Premier League club when it came to off-the-field expenses. But that was only half the story. It's one thing acting in such a way, but it steps up to a completely different level when you get into the areas of alleged transfer bungs.

The FA Compliance Unit demanded that the club hand over certain documents, but they were resistant to that request. In a letter dated 31 August, 1999 Hull City's late Chairman, Nic Buchanan, wrote to me suggesting that my investigation had been unprofessional, that I had embarked on a *"fishing expedition"* and that he was *"greatly annoyed by your reported approach to John Fieldhouse"*. He also stated in the same letter that *"Hull City have nothing to hide nor fear from your investigation"*. He couldn't have been more wrong. Buchanan was a brash and brazen man who tried to impose himself on me. I've no doubt some people would have wilted due to his bullying attitude, but there was no way he would exert that influence on me. I made it clear to him that he was wasting his time. On one occasion, a colleague and I commandeered the boardroom at City's former home at Boothferry Park and started to go through every club document. When Buchanan came in with his usual brash attitude he went behind the bar where he opened a bottle of red wine and start drinking it while trying to get us to share the bottle with him. He was told in no uncertain terms to leave, which led to a heated discussion. He knew we were onto them and we were not going away.

In October 1999 Buchanan did an interview with the *Sunday Telegraph* about me and the investigation in which he said:

> *"We are being hounded by this man. I took over Hull City to help out a football club in trouble and hopefully get a bit of enjoyment from the game. I have always followed football as a hobby, yet my life and those of my staff are being made a misery"*.

The journalist who wrote the story, the late Steve Curry, who I always got on very well with before and after the publication of this article, later told me that he had been taken in by Buchanan's claims and realised he had been used.

You may recall that I had been told by Nic Coward when I had my interview to become the FA's Compliance Officer that the job was *"not about brown envelopes in motorway service station car parks"*. That soon changed. Ferrybridge services sits at the junction of the M62 and A1 and is a rather obscure and small motorway services. Sometime after I had started my enquiry into Hull City I was asked by a contact to park my car up there.

A short time after a car pulled up alongside and the occupant passed a large brown envelope over to me before disappearing into the distance. The contents of the envelope were staggering. Among a number of club documents was one that really took my eye.

During the 1999 season Hull City had signed goalkeeper Andy Oakes on a free transfer from non-league Winsford United. As part of the deal Winsford had wisely negotiated a 25% sell on fee if Oakes was sold. After only making nineteen appearances for the Tigers, Derby County signed him for a fee of £460,000. As is normal in these types of deals, once Hull realised they were about to make a massive profit they set about trying to buy themselves out of the arrangement with Winsford and offered them a payment of £10,000 in exchange for them forgoing the 25% sell on cut of the transfer. Wisely the directors of Winsford United declined this offer and subsequently received over £100,000 when the transfer was completed. The offer of the ten thousand pound buy-out was included in a letter from Hull City dated 20th May 1999 and was signed by club director and company secretary Richard Ibbotson, a solicitor by trade.

That wasn't the only document I was interested in however - another one that caught my attention was one signed on the same date, by the same director on Hull City headed paper and addressed to Terry Savage, the then chairman of Winsford United.

Dear Mr Savage,

As requested should the sale of Andrew Oaks (sic) proceed to completion Hull City will pay the sum of £40,000 to you personally.

Yours sincerely,
R W Ibbotson
Director and Company Secretary

It was there in black and white, the offer of a £40,000 bung.

I later interviewed Terry Savage who stated he had not asked for any payment, that it had been initiated by Hull City and that he had immediately refused it. This was no doubt the moment when Winsford United realised that they were in for a big payday on the back of Andy Oakes, hence their refusal of the £10,000 buy out offer.

I was really on Hull's case now and my enquiries continued until we were contacted by the Humberside Fraud Squad who had taken an interest in the goings on at Hull City themselves. At the FA we were on the verge of issuing numerous serious charges against the club and individuals connected to it, including what appeared to be an offer of a £40,000 bung. However when the Fraud Squad commenced their own criminal investigation into the club we were advised to place our investigation on hold so as not to prejudice any investigation by the police and we had no option but to accede to their request. Unfortunately, by the time the police investigation finished the CPS decided not to take any criminal action. The reason for this was the difference between the burden of proof of a criminal and civil investigation. The police would have had to have proved 'beyond reasonable doubt' the directors had been running the club whilst it was insolvent, whereas at the FA we only had to prove the case 'on the balance of probabilities' and we were looking at the specific rule breaches such as bringing the game into disrepute and the offer of the alleged transfer bung.

After I left the FA it was up to those who replaced me to pursue what I had uncovered, even though the club was under new ownership. The FA failed to do that and it seemed that it all just got brushed under the carpet. That didn't stop Buchanan telephoning me after a story appeared in the *Yorkshire Post* about the CPS not taking any action. As usual he was full of the joys of spring and gloated that no criminal action was being taken. As I have said, I had left the FA by that time, so it really didn't bother me at that moment but I still told him "*What was happening at Hull was bent*" and "*to go fuck yourself!*". After that I strangely never heard from him again.

However it rankled with me that the FA had not taken any action against Hull's former directors or the club itself. I had done my bit, so the ball was then in the FA's court and nothing happened.

My replacement as Compliance Officer was an accountant, David Lampitt, a bloke with the personality of a lettuce. Mind you, I think most accountants have a similar personality. Me and Lampitt had several run-ins over the years after I left the FA. It was my view that my clients were being targeted in disciplinary matters which would normally have attracted nothing more than a warning letter. I confronted him about this and he told me *"It was in my head"*, to which I replied if he carried on there would be *'something in his head'* and it wouldn't be very pleasant. That earned me a letter from David Davies rebuking me for harassing his staff! I pointed out at the time that it was a bit rich sending me a letter like that, when at the around the same time the FA were hanging Sven Goran Eriksson out to dry over the Faria Alam story. Lampitt liked to portray himself as whiter than white in his dealings with me, when at that time he was supposed to be conducting an investigation into the super agents Pini Zahavi and Kia Joorabchian but was spotted in *Les Ambassadeur's* private members club in Mayfair with the both men. Journalist Charlie Sale revealed this exclusive story in his *Daily Mail* gossip column, and a short time later Lampitt was made CEO of Portsmouth FC, a club with connections to Zahavi who had been involved in the recent change of ownership. I was told that the news of Lampitt's defection from the FA broke on Sky Sports News even before he'd had the chance to tell his employers, which would have been highly embarrassing. But it's strange that a man in the responsible position of FA Compliance Officer should suddenly join a club in a senior position which had seen some heavy involvement by the agent he had been investigating. It's fair to say that Charlie Sale, who had some of the best contacts in football, was on his case.

There were some amusing moments at the FA connected to investigations I conducted. I recall the day Ian Wright smashed the referee's room up at Upton Park when playing for West Ham against Leeds in 1999, after he had been sent off by Referee David Elleray. Several days later I arranged to meet the former Arsenal striker to interview him about what had happened. We met in secret at Loftus Road Stadium, the home of Queens Park Rangers, but as soon as I turned the tape on Ian went into a rant about Elleray and tried to justify his actions. I immediately stopped the tape, rewound it, and before I turned it back on I gave Ian some friendly advice on how to answer to get the best possible outcome for himself. He did as I advised and was very contrite and apologetic as we taped over his original outburst so it never came to light. He later appeared before a Disciplinary Commission where he received a three-game suspension and a fine of £17,500 following which an FA Spokesman said, *"He offered a full and frank admission for his conduct and apologised unreservedly for the distress he caused"*. Had I allowed him to say the things he really wanted to say on tape I think the penalty would have been a lot sterner. As we left the Disciplinary Room he came over and thanked me and then said, laughing, *"I hope I never see you again Graham!"*

At the 1999 League Cup Final between Leicester City and Spurs I conducted what was described as *"the most serious and thorough investigation into the misuse of match tickets ever undertaken by the FA"*. Crowd trouble had broken out at the game after Spurs fans obtained tickets for the Leicester City end after a group of Leicester players and officials had supplied them to Spurs fans. At the time we issued the charges Foxes manager Martin O'Neill had gone on a family break to Barcelona but decided to return to the UK to deal with the fallout. O'Neill was fiercely protective of his players and en route to the airport in Barcelona had telephoned me; he was raging and I got a real ear-bashing from him to the point that I was holding the phone away from my ear. He then told me he was going into a tunnel and would lose contact but would call me back when he came out the other end. The phone went dead and, relieved, I put the phone down. Two minutes later it rang again and on answering it was O'Neill again and he just carried on where he left off! He was berating me, he was still raging, as if he had never stopped. I remember thinking how it must be for his players if they weren't performing!

I've always got on well with Harry Redknapp but my first experience of him wasn't particularly cordial. Paulo Di Canio had been involved in some form of misdemeanour on the field and it was decided that rather than issue a charge he would be summoned to the FA to be "advised" about his conduct. Arrangements were made for him to attend my office, but the *Evening Standard* were tipped off about the meeting. After the story had appeared in the paper my phone rang and it was Harry on the other end. Without introducing himself, his opening line to me was *"Have you been fucking talking to the fucking Evening Standard?"* The meeting subsequently went ahead without any problem, but it shows how stressful it can be for people connected to the game when the papers get hold of a confidential piece of information.

Recently there has been a media clamour for a Football Regulator to be appointed. Someone independent of the game's governing bodies to oversee the game, much in the same way that Ofcom oversee broadcasters for example. I'm sure its going to happen, it's just two decades too late!

I remember one day in Lancaster Gate David Davies asked me how I thought the game could be bettered from a regulatory point of view and I told him that the only way forward was a regulator, and this was back in 1999. I now see that in these last few months even he has acceded to my point of view. If only he had taken my advice back then! Any such appointment though should not be a government patsy and should not have any vested interest in the game – they need to be completely independent and they need some teeth. Another thought I had back in my FA days, and it's something I still believe should happen, is that the Compliance Department, or whatever fancy title they give it nowadays, should be housed in a separate building from the main FA offices. This way any of its investigations are away from prying eyes, its members cannot be influenced from within the FA and it's a completely separate entity. This would only be good for the game and the FA.

When I joined the FA it was just me and my PA, Teresa McReady and later Bev Walrond and between us we had to do everything. Looking back, it was a hopeless task, yet despite this we had some successes. Now the department has expanded to contain more than forty people, which is how it should have been from the start. I'm sure that there are still some people inside the FA that view me with suspicion and regard me as the "enemy" but to me it was a role I performed, it was never personal. I don't lose sleep over what they think, and neither should they.

Looking back at my time at the FA I suppose in one sense you could say that David Mellor was right in his comment about me being made "*The Fall Guy*". Somebody had to take the fall, so who better than the man doing the investigations who didn't fit the FA mould?

8 - BEHIND ENEMY LINES

UPON LEAVING THE FA I formed Football Factors and Everton were the first club to sign up. The then Chief Executive, Michael Dunford, who I'd had a very good relationship with over many years, even before I joined the FA, was more than happy to give me a twelve-month "trial run" contract. That twelve months turned into an eight-year relationship where I saw many ups and downs in the life of Everton FC. As a Liverpool supporter, working with the local enemy always led to lots of banter between the senior staff at the club and I - not to mention it guaranteeing me tickets for every Merseyside derby game played at Goodison Park! I never wanted tickets in the corporate area though – I always insisted on being in the Liverpool end. I used to take great delight every season in reminding the club Secretary, David Harrison how generous the Toffee supporters were in the area next to the Liverpool fans when they insisted on throwing chewy sweets of at us whenever Liverpool scored. It meant we never went hungry during a game!

I was at Goodison Park in the Liverpool end for one of the most controversial Merseyside derbies in the Premier League era. It was during the 2007/08 season and led to me representing Everton manager David Moyes following his criticism of referee Mark Clattenburg's handling of a very fiery match. The first Merseyside derby that season took place on October 20, 2007 resulting in a 2-1 win for Liverpool secured by Steven Gerrard with a 90th minute penalty, his side's second spot-kick of the game... but that was only half the story! Everton had taken the lead before half time courtesy of a Sami Hyypia own goal. Liverpool equalised in the second half following a 53rd minute penalty given when Gerrard was fouled from behind by Tony Hibbert, who had chased him from the halfway line and into the penalty area before bringing him down. Clattenburg sent Hibbert off for denying Gerrard a goalscoring opportunity, but this was not before he'd initially taken out a yellow card from one pocket, before putting it back after Gerrard spoke to him. He then brandished the red card and dismissed the defender. It may well be that Gerrard's conversation with the referee was all very innocent but following the game the inference by all on sundry was that Gerrard had 'had a word' with Clattenburg which caused him to change his mind. It was a serious bone of contention in the post-match analysis. This became even more relevant some weeks later when a very interesting paragraph from the Liverpool captain's autobiography came to light.

Later in the game there was a ferocious two-footed challenge by Liverpool's Dirk Kuyt on Phil Neville. Both of the Dutch striker's feet left the floor and there was little doubt that this was a red card offence. Yet Kuyt escaped with a booking, much to the anger and dismay of every Everton supporter in the stadium. Once again it was an issue that dominated the post-match comments and then, as if to rub salt in Everton wounds, Clattenburg gave Liverpool a 90th minute penalty after Phil Neville was adjudged to have handled the ball and was dismissed, leaving the home side with 9 men. Gerrard tucked away the spot-kick in the dying seconds and minutes later Clattenburg blew for full-time.

The Everton manager was understandably upset in his post-match comments. The emphasis from the interviewers was on the controversial performance of Clattenburg rather than the performance of the two teams. The media seized on Moyes' comments and the FA quickly wrote to him asking him to explain the following comments reported in the newspapers:

> *"You wonder whether they [Premier League referees] allow themselves to be influenced by the top four. Didn't Clattenburg go to Hong Kong with Liverpool for the Asia Cup this summer? Maybe he wants to be their friend."*

The reality was those comments were all said at different

The 140 labours
of Mister Bean

p. 70

My appointment as the FA's first Compliance Officer prompted plenty of attention, particularly in the Daily Mail...

Peanut
power

GRAHAM BEAN the

At my desk at Lancaster Gate. We began with a very small staff to cover all kinds of issues across the game.

FERGIE LAUNCHES VERBAL ASSAULT ON 'SINISTER' REF

FROM BACK PAGE

a penalty, and turned down a penalty against Chelsea in the Carling Cup."

England striker Rooney volleyed

night's award ceremony, hours after proving it with his 56th-minute opener.

Ferguson revealed Rooney scored his 30-yard wondergoal

ready to take him off because of his injury. But while he is on the pitch he is always a danger and that is why I kept him on.

"It was very, very important to ...ome harsh words ... Howard, whose ...ed to Newcastle ...'It was a bad kick ...t of slackness," ...r.

FERGUSON: Ref rant

Fergie rant: Ridiculous.. sinister..and sensational

My first case working for Sir Alex Ferguson came following a glut of headlines concerning his post-match interview during which he suggested that 'sinister' refereeing was affecting United's form.

SPECIAL ISSUE JUNE 2008

Football Factors LTD

Disciplinary Consultancy

UNITED BOSS SPARKS CIVIL WAR

FERGIE FIASCO AT THE FA

Sir Alex let-off after rant at ref..but now chiefs are appealing their own decision!

UNITED DUO'S GREAT ESCAPE

FARCICAL!

FA Fury after Ferguson is let off the hook

Issue 5 October 2005

Football Factors LTD

Disciplinary Services

THE MIRROR, 19th July 2005

FA ESCAPE FOR FERGIE

"Clubs can try to force change in this area"

I didn't waste time announcing that Sir Alex Ferguson had become 'Football Factors' highest profile client nor our success in defending FA charges for him.

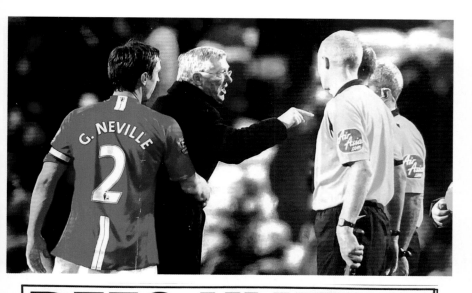

REFS UNITED

v FERGIE

They want FA action

By PAUL JIGGINS

REFEREES urged the FA to throw the book at Alex Ferguson for his attack on Alan Wiley.

The FA launched a probe as the Manchester United manager said ref Wiley was not fit enough after his side's 2-2 draw with Sunderland.

Premier League assessor Dermot Gallagher said: "Alex's comments are laughable. Alan is

Turn to P51

Fergie got in hot water for this attack on referee Alan Wiley following a 2-2 draw at home to Sunderland in October 2009 in which he accused the referee of 'lacking fitness' which led to tabloid outrage.

The FA successfully charged the United boss with 'improper conduct'.

He has goaded referees for years but now they've had enough and are insisting...

SHUT FERGIE UP FOR GOOD

Duncan Ferguson was 'bang to rights' following this reaction to a tackle from Leicester City's Stefan Freund. He saw red in both senses of the word! My defence of his FA charge wasn't helped by his non-appearance at the hearing.

The inconsistencies of the FA: Neil Warnock went unpunished following this gesture made to a referee yet when Liverpool manager Rafa Benitez responded to a question about the non-award of a penalty by Phil Dowd by proffering his glasses to the press he was charged.

Life at Leeds United under Massimo Cellino was never dull. He went through 8 managers during his three and a half years in charge and I was an eyewitness to the behind-the-scenes chaos of his chairmanship.

This notorious 2007 'friendly' between QPR and the China Olympic team went viral when the game descended into a brawl. The FA couldn't charge the Chinese but went after QPR, a club I defended on many occasions.

When Barnsley FC banned me from their Oakwell ground (despite the fact I was one of their sponsors) I went to war with the board - I was determined to unseat Barnsley chairman Barry Taylor from his cushy Divisional Representative role with the FA and ran the campaign of Doncaster chairman John Ryan against him. The resulting election was chaotic to say the least

RYAN VOTE FURY

Doncaster chairman makes complaint to FA over council ballot

JUST NOT FAIR

John Ryan has been consulting his lawyers over the voting

Liverpool boss Rafa Benitez tries to calm Javier Mascherano down after he is dismissed at Old Trafford after which the player was charged with 'failing to leave the field of play'. I represented Javier at the subsequent hearing and, despite admitting the charge his ban went up from one game to three!

Hull City under pressure as FA send in their watchdog

Steve Curry on the case for the defence as a beleaguered club owner and fan deals with the trauma of investigation

GRAHAM BEAN, the Football Association's compliance officer, stands accused today in his investigations of Hull City, one of the smaller clubs fighting to keep professional football alive in their local community. The former Barnsley policeman has become a kind of one-man watchdog for the game since his appointment a year ago.

He has, however, infuriated many people, not least the Players' Union, and there is concern about his all-powerful role as Lancaster Gate's disciplinary master.

Nick Buchanan, the Sheffield businessman who bought Hull City from Davis Cup tennis coach David Lloyd last November, is seeking legal advice about the alleged manner in which Bean has been investigating the running of his club.

"We are being hounded by this man. I took over Hull City to help out a football club in trouble and hopefully to get a bit of enjoyment from the game. I have always followed football as my hobby yet my life and those of my staff are being made a misery," he said.

"When Bean rang up the local sports writer with the suggestion that I had been issuing him with death threats unless he wrote kindly about the club. I was absolutely furious.

"It is a slur on my character and totally untrue, as the journalist in question would swear to, and I don't believe we should be subjected to the kind of treatment being taken by the FA."

The *Sunday Telegraph* has spoken to the journalist, John Fieldhouse, who confirmed that he received telephone calls from Bean along those lines.

Buchanan and a business associate, Stephen Hinchcliffe, bought a 65 per cent interest in Hull City earlier this year, though Hinchcliffe, who is barred from being a director by the Department of Trade and Industry, cannot serve on the board.

It is believed that disaffected former employees of the club may have alerted Bean about the running of Hull City, though the FA have declined to tell *The Sunday Telegraph* the reasons for their investigation.

When he was first informed that Bean was on the case, Buchanan invited the Football League to conduct their own investigation into the club's affairs.

He said this week: "When I was informed of the FA's concern, I was naturally anxious to clarify my own position so that I was not compromised in any way.

"I invited the Football League chief executive, Richard Scudamore, to put in whoever the League wanted to check the club out. He asked if I would have any objection and I said absolutely not.

"I didn't have any idea who they were sending and a women came from Manchester, from De Loitte Touche, and they interviewed everybody in the week they were there. They sent a report back to the League, which I have not seen, but which I am told was not positive.

"This, I am sure, has all come about because I sacked Tom Belton, the chairman I first put in to run the club, and David Bennett, who was a business associate of mine."

Since then, the Department of Trade and Industry have visited the club and they have not found any reason for complaint.

Buchanan believes their interest is in the role Hinchcliffe plays at Hull City but he says: "He never goes to the club unless the team are playing. I ask him to advise me as and when necessary because he has had a lot more experience in football than me. He is an asset to the club when it comes to dealing in players.

"If I say to him that I want him to attend a board meeting, he is written to and it is documented and minuted. There is nothing wrong with that. I have had it screen-tested with my lawyer as to how far I could go."

Bean is also demanding to investigate the purchase from Hinchcliffe of a team bus for £75,000.

But Buchanan said: "I begged Stephen to sell us the coach. He had it sitting in a garage, a great big DAF with only 20,000 miles on the clock with club-class seats, while we were paying £6,000 a month out in coach hire.

"We financed the purchase through General Guarantee and it costs us £1,100 a month, so we are making a big financial saving. It was General Guarantee who made the valuation on the bus. All we have done is a common business manoeuvre, which is saving the club money."

Bean refused to discuss his investigations when approached by *The Sunday Telegraph* this week.

Graham Bean... accused of 'hounding' Hull City

The frustrations of working at the FA was highlighted by my investigation of Hull City. We caught them bang to rights when a letter on headed notepaper signed by Company secretary Richard Ibbotson came into my possession appearing to offer the Witton Albion chairman a bung. Unfortunately my investigations attracted the attention of the Humberside Police Fraud Squad which paused our investigation before the case was quietly dropped after I left the FA.

Mark Clattenburg dismisses Sir Alex Ferguson from the bench during a hotly contested Lancashire derby between United and Bolton at the then Reebok stadium. Clattenburg claimed Fergie called him a 'fucking disgrace' and the United boss was banned from the touchline for the second half. This was one of Football Factors highest profile cases and thanks to my defence he escaped with a two-match touchline ban and a modest fine.

Nathan Tyson got himself in hot water after brandishing a Nottingham Forest flag during a heated East Midlands derby. Sometimes there is no defence for such actions.

stages of an interview but were then put together to give a distorted impression of what Moyes had actually said, so the meaning had a completely different emphasis. It looked like he was questioning the integrity of Clattenburg.

I responded to the FA on David's behalf a few days later, arguing that it was sensationalist and selective journalism. We argued his words had been adapted to give a different picture to the one that had actually been portrayed. But before any further action was taken by the FA, Moyes was challenged again about the performance of Clattenburg in the derby game at a press conference five days later in advance of Everton's UEFA Cup game against Larissa. When the questions should have been about the European game, the press conference turned to a more controversial topic. His additional comments resulted in the FA writing to him a second time in a matter of days, asking him this time to explain himself again after he had said;

> *"At one point it was 12 against 9. The only positive was the game was not decided by the player, but by the referee. I'm confident it will be 11 against 11 with the Swedish referee (who was officiating the game against Larissa)."*

A fortnight later we received a letter from the FA's Compliance Unit and we replied raising the complaint that it had taken them two weeks to write to him about the UEFA press conference comments, which was unacceptable. They had the media reports the day after the press conference, yet they had sat on them, and we wanted to know why. We accused them of waiting for receipt of his first response which had not been sent until after the Larissa UEFA Cup tie, in which we had put a strong argument forward as to why action shouldn't be taken. It appeared that the FA then decided to raise new issues and were therefore, in my view, being unfair to him. My letter to them was very strong:

> *"We consider this to have an element of unfairness about it. It seems to him (Moyes) that this is either a case of*

an uncoordinated investigation and review of the issues at hand by your department, or a witch hunt against him personally. He believes, like many others, that the real issue the FA should be focusing upon is the inadequacies displayed by Mr Clattenburg in his performance on the day."

It made little difference to the FA and over a month later, on November 26, they charged Moyes with two cases of misconduct for his post-match comments immediately after the derby game and then his press conference less than a week later.

"You are hereby charged with misconduct for two breaches of FA Rule E3 in respect of; Your post-match comments immediately following the fixture on 20 October, 2007 and; Your further comments made at a press conference on 24 October, 2007. It is alleged that the comments made referring to referee Mark Clattenburg on each respective occasion amount to improper conduct, as they call into question Mr Clattenburg's integrity and/or imply that Mr Clattenburg was motivated by bias."

I immediately started to put together Moyes' defence and, in doing so, obtained the referee assessor's report on Clattenburg, which was scathing about the official's performance and highly critical about his handling of the game. The report awarded him marks which ranked him as having had a "below standard performance". This supported Moyes' argument that the referee had not officiated the game in a competent way. However at this point we discovered the existence of a previously unknown tape recording made by Liverpool journalist David Prentice, who was the chief sports writer at the *Liverpool Echo,* who had conducted an interview with Moyes after the derby game. On the tape the full extent of Moyes' comments were clear. He had spoken eloquently about the performance of the referee and the way he had dealt with the incidents on the pitch. One of the main points was that the interviewing journalist had said to Moyes:

"Gerrard shook his (Clattenburg's) hand when he left the field, didn't he? Maybe that showed he wanted to be their friend?"

The reply by Moyes was damning and blew the FA's post-match interview charge about his comments immediately after the game out of the water. Moyes had simply replied *"Maybe"*.

Not only had he not said the comment questioning Clattenburg's character, as the FA alleged, but neither had he agreed with it. We quickly obtained a witness statement from Mr Prentice which was then submitted to the FA, backing them into a corner with no way out. We had proved beyond any doubt that he had not made the comments the FA were relying upon. As usual, the FA had taken the newspaper reports at face value instead of using a little more investigative nouse. If they had done, it would have led them to the truth about what had really been said. The FA had no option but to make an embarrassing U-turn on the first charge and withdraw it, meaning no further action was taken. It was a huge blow to them, but it was entirely their own fault because the Compliance Department had not done their job properly. However we still had to face the second charge relating to his press conference a few days after the derby game, although on the plus side it meant the impact of the charge had been significantly diluted.

I felt it was important to refer to the comments that the FA had relied upon about Steven Gerrard in the derby game. The purpose of this was to show that the whole investigation by the FA was flawed and so I prepared a detailed witness statement for Moyes in which it was pointed out that we had uncovered a section of Steven Gerrard's recently published autobiography, in which he had said:

"As captain, I view refs in a different light. It's handy to build a decent relationship with a ref to get him on Liverpool's side. I'm quite cynical about that. It's gamesmanship. A tight decision in the 90th minute may

go my way if I've spent all game being friendly to the ref. He's only human. An official like (Graham) Poll or Clattenburg is likely to be more sympathetic if I work with them, than if I'm in their face like a cheeky Scouser, as I was years ago."

Irrespective of the fact it had been proved Moyes didn't say Clattenburg wanted to be a friend of Liverpool's and therefore was not questioning his integrity, the comments by Gerrard in his book shed a different light of suspicion on what had happened on the pitch when Hibbert had brought him down. It just strengthened the whole case. It was a gift that Gerrard had even mentioned Clattenburg by name. We couldn't have asked for things to go any better for us. When you are dealing with these types of cases, it's always important to look for any piece of evidence that may come back to haunt the FA and damage their case – whether that be an extract from a newspaper from many years earlier, a social media post or, as in this case, the autobiography of an individual connected with the game. We also submitted the damning referee assessor's report on Clattenburg to support our arguments which was critical of the way he had handled the Hibbert sending-off. Although Clattenburg's explanation after the game was that he was taking his notebook out at the time he initially took out the yellow card.

Despite these setbacks, the FA ploughed ahead with the second charge which Moyes denied, and a hearing was held on April 14, 2008 at their offices in Soho Square. I made a very strong submission on behalf of Moyes, who was sat alongside me. I still have the record of exactly what I said to the Disciplinary Panel that day, a section of which was;

"There has to come a time in this day and age of free speech when the FA has to accept that comments in certain circumstances are wholly justified. We say that this is one such occasion, based upon the whole circumstances and not just the small window of opportunity the FA rely upon

from the October 24 press conference. Factually, much of it was correct. At one point Everton did have nine men on the field and the referee, based upon the non-decisions that the independent report that says he made major mistakes in Liverpool's favour, does give an aura that they had a 12th man on the pitch. Nevertheless, the allegation from the FA is that these comments were wrong of Mr Moyes to say - and to question the integrity of the referee. But we reiterate, in the circumstances, that he considers this was a justified remark. And taking into context the passage from Gerrard's autobiography, which the FA didn't seek to question, he does not believe he can be guilty of this matter. Gerrard inferred that the referee could be influenced and was involved in an incident which gave rise to strong suspicions that the referee acted upon the comments of the player."

In a rare case of common sense breaking out, the panel took on board my arguments and despite finding the charge proved against him, decided to give Moyes nothing more serious than a warning as to his future conduct. We had gone through six months of letters, charges and disagreements going back and forth between my office and the FA, only for it to be disposed of in that way. When that happens it makes a mockery of the whole disciplinary system, because it could have been dealt with, as I have said on many occasions, by a simple letter reminding him of his responsibilities. This would have put the issue to bed months earlier. It felt like another victory against an oppressive regime intent on pursuing even the weakest of cases.

David Moyes became a regular client of mine and I found him difficult to work with at times. I don't mean that in a nasty way at all. He was always very courteous and professional, but he was always intense. In my view he is a very honest individual who wears his heart on his sleeve and is honest in his explanations to support comments that he has made in public. He has a lot of integrity and you can't ask for anymore than that in a client.

We'd had more success a couple of years earlier for Moyes following a game between champions-elect Chelsea and Everton in April 2006 at Stamford Bridge, when the home side won 3-0 before they lifted the club's second consecutive league title. Chelsea had been 1-0 up when Everton's Lee Carsley was sent off for a foul on Didier Drogba right in front of both dugouts early in the second half. This is the worst place on the pitch for a controversial incident to occur as it always creates an overreaction, which can sometimes cause officials to be influenced by the occupants of the technical area – as opposed to the initial act. Following the game, in his post-match interview, Moyes spoke about the decision and the performance of referee Rob Styles when he said;

> *"We didn't think it was a red at the time. I think the reaction of the people caused it. It's a yellow card, it's a bit reckless, but it's not a red card. It's not the referee's fault we lost the game, but it played a massive part. It looked as if he was star struck. He was talking to the players at half time in the tunnel. The game kicked off and (Arjen) Robben's come diving on the pitch. My understanding is that no players are allowed to enter the pitch without the referee's understanding - and you can see him (Styles), laughing and joking about it. Maybe he got caught up in the whole day and thought he was going to get a medal as well."*

A few days later the expected letter arrived from former Council Standards Officer Jenny Pyle requesting David Moyes' observations about his comments. As usual we obtained a copy of the match delegate's report, which is an independent observer's report used in Premier League games. This is quite different to the referee assessor's report, which solely concentrates on the official's performance. The delegate's report covers a multitude of different issues associated with the game they are attending.

> *"Chelsea, not surprisingly, changed their goalkeeper at half time, and this was duly dealt with by Rob Styles at the halfway line. Maybe this distracted the official, as Chelsea actually started the second half with 10 men, with Robben of Chelsea being absent. He joined the fray almost immediately, but this was a first for me - and probably Rob Styles as well. The next phase of the game became the pivotal moment, when Rob Styles, who had only given six fouls in the first half, produced a straight red card on the Everton midfielder Carsley, following a tackle on Drogba. My gut feeling at the time was this was definitely a strong yellow, but not a red. A long study of the video leaves me of the same opinion. Lee Carsley had been no trouble to the referee before this incident. He only had his eyes on the ball when he makes his challenge and with the pitch being watered, slides on the wet turf in completing his movement. The geography of the tackle i.e, right on the halfway line in front of the dugout, meant no question of a chance of a goal being denied and I felt the red card was definitely too harsh against an Everton side who had had such a good first half."*

We responded to the FA stating that the comments were not a personal attack on the referee and his integrity, but were based around the fact the sending off was harsh and changed the course of the game. We included the delegate's report, which supported Moyes' viewpoint. The issue of Robben's late entry onto the field was easily dealt with by pointing out that Moyes was demonstrating his own knowledge of the laws of the game and that Styles had not applied these, because he allowed the player to enter the field without permission. For some reason the FA were not satisfied with the reply and on April 28 wrote again, in a letter from the pedantic David Lampitt, questioning, among other things, why Moyes had not used the *"official reporting mechanism"* to raise his concerns. The use of such a technical phrase shows to me just how out of touch some of the people in the FA could be at times. We replied to the effect that Moyes had adequately answered the points raised in the original letter from the FA and that all he had done was answer questions about Robben entering the field, when asked by the media. I then really went in strong on Lampitt, a person who at that time Moyes had little time for. I wrote;

> *"It would appear that the issues you raise are your own personal point of view. Simply because Mr Moyes has given an explanation that you personally are not content with, is not a justifiable reason to demand further explanations. It is a matter of public record that Mr Moyes has questioned the competency of the compliance department and you in particular this season. He believes that you personally are conducting a campaign of victimisation against him and his club, and the fact that you've sought to become involved in this inquiry, which was being dealt with by Ms Pyle, gives rise to that suspicion. He (Moyes) wishes to reiterate that he does question your experience and ability to understand the issues surrounding the industry."*

This was a real put down to Lampitt. Moyes was effectively saying he didn't have a clue what he was doing or understood the game. This obviously upset the FA Compliance Officer, who then went to incredible lengths to try to justify his position. Anybody else would have just let it ride over them, but not Lampitt. He took the bait and sent another letter back in which he said;

> *"Ms Pyle is on annual leave and I have dealt with the matter in her absence, for the sake of expediency. In any event, Ms Pyle reports to me and, if the letter had not been written by me, it would have been approved by me. The suggestion of victimisation is disappointing and groundless.*

Public comments that Mr Moyes has chosen to make about the Compliance Department, or me personally, have no relevance to, or bearing on, the current matter. The FA will contact you again in due course."

Lampitt needed to show how important he thought he was by reiterating his seniority over Pyle. His cage had been rattled and we'd hit a nerve. When I got the response from him I, and others, including even some of his own colleagues who I was friendly with, found it highly amusing. His final line said that we would hear from the FA in due course and we certainly did, although not perhaps in the way Lampitt would have preferred. After his pedantic letters Lampitt was left with egg on his face when he wrote back again on May 12 stating that the FA intended to take no disciplinary action. There was clearly not enough evidence to prove a charge, so all his petty points were to no avail. In his own personal battle with the Compliance Department the score line was now Moyes 2, The FA 0.

The Everton boss found himself in trouble with the FA again following a 3-2 away win at Stoke City on September 14, 2008. He was reported by fourth official Mike Jones:

"On a number of occasions during the course of the game, I had to remind Mr Moyes of the expected standard of conduct inside the technical area. During the game he had thrown a water bottle to the ground in an act of displeasure at a decision on the field of play, as well as publicly berating the referee and assistant for other decisions. Then in the 74th minute of the game, he left his technical area, entered the Stoke City technical area and once more publicly berated the referee and assistant over a penalty claim. At an appropriate point in time, I called the referee over to inform him of Mr Moyes' repeated inappropriate conduct and the referee, Alan Wiley, asked him to leave the technical area."

There had been a number of controversial decisions in the game, including the referee changing his mind about awarding a penalty to Everton after being surrounded by Stoke players. Instead of awarding the penalty the official gave a free kick instead. This had infuriated Moyes, especially as it appeared the foul had occurred inside the penalty area, but it seemed the referee had been influenced by the home players.

On the basis of the official's match reports, the FA charged Moyes with misconduct and once again he called upon my services. As normal, we obtained the match delegate's report and the first line summed up the referee's performance:

Major Decisions

In this department, I did not think that Alan (Wiley) had one of his better days."

Because Moyes had gone into the opposition's technical area, he had no choice but to admit the charge, which he did immediately, especially as Mike Jones, the fourth official, had responded to an FA request for more details about Moyes' behaviour. In an additional report Jones claimed that Moyes had said he was going to give the referee a *"full volley"* in the tunnel at half time, as well as making general complaints about the referee's decision-making. In his submissions to the panel, Moyes played heavily on the fact Wiley had changed his decision under the influence of the home team, despite the incident having taken place inside the penalty area. But what was really important to us was that at no time had he used any offensive language to any of the officials, which is always an aggravating feature in incidents such as this.

The hearing was held at Manchester City FC two months later and Moyes was fined £5,000, but did not receive a touch line ban. So once again we were generally satisfied with the outcome. In our eyes it was another victory.

Another intense Scotsman I encountered while working for

Everton was Duncan Ferguson, who I represented on two occasions. The first time was following a game between Everton and Leicester at Filbert Street in 2004 when referee Barry Knight sent him off for a second bookable offence. But the scandal wasn't the red card, it was what 'Big Dunc' did before leaving the pitch. It was one of the most memorable incidents of a season – but for all the wrong reasons. As Knight reported:

> *"After showing Ferguson the red card, he proceeded to run to his opponent, Mr Steffan Freund and violently and aggressively grab him round the throat with both hands and shook him. He was eventually separated from Mr Freund by the players and left the field of play. As he left the field, he made an offensive gesture to the crowd."*

The whole thing was captured on TV. The FA didn't hesitate in issuing two charges of misconduct three days later against Ferguson. The first charge related to his violent conduct towards Freund after his sending off and the second related to a gesture made towards the supporters as he stormed from the field. Sometimes you just have to take your medicine because there is no way out – and this was one of those cases. I advised Ferguson that he had no option but to admit both charges as soon as possible, which he did.

In his witness statement, which was placed before the disciplinary panel, Ferguson asked them to take into consideration the fact that his physique and him also being six-and-a-half feet tall sometimes gave a misleading impression to referees that he was committing a foul, when he was actually playing in a fair manner. He felt that during the game he was being unfairly punished by the referee when making genuine attempts to gain possession of the ball, and in his view had been unfairly booked for persistent fouls. In reality we were clutching at straws but trying to make the best of a bad job.

When his second booking happened meaning it was a red card, Ferguson thought Freund had been impeding him, as opposed to the other way around. His statement read:

> *"I would wish to be totally honest with the commission judging my case. I don't want to make various excuses about my behaviour. As I began to walk away from the referee and towards the tunnel, my opponent, Steffan Freund, was standing directly in my path. As I approached him, he did not move out of the way. The best way for me to describe what occurred next was that the "red mist came down". As I passed him, I grabbed at him around his throat. I held on momentarily before letting go. Many newspapers printed a photograph over the next few days, which in reality gave a distorted view of the manner in which I grabbed at the player. It seemed in the photo that I was trying to strangle him. But this was most certainly not the case. On grabbing the player, I instantaneously realised that my actions were wrong and let go of him and carried on walking towards the tunnel. As I continued walking I was aware of the strong animosity and anger of the crowd. I was angry at myself being sent off and made a hand gesture towards the angry crowd. I regret both my actions now."*

It was the best he could do. We had to try and limit the damage but knew this would be very difficult. The publicity around his behaviour had made it difficult and we knew the FA would have to come down hard on him.

Moyes provided a witness statement in which he outlined disciplinary action the club had taken. He also offered his apologies to all concerned on behalf of the club. We'd also obtained a copy of the match delegate's report, which was highly critical of Ferguson and very supportive of the referee, so we couldn't even use that because it would have made matters worse. We knew it was an uphill battle.

The hearing was held at Birmingham City on April 5, and the FA didn't disappoint in their judgement. The video footage of what happened was absolutely damning. He was lucky to be banned for only four games and fined £10,000.

Yet Duncan was never far from trouble. To describe him as a no-nonsense centre forward would be one of the great understatements. His reputation as a hard man was legendary and I found myself representing him again following a Premier League game in January, 2006 between Everton and Wigan at the JJB Stadium.

Ferguson was charged under the FA's new "fast track system" after being shown a red card by referee Mike Dean for punching Paul Scharner in the stomach. This was within minutes of him being sent on as a substitute! However the charge didn't relate to the red card for punching Scharner. In typical Duncan style – and to make matters worse – he didn't go quietly! Following his altercation with Scharner, he then got involved with Wigan's Pascal Chimbonda by pushing a hand into his face, right under the nose of Dean. Following a request from the FA, Dean then stated that he hadn't seen the incident involving Chimbonda, despite the photographs of the incident showing Dean standing right next to the pair.

There was a point of contention about at what juncture Dean had decided to send Ferguson off. The FA raised this with Dean to clarify the situation, as it was unclear from the reports he had submitted. In answer to the FA query, Dean went on to explain that he had decided to send off Ferguson prior to what took place with Chimbonda. In effect he had seen Ferguson punch Scharmer and at that point had decided Ferguson had to walk but had not had the opportunity to advise Ferguson of his impending sending off before he got involved with Chimbonda. By doing so this opened up an opportunity for me to challenge the FA's new system and I got to work on the case. I intended to submit that Ferguson had not been advised he was being sent off at the point of the Chimbonda incident, and was therefore still under the jurisdiction of the referee, as opposed to the FA's new fast track system. On the basis of the fact Dean had not dealt with

Ferguson's second offence at the time, we felt it unjust the FA had decided to intervene and charge Ferguson retrospectively, but they used the argument that Dean had said he had not seen the incident.

Over the coming years the instances where a referee would say he had not seen an incident, despite video footage or photographs suggesting that he had, has been the cause of many disputes in the regulatory system. It annoyed players and managers alike. It was a very controversial introduction to the game. It was seen as a "Get Out Of Jail Free" card for referees who had missed glaringly obvious incidents on the pitch. It was felt that the FA had given them an extra level of protection, while at the same time allowing the FA to re-referee a game by taking retrospective action. In fact the FA wrote it into their rules that where a referee stated that he did not see an incident, it had to be taken as a fact. This meant you could not challenge the claim by the referee, even if the video or photographs of the incident suggested otherwise. In my view that was a stitch up by the FA to railroad these types of incidents through the system. Nowadays it's just an accepted part of the game, but back then it was new and open to all sorts of challenges and allegations that referees had actually seen the incident but ignored it - and only claimed they had not seen it when the FA came calling or the media publicised it.

We knew that if any challenge to the rules failed, Ferguson would have to admit the charge. But we felt we had to have a go at challenging it on a technicality, just to test the water. We requested a pre-hearing to discuss the legality of the charge and for a disciplinary panel to make a ruling on it. Our submission was very straight-forward and we asked the simple question, *"At what point does the player concerned leave the jurisdiction of the referee?"* To support our argument we raised it with FIFA, who responded to our email query. The Referees Department at FIFA, in answer to the same question, said:

"A player who has committed a sending off offence is still

under the jurisdiction of the referee, even after the match. "

This was a supportive answer to the point we were trying to prove, that the FA didn't have jurisdiction to re-referee the game, and we put it before the panel. But it made little difference and they backed the FA in the argument. Then again, it would have been embarrassing for them if their new system was suddenly exposed as illegitimate, I suppose. This meant Ferguson had no option but to admit the charge, and a full hearing was held only two days later in accordance with the new fast track system procedures.

At the last minute Duncan decided not to attend the hearing, which didn't exactly help matters. The commission were not impressed and even though the rules say that a person charged must attend if he has requested a personal hearing, as Duncan had done, the panel decided it would still proceed without him. His disciplinary record was such that we were once again fighting a losing battle. He was given an additional four-game ban and £5,000 fine, on top of the automatic three-game ban for his initial red card for the punch on Scharner.

It was unfortunate that I couldn't do better for Duncan, but sometimes the evidence is so overwhelming that you just have to take a hit on it and try to limit the damage to your client. But Ferguson's actions in the two instances I dealt with made it very hard to get any good outcomes.

It was soon after these Everton cases that the FA put a stop on representatives gaining access to the referee assessor reports. It appeared that we were using them too much as an effective tool to fight cases. They had closed another loophole to the detriment of those charged.

I was not a fan of the new fast-track system introduced by the FA, mainly because it didn't work fluently with my *Football Factors* business model. It meant that the work I did over a period of weeks or months for clients was reduced to having to being completed in a matter of days. In effect this meant fewer fees and more intense work over a much shorter period of time. Looking back, I didn't adapt the business to suit the new systems that were put in place. That was a mistake by me which ultimately placed pressure on the viability of the business. In hindsight, I should have done one of two things at that point. Either adapt the business model to be more effective to the FA's new systems, or cash in and sell the business to a legal company wanting to get involved in sports regulation and representation. I did neither – and I regret the fact I just carried on, which ultimately was to my detriment.

9 - *ONE RULE FOR THE FA...*

NOT EVERY CASE I HAVE undertaken against the FA has involved household names such as Sir Alex Ferguson, Rafa Benitez or Duncan Ferguson. The name Ezekiel Teya won't attract the attention of tabloid sports editors but a case I made against him was arguably more important than those stellar names as it highlighted the manner in which the FA looked after its own and the type of cover up that the Nottinghamshire FA became embroiled in as it tried to save Teya's skin.

Teya was a Football Services Officer (FSO) in charge of the Discipline Department at Nottinghamshire FA. It is a senior role in the organisation. He was responsible for the issuing of disciplinary charges and arranging and overseeing disciplinary hearings. It was a job for which a person of the highest integrity was needed. However a case which Teya was involved in brought about one of the most important ones I have ever had to deal with. This was because it reinforced to me how protective the FA can be towards their own employees – even when they are blatantly wrong and dishonest. The events which I am about to recall are staggering, to say the least, and in any other workplace would lead to instant dismissal... but not at the Nottinghamshire FA.

I make no apology for the heavy detail, but I felt it was so important to outline this case, such was the way Teya conducted himself. It went to the very heart of transparency and honesty in regulatory issues.

As well as dealing with professional clubs, I have on many occasions assisted non-league and junior football clubs with disciplinary matters. In late 2020 I was contacted by a man called Anthony Spencer who was a part-time academy coach at Ilkeston Town and a voluntary senior official at a junior club called Nottingham FC, which fell under the jurisdiction of the Nottinghamshire FA. Anthony had been advised to contact me regarding a three-year suspension from all football activity he had received following a disciplinary hearing at the Notts FA. The issuing of such a draconian penalty would have had a serious impact on his employment and he desperately needed my help.

On the face of it, it seemed to be a fairly straightforward case for the Notts FA. In May 2020, at the height of the Covid lockdown when there was no football taking place anywhere in the country, Anthony and his brother had been carrying out some work on a plot of land that he owned, which was used by local football clubs during the season. This had nothing to do with his employment in football. He was just carrying out some maintenance to the field, along with some administrative work in his office. Some lads were having a kick around on the field, when suddenly a group of youths turned up in a car and began driving round the field doing handbrake turns. A young woman with her baby in a pram was worried about the safety of her and the boys who were playing football and raised this with Anthony. He immediately approached the youths in the car, who by this time had parked up, and asked them to move the vehicle off the field but they refused to do so. It was not the first time it had happened, and Anthony had warned them about doing this on a previous occasion. An argument developed resulting in a fracas with the youths from the car. All this was captured on one of their mobile phones and it found its way into the hands of the Notts FA, following a complaint to the police about Anthony.

Following its own investigation on September 17, 2020 the Notts FA issued a charge of assault against Anthony Spencer by a "*Participant upon a Participant*". In football terms, if you are under the jurisdiction of the FA for any reason, you are referred to as a 'participant'. The Notts FA claimed the youth Anthony was alleged to have assaulted was a player for a local team and, on that basis, despite the fact it had no relevance to football, a charge was issued.

In normal circumstances someone would have seven days to reply to the charge, but due to a computer malfunction the charge letter sent to Anthony indicated a date of October 1, 2020 as the final date to reply to the charge, which was fourteen days rather than the usual seven. As it turned out, these dates were highly important in the whole process.

A few days after October 1 Anthony received notification that he had been banned from all football, but he complained to me that something appeared to be very wrong with the whole process. He explained that he had not responded to the charge, as he was still collating his evidence and had intended to deny it. He went on to say he had been told that the Disciplinary Panel had considered his case, had sat and decided upon his guilt on the September 29, 2020. This was two days before the deadline expired for his response on the basis that he had failed to reply to the charge.

I realised that, if what he was saying was correct, the Notts FA had dealt with this matter in a wholly inappropriate way. You cannot deal with a case until either the participant has responded within the time limits stated, or the deadline date for replying had passed. If we could prove that the case had been dealt with before the deadline date, then it was a chance for him to appeal against the ban. I have to say that at this point I was dubious about his claim, because I couldn't believe for one minute the FA would deal with a case before the deadline to respond had expired but Anthony was insistent this was what had happened, and that his information had come from a man called Andrew Harland who had sat in judgement on the case. I asked Anthony to send me the papers to review it all.

Contained within the papers was an email trail between the chairman of the Nottingham FC club, Janade Aktar and Elaine Oram, the CEO of the Nottinghamshire FA, in which she repeated that the hearing had taken place on October 2. The only way I could ascertain the truth in the case was to contact the Disciplinary Panel Member, Andrew Harland, directly. In normal circumstances this is something I would never do. In fact, in over twenty years of being involved in the FA's disciplinary systems, it was the first time I had ever contacted a panel member about a case outside the official channels. But the more I spoke to Anthony and Janade, the more it appeared that something was very wrong with the whole process.

I bit the bullet and telephoned Andrew Harland. I immediately made it clear I did not want to discuss the case details but simply wanted him to confirm when the hearing had taken place. He told me that it was held on September 29, 2020 and that Teya had been present and overseen the administration of it. I explained to him that the Nottinghamshire FA were claiming the hearing had taken place on October 2 and he immediately said this was not correct. He added that if the Nottinghamshire FA had said that, then in his words it was *"indefensible of them"*.

Armed with the confirmation I required, I then agreed with Anthony that I would assist him and set about putting a detailed appeal document together. I cited that the FA had failed to give Anthony a fair hearing because they had heard the case before the expiry date had passed and by doing so they had reached a decision that no reasonable body could have come to, as well as various other reasons surrounding the date it had been held.

Any appeal against a decision of a County FA has to be made to the main FA, but Teya was also responsible for handling the appeal process on behalf of the Notts FA, along responding to our written submissions. The right and simple thing for him to do on receipt of it would have been to admit that an error had been made in hearing the case early, and that a re-hearing should be scheduled. Had he done this, it would have been a much fairer process and avoided any further scrutiny of his actions. However, when we received the response to the appeal from the Notts FA, I was staggered by what I read. Teya had prepared the response, in which he stated that:

> *"The NFA convened the hearing on 2/10/20 in line with FA procedures and heard the case after no response*

was received from Mr Spencer by 1/10/20".

This was a blatant lie. He was deliberately misleading the FA appointed Appeal Board to cover up his mistake. I responded immediately asking for a pre-hearing to get an order for the disciplinary panel member Andrew Harland to be instructed to give evidence at the appeal hearing, whilst at the same time registering an official complaint with the FA Disciplinary Department in London, asking them to conduct their own investigation into their employee, who in our view was acting dishonestly.

Unbelievably the FA refused to conduct an investigation until the appeal process was completed. They were saying that my complaint formed part of my grounds of appeal, so it was not appropriate to investigate the matter at that stage. This was a fudge and dereliction of their duty. We were making a serious allegation that their own employee was telling lies that could be proved by making some very simple enquiries. All it needed was for them to make one telephone call to Mr Harland, or any of his fellow panel members, to obtain the truth. Yet they were refusing to look at it. They were throwing a protective bubble around Teya. It was disgusting – but that just made me even more determined to prove that Teya was a liar.

The pre-hearing in which we were asking for an order for Mr Harland to give evidence was overseen by the chairman of the appointed Appeal Board, Peter Powell, a solicitor by trade and a former director at Colchester United. I felt reasonably confident that we would succeed in getting an order in our favour, but I was wrong. It was clear that even Powell was initially against us, especially when he asked Teya to confirm when the hearing had been held and he repeated falsely that it was on 2nd October. Teya also claimed that it was *"impossible to discount"* that Mr Harland may have been pressurised into giving false information – and he made this allegation without a shred of evidence. It was clear Teya was getting desperate, even at this early stage. This was now the second time he had told lies and misled the Appeal Board.

Powell asked him if he was willing to state that in evidence, which he said he would do and that seemed to convince him.

The Chairman ruled that:

> *"There is no need to grant that application (for Harland to attend) as in my view nothing turns upon the date. I do not accept that Mr Spencer was about to put in a response on or before 1st October so was not prejudiced".*

In my view Powell got this so wrong. The issue was all about the transparency of the process. It was irrelevant at that point whether Spencer intended submitting a response to the charge. I was determined not to give up on this because I knew the Nottinghamshire FA were now involved in a cover up by telling lies and were even willing to see Anthony suspended for three years on the basis of their falsehoods.

My next move was to request that the Appeal Board be adjourned, pending any investigation into Teya's conduct, as I felt it would be prejudicial to Anthony to proceed with the appeal until it was determined one way or another whether Teya was being truthful. The reality was I was gambling with high stakes, because I knew if any investigation proved Teya was telling the truth, then Anthony's appeal would fail but I was convinced the truth would come out and we would be proved right. Anthony was fully behind me with the advice I was giving him. He had nothing to lose. Once again Powell ruled against me when I asked for the adjournment, clearly stating that he believed Teya about the date ruling as follows:

> *"Mr Bean gives 2 reasons for his application. First, he says the hearing was 29th September not 2nd October and has applied to the FA for an inquiry. But as I am satisfied Mr Spencer was not going to submit his response on or before the 1st October he was not prejudiced by the hearing being held before then, even if indeed it was (and at present I do not accept it was). There has been no evidence, other than hearsay, that the hearing was early."*

My view was the hearsay evidence he referred to could be confirmed as factual evidence, just by making one telephone call. Powell was completely missing the point. It was a red herring he was using to cover up why there shouldn't be an adjournment. The point was that it could not be ruled out that he was going to reply, and this being the case, the FA had not dealt with the matter properly and in accordance with their rules. However they were riding roughshod over their own rules and effectively protecting Teya. I refused to let this put me off and stuck to the task in hand. We were being obstructed from finding the truth at every possible juncture. It was a cover up, plain and simple.

By this time we had learned that the original disciplinary panel member, Andrew Harland, had emailed another FA employee called Fraser Williamson, who was the Grassroots Discipline Manager based at Wembley Stadium, confirming that the hearing had taken place on 29th September, yet they were still sitting on that information and not disclosing it to anybody, in the full knowledge that it was the most important issue of the appeal. I really went on the offensive and emailed the FA in the following terms, which I then followed up with a formal application;.

> *Our client is deeply concerned at his perceived fairness of these appeal proceedings. We would raise the following issues: The failure of the FA to investigate the complaints regarding Mr Teya and the Notts FA is nothing short of a "cover up". The FA state they will not conduct an inquiry until the completion of the Appeal. This is no more than a "fudge" of the issue and simply a tactic to "kick the can further down the road". In Mr Spencer's view, it is to protect the embarrassment that the FA will obviously suffer from if it is shown that one of their employees (Mr Teya) has engaged in a course of inappropriate conduct. Furthermore, if that is shown to be correct, then given that the Chairman has already inferred that he leans towards Mr Teya's version of events, then his further involvement in*

these proceedings would become untenable.

We understand the FA are in possession of information from Mr Harland which in our view will prove that Mr Teya has deliberately misled all concerned in regards to these proceedings. If that were to be shown to be the case, then the whole integrity of the process is in question - along with that of Mr Teya. There is absolutely no justification in the FA shelving this matter pending the appeal, particularly as the date of the hearing is a core issue in our view and central to the appeal.

If the FA are not prepared to conduct an immediate investigation into one of its own employees, then at the very least they should have the courtesy to independently confirm when the hearing took place (with supporting evidence) - and it is within the remit of the Chairman to order this to be divulged in the interests of fairness, transparency and natural justice.

Additionally, it has been made known to us that there is now a clear effort by the FA to obstruct Mr Spencer in pursuing this angle and presenting such evidence at the appeal. We understand that Mr Harland has been instructed by Mr Teya and the FA not to converse regarding this matter. If they are making such orders/instructions on Mr Harland, then it is clear that Mr Spencer is being denied the opportunity to obtain evidence to support his case - and justice is being actively prevented from being done. We have already seen in the first application hearing that Mr Teya has alluded to the fact, wrongly and without proof, that it is "impossible to discount" that Mr Harland has been pressurised into his current position. This, in our view, shows that he is willing to go to any length to cover up his own misgivings.

In any event, such is our concern of a perceived "cover up", it is now our intention to raise this issue as soon as possible in writing with the Chief Executive Officer and

Human Resources Department of the FA, in the form of a formal complaint and concerns against both Mr Teya and now also Mr Fraser Williamson (Senior Discipline Manager – Grassroots Division). Mr Williamson is the FA employee handling the original complaint against Mr Teya and in possession of information from Mr Harland.

It is our view that until these processes are exhausted, then it would be inherently wrong to hear the appeal, unless of course there is some concession by the FA regarding the disclosure of the date of the hearing (and evidence to support it). As we have previously stated, if the hearing took place on October 2 it would be a simple process to exhibit this, remove any suspicion from Mr Teya and the Notts FA, whilst at the same time dilute the grounds for Mr Spencer's basis of appeal. The silence is deafening and in the absence of any credible evidence or response from the FA, can only point to one reasonable conclusion at present.

These issues are further compounded by the Chairman's response to the original application, in that it is not relevant to the proceedings as he reached the conclusion that Mr Spencer would not have submitted a response by October 1. We fail to see how he can reach this conclusion without listening to full submissions at any full appeal hearing.

The perception gained by Mr Spencer is that the Chairman has ignored the fact that there would be very little point in making any submissions by October 1, if the hearing had already taken place on September 29. It is his submission that this is a matter for a full Appeal Board to consider and reach a conclusion on, and by pre-empting this it has placed Mr Spencer at a serious disadvantage and is unfair and potentially prejudicial to him.

As the Chairman will understand, as well as justice being done, justice must also BE SEEN to be done, and there must be a clear and unequivocal perception and belief that justice is being done. Any person charged must be

*fully comfortable and have confidence that the proceedings
he is facing must be done in a fair way, with all issues
being dealt with transparently irrespective of which party it
assists. It is Mr Spencer's strong view that this is not being
done at present.*

*If it could be independently established and divulged,
with supporting evidence, exactly when the hearing
took place, then this perception may be removed. It is a
simple request that will have a significant impact on the
proceedings one way or the other in respect of Mr Spencer.*

*In the circumstances we would ask that consideration
be given to the following;*

*1.   The FA divulging the information they are in
possession of regarding the date of the hearing with
supporting evidence and/or*

*2.   The Chairman make an order for that
information to be furnished to us within a set timeframe.*

*If we are denied this, then in our client's view it
reinforces the fact that he is not being afforded a fair process.*

*If that is the case, then it is with great reluctance and
regret that we are left in a position where he believes that
it is in the best interests of all parties that the present
Chairman of the Commission be invited to withdraw
himself from any further involvement in this matter.*

It was shit or bust, because we were now questioning the
fairness of the Appeal Board Chairman. It still didn't make any
difference at all and the FA still refused to confirm the details
of the information they were holding, while Powell refused to
stand down from the Appeal Board. To say we were really up
against it was an understatement, but we were not giving up. It
had become a war of attrition, but we had come so far we just
couldn't back down now. At no point did it ever cross our minds
to do so.

I decided on one last roll of the dice to try to force the FA
and Powell's hand, and took the very unusual step of writing to

Christopher Quinlan QC, the Chairman of the FA's Regulatory Panel. This was the very top man of the disciplinary system at the FA, someone who was an independent barrister and Queen's Counsel. In my application to him, I explained the issues and difficulties we were facing and the importance of the date of Spencer's original hearing. Whilst he could not make a ruling and interfere with the process, he did respond to everyone involved and wrote;

> *"These are appeal proceedings. Paragraph 15 of the Disciplinary Regulations does not apply to appellate proceedings. Therefore, and regrettably, I do not have power to adjudicate upon the said application. I say regrettably as I have sympathy for and see the force of the application and submissions made in support hereof. The application should be referred to the Appeal Board Chairman immediately, with a copy of this ruling. I would respectfully invite him to consider again the rulings hitherto made, given the centrality of the issue to which they relate: the day upon which the hearing took place."*

It was the breakthrough we needed, despite being less than twenty-four hours before the main Appeal Board hearing was due to take place. Without making a formal decision, he was backing our requests and was effectively telling Powell to reconsider what we were asking. That was tantamount to telling him to do the right thing and get the information that we were asking for. Our tenacity looked like it was paying off and it was becoming embarrassing for the FA.

Within two and a half hours Powell ordered the Nottinghamshire FA to hand over all emails between themselves and members of the original disciplinary panel that had overseen Anthony Spencer's hearing before 1.30pm the following day. It was hoped that this would confirm when the hearing had taken place. This meant that the Appeal Board would have the opportunity to read all the email trails before the main hearing was due to be heard at 2pm. This was a massive moment in these proceedings and when Teya got notification of it he must have shit himself. He would have known the game was up and his lies were about to be exposed.

However, there was another twist in the tale. At 1.24pm on the date of the Appeal Board and just six minutes before the deadline for handing over of the email trails, the FA received one from Teya which read as follows:

> *"The NFA office does not keep months old email correspondence from customers, panel members and stakeholders stored in our inboxes, as we like to keep fresh disks. We do however save all discipline case folders on our shared drives which contain charge documentation, evidence, and participant responses and appeal submissions; all of which have been shared with all parties."*

In effect Teya was now saying that they did not have the emails. He knew he had been rumbled, but the problem he had was that the FA did have them, having been provided them by Andrew Harland on December 5 some six weeks earlier. The FA had sat on those emails knowing full well that Teya had been misleading the Appeal Board – and had not disclosed it.

It was a scandal.

The Appeal Hearing went ahead, commencing 30 minutes later, when Teya came under some fierce questioning by the three Appeal Board Members. Initially he said he was the only person available to attend from Nottinghamshire FA, and then went on to continue with the pretence of the false date of the hearing and the fact that all emails had been deleted. It was all just too convenient and at long last the panel saw straight through him. The panel were not impressed and adjourned the hearing for a week, ordering that the CEO of Nottinghamshire FA attend as well as the three members of the original disciplinary panel, including Mr Harland. It had taken us almost four months to get to this point and we were finally getting what we had requested, in that Mr Harland should give evidence.

Forty-eight hours later, on January 23, 2021, Teya sent another document to the FA in which he admitted for the first time that the hearing in respect of Anthony Spencer had taken place on September 29, 2020 and not October 2, as he had told the panel on numerous occasions. In effect he was admitting to misleading the panel and telling lies. In the meantime, it transpired that one of the original panel members could not attend the hearing, so he sent a report in confirming that he had sat on the hearing on September 29 . The whole thing was caving in around Teya, but worse was still to come.

On January 28 2021 the hearing was reconvened. The first witness called was Elaine Oram, the CEO of Nottingham FA. She stated that Teya had told her that Spencer's hearing took place on October 2, but when pressed by the panel members she admitted that around Christmas time 2020 she had been made aware of the appeal proceedings and had learned that the hearing actually had taken place on September 29, as opposed to October 2. But despite being in possession of that information, she did nothing at all with it and made no attempt to correct the story that had being concocted by Teya! It was astounding that the CEO of a County FA had been aware that the person in charge of disciplinary matters was deliberately misleading some appeal proceedings, but had then done nothing about it. She was part of the cover up. She then went on to admit that she was available to attend the hearing the previous week, when Teya had misled the Board again by saying he was the only person available. Oram's evidence was even more astonishing when she claimed that there had been no deliberate attempt to mislead anyone by Teya – despite the fact that he had lied on numerous occasions. She was more concerned that there appeared to be a lack of confidentiality from the original disciplinary panel. In effect she was complaining because the Nottinghamshire FA had been found out.

It was then Teya's turn to give evidence. He was asked

directly by the panel if he had lied to them previously, and amazingly he answered "*No*". Even then he still wouldn't admit it. Following on from him was Andrew Harland, who buried Teya by confirming the date of September 29. My job was done, without me even having to ask any questions! My tenacity had paid off. I had exposed a major cover up from the very top of the Nottinghamshire FA, which had even extended into the main FA.

The Board quickly ruled in Anthony Spencer's favour and referred the matter back to be reheard. When the written reasons were produced, they were absolutely damning:

> *"The Appeal Board took the unusual step of requesting an FA investigation because in their opinion Mr Teya deliberately misled the Chairman at the original Application Hearing on 2nd December 2020; he deliberately misled the Board again on the 21st January and all written submissions throughout until the 23rd January 2021 when he changed his account regarding the date of the Hearing. Ms Oram has been aware of the falsified date submission by Mr Teya for several weeks, but has made no effort to obtain any independent corroboration of what Mr Spencer was apparently telling her and still supports Mr Teya fully. "*

Finally the truth had been exposed and an investigation was ordered into what the Appeal Board described as "*The wholly unacceptable behaviour and conduct of Nottinghamshire FA*". Some weeks later a rehearing took place, where we proved that at the time of the incident in May 2020 it was not football related. Anthony Spencer was not working in his capacity as a football coach or administrator and no evidence was provided by the FA that the other youth involved was a participant. So the disciplinary panel dismissed the case very quickly. The charge should never have been issued in the first place because it was never a football-related matter under the jurisdiction of the FA.

But that wasn't the end of the story. The FA Compliance Department investigated the whole thing. Amazingly, it concluded that no action was to be taken against Elaine Oram even though she had been deeply involved in the matter and knew that Teya was misleading the panels. Teya himself was charged by the FA with "*knowingly providing a false account which was deliberately misleading*" and appeared before a disciplinary panel to answer the charge.

So, to put things into context, we had the CEO and the Head of Discipline working together, bringing shame and disrepute onto their organisation. Teya was responsible for running the disciplinary department and was caught out telling numerous lies. He was happy to see someone banned from football for three years due to those lies. His integrity was shot to pieces and you would ask yourself how can he possibly remain in such a position of responsibility, where honesty and integrity are paramount qualities? You would have fully expected him to be the subject of a suspension himself for his odious and disgraceful behaviour but instead he was looked after by the FA. Unbelievably, he received just a warning and was fined £375. You couldn't make it up. I understand that he was disciplined by the Notts FA afterwards, but then left the organisation of his own accord later. Maybe he jumped before he was pushed? But it shouldn't have come to that. His conduct deserved an immediate dismissal in my opinion.

We raised the issue with the FA about the leniency of the penalty against him. They did not even submit an appeal against the leniency of the penalty issued and sent us a standard letter back, telling us they no longer intended corresponding with us about it all. Had Teya acted like this in any other organisation, or had it been a player or manager who had behaved in that way, they would have been suspended or sacked. They most certainly would not have received a minor slap on the wrist for it.

The FA look after their own. In normal circumstances they cannot wait to publish written reasons on the FA website about matters of such seriousness, but they ensured that details of this case were not made public to avoid any embarrassment on their employees.

It's pretty obvious that there is one rule for the FA and another for everyone else in the game.

Another example of the FA's ability to turn a blind eye to serious wrongdoing by one of their own happened right on my doorstep. I have never seen eye-to-eye with former Barnsley FC director and FA Vice President Barry Taylor. To say we don't get on is putting it lightly. However I will just concentrate on when the FA bailed him out in an election when it looked like he was going lose his precious seat on the FA council and all the little extras that came with it.

I have always had an affection for the Tykes and for several years I sponsored the team sheets handed out at home games. The sponsorship was only worth £1500 a year to them but prior to me doing that they were getting nothing for it and as they say 'every little helps'. I was fairly close to former chairman John Dennis, a true football man, who always made me feel welcome whenever I went down to Oakwell. Although once he left, and Peter Ridsdale went the same way, my visits attendance there was considerably reduced as I was none too keen on the new regime which included Taylor, who was keen to keep his place on the board to maintain his FA position.

Taylor was what is called a 'Divisional Representative', which is a position on the FA council where the elected person looks after the organisation's interests in his local geographical area. Taylor had made himself a nice little position out of it without really being challenged. He had found himself on two 'plum' FA committees: the FA Cup Committee and the International Committee, and regularly represented the FA abroad at tournaments. Like I say it was a plum position. Who wouldn't like that type of experience?

When an FA councillor has completed twenty-five years of service they are elected as a honorary vice president to the FA, meaning they are there for life with all the freebies and trappings that come with it. Taylor was close to reaching that milestone, but following a bust up we had I went out of my way to try to stop that. My mission was to make life uncomfortable for him in his normally unchallenged position.

Our dispute started over some comments I had made to our local paper, the *Barnsley Chronicle*. In the autumn of 2008 in a game against Sheffield United Barnsley striker Ian Hulme suffered a fractured skull in a challenge with the Blade's Chris Morgan, when he was elbowed in the head. Referee Andy D'Urso only booked Morgan, when in reality he should have got his red card out. These were the days when the FA did not take retrospective action so that was the end of the matter. But that didn't stop Barnsley FC encouraging local MP Eric Illsley, who was later convicted in the MP expenses scandal, raising the matter in the House of Commons asking for support for action to be taken. It was a ridiculous thing to do. The country was in the middle of a recession and people in Barnsley, who Illsley purported to represent, were fearing the worst due to the state of the economy following the collapse of several banks in Europe and America. Yet here we had the local MP acting on the whim of a club director raising such an inappropriate matter in the Houses of Parliament! There were far more important things to discuss at that time. In answer to a question from a reporter I said as much – that it was wrong of him to be used in that way, especially as Taylor was on the FA Council and in an ideal position to make his concerns known and to lobby for some form of action to be taken.

It didn't take long for me to receive a letter signed by my good friend, the General Manager at Barnsley FC, Don Rowing on behalf of the directors complaining about my comments. After noting my objection to the co-ordinated attempt to bring the issue of a red card in a Championship game to national attention, the last paragraph read as follows:

> *I am sure you will understand therefore our resentment on reading your comments in the* Barnsley Chronicle *when you openly criticised Eric Illsley for raising the matter in the House of Commons in an effort to reflect the views of both Barnsley FC and its supporters. The nature of your comments prompted a meeting of Directors ,following which I have to inform you that due to your stance on this issue we are unable to offer you hospitality at Barnsley FC in the future.*

So I was barred from the club, despite sponsoring them!

It was trivial, petty and lacked any foresight. Don phoned me about it and was very apologetic. He told me that it wasn't a concern to him, but it was Barry Taylor who had been party to instigating the ban. I decided there and then that I would target Taylor's FA spot. Like any plan for revenge I had to bide my time. In the meantime I ended my sponsorship with immediate effect and withdrew permission for the *Football Factors* logo to be used on the team sheet, threatening them with legal proceedings if they used the logo again. This put them in a hole because I waited until the Friday evening before a Saturday game to inform them, thus make things as awkward as possible for them.

I was aware that Taylor was up for election was again in May 2009 and as the date approached I called John Ryan, Chairman of Doncaster Rovers, to see if he was interested in standing against him. John was well up for it. As far as I am aware it was the first time in over twenty years that Taylor had actually been challenged – he was shocked. I ran John's campaign and began by contacting all the clubs eligible to vote which in effect were the Yorkshire clubs and a few in the East Midlands, including some amateur clubs. There were a total of eighteen votes up for grabs and by the voting deadline of 3pm on May 30, 2009, we felt that we had done enough to get the ten we needed to win the election.

However later that afternoon we were contacted by the FA and advised that Taylor had won the election by nine votes to eight. We were dumbfounded, as we felt we were in a very strong position. Something didn't feel right about it, especially after Charlie Sale of the *Daily Mail* and a long-suspected favoured 'contact' of Taylor's, telephoned me gloating that we had lost. Charlie didn't disappoint, because the following day he wrote a piece in his gossip column that I had *"failed in a disturbing attempt to oust one of the FA's most senior counsellors in a personal dispute"*. Sale went on to add that we were making a *"frivolous objection"* to the outcome, but he was made to eat his own words when following that *"frivolous objection"*, the FA had to have a re-vote due to serious discrepancies in the voting process.

Alistair Maclean, the then FA Company Secretary, was the person responsible for overseeing the election process. Maclean, acting for the FA, was the only person authorised to circulate the voting papers and he did this to all the clubs eligible to vote on Thursday, May 21, 2009. He confirmed he had done this in a letter to John Ryan on May 27, following a complaint we raised about how Taylor had conducted himself in the voting process. We discovered that Taylor had circulated a covering letter written by himself together with a copy of the voting paper. It was like going to the voting booth on General Election Day and finding a leaflet from one of the political parties attached to a facsimile voting paper! Not only would you assume that the letter was an attempt to persuade you to vote for that particular party but you would be completing a fake ballot paper!

When challenged by Maclean, Taylor admitted to it but claimed that "some clubs" had not received their voting paper from the FA, although further investigation failed to identify which "clubs" these were. It was underhand of him, and not a little desperate, but as expected his mates at the FA stuck up for him with Maclean going on to claim Taylor had *"not done anything untoward"*. If that was the case, then why did Maclean continue in his letter to John Ryan by saying:

"I have told Mr Taylor that I believe that it is only appropriate for voting papers to be sent out by the FA and if a club has not received the information for any reason, then they should contact the FA to receive it". He was contradicting himself in his attempt to cover for Taylor's improper act. The rules surrounding FA elections are quite clear - and he had broken the rules.

Simon Mullock from the *Sunday Mirror* picked up on the story and obtained an exclusive interview with John Ryan a few days later which began:

Ryan is demanding that the election is held again after discovering that the long-time Yorkshire and Derbyshire divisional representative Taylor sent out literature promoting his own campaign, along with photocopies of the official ballot paper, contravening FA Rules.

John went on to say:

I believe what Taylor did, sending out a photocopied ballot paper along with leaflets promoting his own campaign, made it appear that he was the FA's preferred choice. In my view it wasn't a fair election, and the vote should be taken again, especially as it was so close. I believe Taylor has behaved improperly and action should also be taken against him.

On 1st June 2009, I fired off a letter to Maclean pointing out that Taylor had gone beyond the simple process of lobbying for votes and had interfered with the election process, something that had been confirmed by him in his own letter to John Ryan, despite the fact that Taylor had gone on to deny it in the *Sunday Mirror* story.

The election process then got murkier because in a conversation with Maclean he advised me that both Rotherham

United and Leeds United had not been allowed to vote. Due to recent financial issues affecting the clubs, their votes were ineligible. I raised the question that if this was the case, then why were ballot forms circulated to them? I didn't receive any satisfactory answer, but the issue now reached the Chairman of the FA, Lord Triesman, who requested an independent lawyer with electoral law experience to examine the conduct of the election. His findings were startling, as it was discovered that in the final few minutes of the vote the FA were ringing clubs telling them to submit their voting papers, when there was no mandatory rule saying requiring them to vote. The only conclusion could be that Taylor was behind and needed these votes. Then, it was revealed that Sheffield Wednesday had made two votes, one for each candidate! The incompetence in the election organisation was staggering.

The independent lawyer advised that the results should be overturned and the election should be re-run for the first time in the history of the Football Association. In fairness to Charlie Sale he did even things up by writing in beneficial terms about our efforts in challenging the outcome and admitted that the *"frivolous complaint"* to which he had referred was proven to be serious and legitimate.

Then, much to my delight, Barry Taylor and his wife were banned from attending the FA's annual summer meeting, which was a freebie weekend in Torquay, on the basis that he had not been elected formally and that a re-run of the election was to take place.

As they say, every cloud has a silver lining!

The rerun of the election took place in the following September and this time Taylor won by several votes. However in our view it shouldn't have got to that stage, because when the original legitimately cast votes had been counted in the May election, John Ryan was the clear winner. Some days after the election Taylor had the audacity to circulate another letter to all clubs who had voted, including addressing one to John Ryan himself in his capacity as chairman of Doncaster Rovers, with the opening paragraph brazenly stating;

"It was an unusual situation to have to win the same election twice".

Once again, he was wrong; he didn't win an election twice. The independent review of the election process proved that. But more importantly, it was clear from the rules relating to FA elections that he had broken them – and unsurprisingly the FA did absolutely nothing to him despite such a serious rule breach. As I have said, there's always one rule for the FA, and one for everyone else.

They look after their own.

As a footnote, on September 10, 2009, Charlie Sale wrote another piece about FA elections in his column:

The FA are facing questions as to how they administer their own council elections, with in-house lawyer Alistair Maclean in the firing line. There were calls earlier this summer for company secretary Maclean to be sacked following his criticised handling of the botched election between Doncaster Rovers chairman John Ryan and Barnsley's Barry Taylor for a regional representative place on the council. This needed to be re-run following complaints from the Ryan camp over the flawed way Maclean had collected the votes. Ryan, who lost to Taylor in the re-vote, is still waiting for a proper explanation as to why the FA process was riddled with irregularities.

So much for the *"frivolous complaints"* to which Charlie had previously referred!

10 - *THE POISONED CHALICE*

IF YOU WERE TO LOOK AT the 'charge sheet' against Chesterfield Football Club over the last ten years or so you would see a club that has been so badly run it's a miracle it still exists. The roll of shame has seen a revolving door of managers, boardroom unrest, alleged financial irregularities over a football development school associated with the club, a fake raffle to win a place on the club's pre-season trip to Hungary in 2016 won by a non-existent fan after only four tickets were sold, players playing under false names, an FA cup tie having to be replayed due to fielding an ineligible player and then, to top it all off, using a player in 39 games whilst he was unregistered. Add to that serious supporter discontent by a troublesome section of the fans that were unrelenting in their attacks on the club and its staff, coupled with the club's relegation from into the National League at the end of the 2017/18 season, and the role of Chief Executive of Chesterfield was not exactly an attractive proposition.

Housed in a comparively new stadium, which is better than many grounds in the Football League, the only thing that was keeping the club going was the goodwill and financial support of owner Dave Allen, a former chairman of near neighbours Sheffield Wednesday and the proprietor of a nationwide chain of casinos. Given the financial support Dave gave the club in turbulent times, they should erect a statue of him in the town in recognition of his contribution to ensure professional football continued to be played there. Put quite simply, if he had not put his money where his mouth is then Chesterfield FC would not exist in its current form. One of the main problems the club had, however, was that Dave insisted on his good friend and business associate, Ashley Carson, having a major input into the overseeing of how the club was run, which is what caused much of the problems and discontent. Carson was Assay Master at the Sheffield Assay Office and a very well-respected businessman in that city who had been involved with Dave during his time at Wednesday. It seemed a natural progression that he would carry on in a similar vein at Chesterfield. Unfortunately it proved to be a disaster with Carson becoming the focus of supporter criticism and abuse for anything and everything that went wrong there.

While some of that criticism was justified, most of it seemed to be a case of using Carson as a scapegoat by supporters simply because they disliked him. Ashley is an amicable and charming man with a great sense of humour but he also has a dark side to him as I discovered once I accepted the 'poisoned chalice' of Chief Executive at the Spireites.

It proved to be an eye opening experience, one plagued with infighting, backstabbing and unrest and in hindsight, I wish I'd never taken the position. If I could turn back the clock, I wouldn't go anywhere near it. But you live and learn I suppose. It was also a surreal appointment because 18 years earlier I had lead an FA investigation into serious financial irregularities at the club, which was the catalyst for the then chairman, Darren Brown, being sent to prison. The club had been deducted points when it appeared before an FA Disciplinary Panel following that investigation. From the moment I took up the position at Chesterfield FC I was viewed as the 'enemy' by fans who tarred me with the Carson brush. They quickly forgot that had I not stepped in all those years ago, there would not have been a Chesterfield FC for them to even complain and whinge about! However fans are fickle and some of those at Chesterfield were among the worst I have ever encountered in football. Which is saying something, given the issues Leeds fans had to deal with at Elland Road in the Cellino era!

In the autumn of 2018 the club had been charged by the Football Association with fielding an unregistered player called Joe Rowley on 39 different occasions over the previous 18 months or so. To field an unregistered player on one occasion is a cardinal sin in football and brings into question the ability of the club secretary, who is responsible for ensuring all registrations are completed correctly. But for a player to accumulate so many illegal appearances is utterly ridiculous and shows a level of incompetency I have never experienced before in the game. Not only does it show an exceptionally poor level of administration, with no grip on how to do the job, but it also shows just how poor the management of the club secretary was during that time. I have never heard of an unregistered player playing as many times without being found out. It must be a record in British football and was typical of the way the club lurched from one crisis to another. It's little wonder that supporters were so fed up with what was happening to their once proud club. Thankfully the club secretary responsible for the 39 illegal appearances had been replaced by former Derbyshire FA employee Nigel Smith. I would like to go on record as saying that Nigel is one of the best secretaries I've ever worked with. He is organised, highly competent and was a real asset to have around during my time at the club. He should have been working at a much higher level.

I was initially approached by club director John Croot, who I had known since the time of my FA investigation, who sounded me out about representing the club in the Joe Rowley affair and then put me in touch with Carson. In November 2018 I represented the club before the FA and astonishingly managed to secure a fine of only £5000 as punishment for this unbelievable breach of the rules. To describe that penalty as lenient would be a huge understatement. I expected a fine of at least three times that and could not rule out a points deduction, so once again I had come to the rescue of the club.

I had never met Ashley Carson before the Rowley case but I'd got on well with him but I was still very surprised a few weeks later to get a call out of the blue from him asking if I was interested in taking up the role of CEO at the club. From the initial conversation I had with him it was clear that he was coming under intense pressure from the fans about his involvement and, on reflection, he needed someone to take the heat off him. That should have been a red flag, but I was keen to get back involved working inside a club, so I agreed to meet with him.

I met Carson at his plush Assay office several days later and as I drove there, I was considering what type of salary the position would attract. Given that Chesterfield were now a National League club, I had decided to wait for Ashley to pitch an offer of around 40k and I would then hold out for £45k and a company car. It was a couple of weeks before Christmas 2018, but I hadn't anticipated that Santa Claus would come early that year! Ashley explained some of the issues he was experiencing from the fans and also the precarious position of the club, both in terms of its on-field performances but also its financial difficulties. He said the fans would never accept him, so perhaps it was time for him to take a step back but as time went on this proved to be impossible task as he enjoyed being in the limelight and perversely I think he enjoyed being cast as the pantomime villain.

When he turned to incumbent team manager Martin Allen, I immediately got the impression that he was very difficult to work with and that Carson felt a little intimidated by him. We then got down to the issue of salary. It was soon agreed. In fact, it was agreed within about a minute when he said that the previous CEO was paid £65k when they were a league club, so he would offer me £60k and a car. Given that I was only expecting £40k, I didn't need prompting to ask for more. Carson may as well have dressed up in a red suit and put on a white beard!

This slap dash attitude to finance was the club's undoing, as I was later to discover when I saw the size of wages in some of the player contracts. They were completely out of sync with what they should have been paying at that level. Some of the contracts just didn't make sense. One player was on £1,000 per week, but if they got promoted it got reduced to £900 and if they got relegated it increased to £1,100. It was bizarre and there didn't seem to be any structure to the pay scales there.

It was as if they had thought of a number, doubled it and then agreed it. Agent payments were also through the roof. To me, it looked like players wages were just agreed on a whim. I think the club was gambling on getting back into the Football League immediately, but history tells us that very rarely happens when a club drops into the National League – and it certainly wasn t going to happen in the case of the Spireites that season. I believe the club made a major mistake when it was relegated into the National League. They carried on as if they were a Football League club in terms of player wages, but they compounded the issue with player wages by lowering match day admission prices to placate the fans. This was a recipe for disaster, especially after I worked on the following season's admission prices when we had no option but to increase them again to try to make the club viable. Had they not reduced the ticket prices so much at the time immediately after relegation, then they would not have suffered the abuse they got for increasing them twelve months later. It was exceptionally poor planning by the club. As CEO I took a lot of the flak for that, but the reality was that it had to be done because of the mistakes made twelve months earlier.

From day one there were problems for me at Chesterfield. Firstly, I was not allocated an office. The CEO's office had been commandeered by Dave Allen's son- in-law, Paul Roberts, who was supposedly involved in the catering and hospitality side of the club. He thought he was a 'whizz kid' in this field, but I formed the impression that the only whizzing he did was the speed at which he moved to get out of the way when there was some real work to be done. He had taken residence in the office normally used by the CEO a few days before my arrival on December 17, 2018. According to staff, before that he just locked himself away in what was the police control room, and nobody ever saw him but he obviously saw me as a threat and tried to impose himself on me straight away. I suppose being the son-in-law of the owner made him think he was untouchable, but that soon ended following what was a very strained relationship between us that resulted in Dave Allen making him redundant. One of the reasons for this was because he was just too much of a problem when it came to the way in which I was trying to do things. He was obstructive and it wasn't good for staff morale. Ashley eventually booted him from the office but within weeks of my arrival we'd had a stand-up row when he discovered I intended interviewing one of his favourite staff members over a sensitive allegation that had been made about their conduct. Roberts bounced into my office with a face like thunder and told me he had spoken to the staff member, so there was no need for me to do so. I told him straight it didn't work like that, and a formal interview in accordance with employment law and their contract would take place.

It ended up with us going toe-to-toe as I stood my ground, before telling him quite loudly that *"It's fucking happening and that's it, so keep your fucking nose out"*, before he stormed off with his tail between his legs. Apparently, the row was heard through the walls of the office so all and sundry knew about it. The interview did take place without any further intervention from him but once Dave Allen showed how ruthless he could be by making his own son-in-law redundant, I didn't need telling that my position, or indeed that of any other staff member, could easily be next.

On my first day at the club I had been interviewed by the local paper, in which I made a harmless comment that the manager, Martin Allen, was not in work that day as it was his day off. The following morning I walked down the cold concrete-walled corridor to Martin's office to introduce myself as we had not crossed paths before. The sign on his door told you everything you needed to know about his ego. It covered almost half of the door in big blue capital letters with the words **"MARTIN'S OFFICE"**. I knocked on the door with slight trepidation and entered. Martin was sat at the first desk right next to the door and his assistants Adrian Whitbread and Carl Muggleton were sitting on a sofa to the side of him. Following introductions Allen immediately tried it on, as if he was trying to mark his territory. I had made some background enquiries about Allen before I started the job, and I had been told to expect an egotistical attitude. In my view his immediate intention was to try to try to get the upper hand and he sought to belittle me in front of his colleagues by making reference to my claim he was on a day off with the local paper, when he claimed he "*never had a day off*". He then went on to tell me what he had done on his "*day off*" as if it was some sort of mind blowing experience, when in fact it was just hot air and bullshit. He was trying to demean me in front of his buddies, so I let him have his say and said I would speak to him later. As first impressions go, he'd made a big mistake, but he obviously didn't realise because in my view he had not even made the effort to welcome me to the club. We had got off on the wrong footing straight away. We never bothered with each other again. I think we had both made up our minds about each other. As they say, first impressions count for a lot and on this occasion that certainly rung true, I thought his head was stuck up his own backside!

Nevertheless Allen probably felt he'd got one up on me but given the club's position in the relegation places and the poor standard of football described by staff and fans, I knew it was only a matter of time before he'd get sacked. His attitude that morning made me determined to get him out of the club at the first opportunity he gave me. It didn't take long. I immediately knew that I would not be able to work with him. He just wasn't my type of person.

The following Saturday the team played away at league leaders Leyton Orient and lost 3-1. The performance was abysmal. To me, given the league position and results over the previous months, it was obvious that things were not going to improve. The one thing Allen was good at though was PR. He can talk a good game and get the fans onside with his goodie two shoes act. After the game I called Ashley Carson, who had not been at Brisbane Road that day, to give him an overview of the afternoon's 'entertainment'. I told him straight, "*This is not going to get any better. The team are as good as down if this continues. I think he (Allen) has to go before it's too late, the sooner the better*". Ashley was sympathetic with my view but given that there were all the Christmas and New Year fixtures coming up over the next ten days, he thought it would be better holding fire until those games were over with and then review it. I could see the logic in that thought process, but I knew it was only a matter of time.

To say my first two home games at Chesterfield were eventful is the understatement of the year. In the Boxing Day fixture we played Solihull Moors, who were going well in the league. The mood around the ground was already hostile and that was even before kick off. The fans had really had enough and throughout the game there was 'anti-board' chanting from the Kop end of the stadium, where the home fans like to congregate. Ashley must have looked in a crystal ball that morning and saw what was going to happen because he didn't attend the game. I was there, together with a couple of the other directors. The directors' box at Chesterfield is not an enclosed area and in effect is an extension of the stand. It's just that the seats are a little bit comfier than a bog standard seat. That meant that you were open to full on face-to-face interaction with those supporters who sat in the immediate vicinity.

The game started badly, with Solihull going 2-0 up within the first half hour and once again the performance from the team was dire. The crowd were getting restless, they were revved-up and very antagonistic. Given my seating position in the directors' area you could hear every single comment around you being critical of the team, the board and everything connected to the club. And the truth was the supporters were not wrong. In the 70th minute things took a sinister turn after Solihull went 3-0 up. In the stand opposite me a small group of supporters came over the fence surrounding the pitch and started a pitch invasion, with their protests being aimed at the board. Within seconds those half-a-dozen fans on the pitch had turned into a massive throng, with over 100 supporters on the playing surface and mainly gathering in front of the main stand where we were sitting, chanting their clear dislike of the board. One supporter even sat on the centre circle and refused to move. The stewards were caught completely unaware and were unable to do anything about, such was the speed of the invasion and they struggled to bring order to the proceedings. The fans who were sat around us also turned, with abuse and swearing aimed at all of us about the state the club. The supporters were singing continually "*Get out of our club, get out of our club, Ashley Carson get out of our club*". The scenes were absolutely chaotic and the players were quickly taken off the field for their own safety. It was a bitterly cold day and at that point I pictured myself in the pub having a pint by the open fire, instead I was facing a baying mob thinking, "*What the fucking hell have I walked into here?*"

I knew the fans were upset about the running of the club, but I never realised the depth of anger and hatred. It was becoming a very scary situation and I genuinely thought we were on the verge of being attacked but I was determined not to hide from the incident and retreat to the safety of the nearby boardroom. I had to watch and listen to what was being said, as I wanted to make a difference with those fans if possible. But ultimately it became an impossible task, such was the deep-rooted hate for the owner and Carson. Order was eventually restored, and the game restarted, with Solihull going on to score again and record a 4-0 win.

By full-time Carson had been made aware of what had happened and rang me. We had a lengthy conversation about the events of the afternoon. He was rightly fuming about it and questioned the lack of action by the stewards, but the reality was that it was an impossible situation for them. The club had declined so much in recent years and the fans were now in full rebellion mode. I pointed out that we could deal with the aftermath of the pitch invasion quickly over the next few days, but I felt that Martin Allen had run out of time. He had to go, pronto. I told Carson this and said if we didn't get rid of him now then it was only going to get worse. We needed to do something to deflect attention from the pitch invasion, to allow us some breathing space. He said he would speak to Dave Allen that evening and a few hours later a telephone call took place between the three of us by which time Dave had decided that the manager would be sacked with immediate effect. It was the correct decision from a football perspective.

The following morning my first job was to relieve his two assistants, Whitehead and Muggleton, of their duties, which was done within 30 minutes of me arriving at the stadium. Then I set about dealing with the pitch invasion. Overnight I had received information about some of those involved and the club photographer had done an excellent job in getting numerous pictures of the offenders, which we shared with the local police and newspaper. As a result we were inundated with information identifying the people on the pitch. It seemed that despite the antagonism felt towards the management of the club, some supporters still felt the actions of a few could not be justified and were happy to help. I then set about putting together a tariff of penalties for supporter misbehaviour. This included a ban of three years for entering the pitch and a ten year ban for doing the same thing where contact was made with a player which was prescient considering what happened at the next home game a few days later!

I knew the FA would be on the case straight away and so the club had to show we were acting tough and took the matter seriously. We announced the penalties we intended to impose and were going to issue them retrospectively on anyone who had been involved in the disorder at the Solihull game. This caused a major outcry by the keyboard warriors on the local Chesterfield FC "Bobs Board" internet fans forum. This small group, some of whom were odious individuals who made up conspiracy theories about goings on at the club, were incredulous. To see some of their postings, they genuinely believed that they should be privy to every bit of information relevant to the running of the club and thought they could do or say whatever they wanted. They were up in arms and were filled with vitriol. But I didn't give a flying fuck what they thought. The problem was that the club had just allowed this group to run riot over a number of years without ever challenging them. The staff moaned constantly about them, but nobody had ever done anything to either challenge them or seek to build bridges with them. The other big problem was that Ashley kept going onto the board and which only wound them up even more. It was stupid of Ashley. He was fanning the flames and it just made him look silly and didn't help his cause. I'm sure looking back now if he had his time again he wouldn't do it. But not only that, he was in contact with one of the main people in the group and was forever speaking to him off the record – and as such the group used this to their advantage to undermine the club. As is normal on these types of social media sites, the group were hiding behind aliases and believed they were untouchable, when in reality they were, and still are, with the odd exception, a group of cowards. I decided to front them up, but to be able to do that I needed to identify them and let them know I was on their case.

For me to put my plan into action I had to do something which I knew would leak out from inside the club. I knew that wouldn't be a problem, because I had already realised the club had more holes than a sieve. So I listed the aliases of the main protagonists from the "Bobs Board" site on the wipe board on the wall in my office, in full view of everyone. Alongside their "alias" I'd discovered their real names and listed those alongside it, so I could identify them. The results were revealing, because I then researched each person's background. One of the most surprising discoveries was that they were not young, spotty-faced kids, but grown men, many with professional careers. For example, we discovered that one was a senior bank manager. I immediately checked if Dave Allen banked with this individual's organisation because if he did, we were about to cause him some real problems with his employers. Very fortunately for him Dave didn't bank with them, so he had a very near miss, but I'm sure his employers wouldn't have been too happy had they realised how crass one of their senior employees had acted on occasions if they read some of his posts. There was another who used the alias of "*Dim View*". I couldn't have named him better myself if I'd tried. Going back to the wipe board list, it worked a treat and as it filled up, within days "*The Earl of Chesterfield*", a guy called Chris Snell, contacted the club concerned that he'd been tipped-off that I was compiling the list and wanted to know why? He made it known that he was seeking a meeting with me on behalf of his fellow keyboard warriors. They were rattled, but in fairness to Chris, he was one of the more sensible posters and is actually a very fair-minded and decent bloke with whom I had many constructive and helpful conversations over the ensuing months – our working relationship helped bridge the gap between club and fans. We could speak quite freely without issue. Chris never betrayed his fellow posters and was always protective of them, unlike some others who were happy to divulge the identities of people on there to me.

Through Chris a meeting was set up with about a dozen of them, so that I could look them in the eye and put a face to names. It seemed to do the trick and we had a very open and honest meeting at the club. After years of antagonism it seemed that at least a little progress was starting to be made. I still received criticism on occasion from them, and in this industry you have to be thick-skinned, but I think that meeting took a lot of the heat off me and strategically it made things a little easier for me. It was progress. The ice had been broken with a group who the club had not tried to work with for many years. I think that is where my experience of working with fans organisations came to good use. They could see I was a straight talker and after years of not having this, it was welcome.

Going back to the Solihull pitch invasion, we identified in

excess of thirty people who had gone onto the pitch and hit most of them with the three-year bans. It was draconian, but it was the right thing to do at that time, simply to show the FA we were taking the issues seriously. We gave them all the right of appeal and in some cases where an appeal was made, the ban was reduced to a six month period which, unsurprisingly, they were content to accept. But I had laid my marker down that I would not cower to troublesome supporters. In fact, that incident led to many supporters contacting me on a more amicable basis, including the guy who had sat on the centre circle during the pitch incursion. He called into my office to see me and once in, I couldn't get him out, such was the way we got on!

If I thought the Solihull game was a baptism of fire, it was a picnic compared to my second home game against Ebbsfleet United on January 5, 2019. The referee for the game was Rebecca French, who later became the first woman to referee a Football League match. But following her performance in the Ebbsfleet fixture you would never have thought that she would have attained that status. She lost complete control of the game. John Pemberton, the former Crystal Palace and Leeds player who now headed up the Chesterfield Academy, had been placed in temporary charge of the team following Allen's sacking - and things didn't get off to a brilliant start. By half time the team were 3-0 down and the crowd were restless again. However, the team had a totally different mindset in the second half with goals in the 64th and 83rd minutes making the score 3-2 as the game headed into nine minutes of injury time. By this stage Ebbsfleet keeper Nathan Ashmore was testing the patience of the home crowd with his time-wasting antics, and a bottle was thrown towards him. Once again supporters began encroaching towards the playing area without actually entering the field, with the stewards struggling to keep a lid on it even though we had beefed up the security. The game was held up while things calmed down but in the

95th minute the stadium erupted after captain Will Evans headed Chesterfield level prompting another mass pitch invasion which included some supporters striking Ebbsfleet's keeper as he laid on the floor in the goalmouth. Incredibly the drama wasn't over because straight from the restart Ebbsfleet went back up the field and following an altercation between the Spireites goalkeeper and an Ebbsfleet player, our keeper was shown a red card and a penalty awarded to the visitors. Captain Evans then went into goal as Chesterfield had used all their substitutes and against all the odds, he saved the penalty. It was real *Roy of the Rovers* stuff and meant that the fans went home happy for once.

I knew we were now in very serious trouble now. Two pitch invasions in consecutive games, an opposition player struck and then, to cap it all off, Ashmore made allegations that he had been subjected to racist abuse by some supporters, which meant we were being investigated for that as well! I knew it would take all my skills at preparing defence papers for the inevitable FA investigation to get Chesterfield cleared. We immediately set about tracking down the supporter who had struck Ebbsfleet's goalkeeper. We did that relatively quickly and issued him with a ten-year ban. We then went on to identify the other supporters involved and issued the three-year bans again, which seemed to placate the FA following the submission of a seventy-page file of evidence. The allegation of racist abuse could not be proved and no further action was taken in that regard either. Nevertheless, there were serious financial implications for the club, because the local Safety Advisory Group who are responsible for the licensing of the stadium to host events, came down hard on us and insisted on various changes being made which impacted on the costs of running games.

One of the main problems at Chesterfield was the backstabbing and tale telling by staff who were constantly running to Carson. He had been there that long he'd developed an internal network of spies and I realised that nobody could be trusted. He had this hold over people, meaning that whilst I was working on a specific project I was always conscious there could be someone whispering in his ear from the staff due to the web that he spun within the club. It pissed me off so much at times. People were fine to your face, but then as soon as your back was turned they would be on the phone to him with their version of events. He would then shoot from the hip, knowing only half the story. It became tiresome and repetitive.

Just before my arrival at Chesterfield the club had introduced a policy of having three 'Associate Directors' who supposedly came from the fans' groups. This was an effort to try to give the board some respectability in the face of the discontent from the supporters. But I realised it was all a facade. The three appointed people, Steve Coe, Lesley Brentnall and Alison Richardson all had different skill bases. Coe was a club sponsor and very close associate of Carson. I found him to be a bit of a 'know all' and despite his success as a local businessman in IT with a lucrative contract with the club to service its IT systems, he thought that whatever anybody did relating to the running of the football club, he knew better. He was actually nicknamed "*Snitch*" by the staff and I'll let you work out yourself why that was. Then there was "fans favourite", Lesley Brentnall, who for years had admirably been involved in arranging the 'Blues on the Move' official away game travel. Lesley was okay, but the longer I was there the more I realised she was very much a mate of the *"Snitch",* so over time I came to distrust her. Then there was Alison Richardson, a successful local businesswoman who was by far the most trustworthy and capable of them. Her ideas were very good, and she wanted to help the club, but she was hindered by a disliking of her by Carson and Coe, who both did anything they could to undermine her. She was treated shabbily by certain people at the club. It was petty and unfair how she was singled out. She had so much to give to the club and was very good in promoting the women's game. It was the view of an element of the fans that Coe had only got the gig because he was Carson's mate and Brentnall because she ran the travel club, but Alison went through the full procedures to get appointed. It was no surprise that she resigned within a few days of me leaving the club. She had lost her best ally once I'd left.

It's very fair to say though that Steve Coe did put a lot of his own time into the club affairs. It was as if he was never away at times which in itself caused problems because one was always on guard that yet another titbit of gossip would be fed back to Ashley Carson. Coe's area of responsibility was overseeing the academy and he had become a Siamese twin to John Pemberton, it was as if his role was of the utmost importance. In reality, the academy operations should have come under the jurisdiction of the CEO, like it does at other clubs, but he treated it like his own little fiefdom. It certainly wasn't a team effort. They may as well have renamed it 'The Steve Coe Academy'. But, like I said, him being involved in the academy was only half the story because he wanted to poke his nose into just about every other area of club life. Steve may have thought he was helping the situation but it was having the opposite effect much of the time. Several times I had to tell him to keep his nose out. Little did he know, though, that given the "tell tale" regime at the club, some of the texts he was circulating about me were always fed back to me. It really was like being at school at times, dealing with naughty kids. The tittle-tattle atmosphere was draining. I don't want to sound bitter about it but I think it's important to get over how febrile and juvenile it was at times from people who should have known better. The thing is it wasn't only me thinking this about Coe. It seemed many supporters felt the same way. But this is Chesterfield we are talking about – a small time club but a place where egos ruled the day.

11 - *EVERY DAY, A CRISIS*

EVERY DAY WAS A 'CRISIS DAY' at Chesterfield. It seemed there was a never ending list of problems caused by factions, favouritism and a lack of co-ordination. Too many people had their own agendas and kept things to themselves, which was usually to the detriment of the club. I'd tried to make things more transparent by holding staff meetings so that people knew of our plans. I hoped engaging the staff made them feel valued and we introduced appraisals for staff – something which had never been done before. It was mind boggling just how lax the club had been on customer service and helping staff develop, and this caused so much in fighting with factions developing within the different groups. Each department viewed themselves as having their own little empire and there was little, if any, co-ordination between them. When there was, it was always done with a degree of reluctance and suspicion by members of the departments.

A typical example of how things were being done was when "Snitch" Coe got his comeuppance for all his posturing while revelling in his "important" position as "Associate Director". The role carried no weight in terms of status, but he felt it did, so I just let him get on with playing at being a football club director. In early 2019, and together with John Pemberton, they decided to sack an academy coach called Miguel Llera, a former Sheffield Wednesday centre half. By all accounts Miguel was a good coach and well-thought of by the players he supervised, but Coe and Pemberton made a decision to end his employment. Llera and Pemberton had both applied for the role of academy head some months earlier and before my time at the club, with the latter being successful, so I think there was a bit of antagonism in the air.

The trouble was that they told nobody about what they

intended doing until a few minutes before it happened. The first I knew about it was when Coe popped his head around the door one morning to tell me what the plan was, and a short time later he returned to confirm that he had terminated Miguel's contract. Before they made the final decision, I believed they should have had the courtesy to tell me of their intentions and let us talk it through, but they didn't, which was their undoing. Like I said, some people were just intent on empire building. When Coe told me how Miguel had reacted to the unexpected news, I sensed it would bring trouble for the club. I wasn't wrong and within days a complaint was registered by Miguel alleging discrimination and bullying, as well as the club failing to adhere to employment practices relating to his dismissal.

Some days later Carson and Coe called to see me about it, upset at what was being alleged. My advice to them was very short and simple – pay him off. Settle it as soon as possible and get an NDA (non-disclosure agreement) signed by him. They both immediately refused. I told them that they just needed rid of it, the sooner the better. That would be much easier than taking him on. I told them the last thing the club wanted was it leaking out because if it did, it would bring more unwelcome pressure and publicity for the club. But still they refused. From my experience of working in clubs, I just knew that the practical way to deal with it was to just get rid of it and move on.

In the meantime Richard Jobson of the PFA was in contact with me and I was trying to work with him and smooth it all over. Richard is a sensible individual who you can talk to on and off the record. He's easy to work with when it comes to disputes and complaints. I've encountered him several times and always found him amicable to work with.

Due to the nature of what was being alleged by Miguel, we had to set up a two-pronged internal enquiry. I was handling one, which was the allegation of discrimination and bullying against him, while a sub-committee of club director John Croot and associate directors Alison Richardson and Lesley Brentnall dealt with the employment law issues. I acted as secretariat to the committee, but was not involved at all in its decisions or considerations. I was merely a minute taker and arranged the meetings.

The first meeting of that committee was explosive, with Miguel and Richard Jobson presenting their case. They were damning as they explained how Coe and Pemberton had handled the dismissal and they provided written evidence in the form of texts and letters that supported Miguel from players under his care, which completely undermined the reasons Coe and Pemberton stated for letting him go. But that wasn't the end of it. As the end of the three hour meeting neared, Llera waited until the very last moment to drop an atomic bomb into the proceedings which exposed the underhand way in which the club had appeared to operate under Carson during the recruitment process of the academy head position. Coe had handled the interview process and he subsequently selected Pemberton for the job. Llera handed over a copy of an email which Carson had sent him from his official Chesterfield FC account a few days before the interviews which read;

> *Hi Miguel,*
>
> *Please keep very private, do not reveal these to anyone, but these are questions you will be asked. I hope this helps you to prepare and give some thought to your answers.*
>
> *Good Luck, I have decided not to be part of the interview panel but I really hope you a (sic) successful interview.*
>
> *No one else will get to see these questions in advance.*
> *Kind Regards*
>
> *Ashley.*

Attached to the email was a list of the questions to be asked in the interview, together with a copy of the scoring technique paper. He also produced a screen shot of text messages between him and Carson after the interview had taken place, in which

Carson said he was sorry that Llera had not got the job and arranging to meet up.

It was explosive stuff. He was producing evidence which showed that a director of the club had been providing him with the list of questions to be used in the interview to give him an advantage over everyone else in the process. It was wrong and immediately would have undermined any defence Chesterfield would have had at an employment tribunal proceeding, which Miguel and Jobson were threatening to commence. The three committee members were fuming about it. It was a real ambush from Llera – and Carson's underhand action, even if well intended, had come badly unstuck. I contacted Carson and told him we were now in really difficult waters because of what he had done. The committee later went on to speak to Coe and Pemberton about what had happened relating to the reasoning behind Llera's dismissal, in which they claimed they had acted properly, but the reality was that the damage had already been done.

My enquiry into the allegations of discrimination and bullying was thorough with interviews taking place, but there was absolutely no independent evidence to support them so it could not be proceeded with any further. But it was a different ball game altogether with the employment issue. As threatened, the employment proceedings were starting to be put into action and once again I told Carson that we should strike a deal with Llera and get rid of it. As it happened, and fortunately for Chesterfield, Llera was close to being appointed as head of the Walsall FC academy and needed a reference, so was open to a settlement. When we got to know about this, I quickly agreed with Carson we would do a settlement on it. That was then done very quickly, to the satisfaction of everyone involved. However, had Coe and Carson taken my advice right at the start, the embarrassing email and text would have never seen the light of day and the issue could have been dealt with much more quickly. But as I said, Coe seemed to think he knew best all the time…

John Sheridan was the appointed the new manager at Chesterfield, replacing Martin Allen. He had enjoyed much success in his first stint as Chesterfield boss several years earlier and brought with him a backroom team of Glyn "Snods" Snodin as his assistant, and two coaches, ex-Sheffield Wednesday teammate Charlie Williamson along with ex-Nottingham Forest goalkeeper, Mark *"Norm"* Crossley. As usual I did my homework on *"Shez"* and was told by several people he was a "cold fish" and difficult to get to know. They could not have been more wrong. We had a great working relationship, and I can say he is one of the best managers I have worked with. He has a cracking sense of humour, will listen to what you have to say, and is willing to help in any situation. It was the same with the rest of the backroom team and we all worked well together. They put lots of hard work in behind the scenes, but in the long term it just didn't work out for them and they were let go a few months after I left the club.

One thing I had to do while John was manager was discipline a couple of his players in matters which were beyond the normal club discipline issues. Sheridan was fully behind the decisions I took and was very supportive throughout. The first involved striker Tom Denton, who had gone on honeymoon during the summer break while at the same time recovering from a leg injury which meant he was not available to play until a few weeks into the new 2019/20 season. One day, after the season had started, he contacted the physio saying he had aggravated the injury and news of this was relayed to the press in a weekly press conference. Unfortunately for Tom, a former Chesterfield player in the shape of Chris Marples tweeted that Denton had been playing cricket for his local team a few days before, hitting a score of 46. I quickly did some investigations and found a photograph on the internet of the cricket team, with Tom in all his glory standing there with a beaming smile in his cricket whites and cap on his head, together with a match report of his great innings, which would have obviously meant him having to run between the wickets! I relayed it back to Sheridan and said we had to discipline him. Shez agreed – and told me to do whatever was necessary. I interviewed Tom and he was very humble about it. He fully admitted he'd been playing cricket while injured. We gave the matter some consideration and there were even discussions about whether he should have his contract terminated. I know that Tom feared this was going to happen, but in the end it was decided that a fine of two weeks' wages was appropriate. Tom knew he'd had a near miss and was grateful for the way it was dealt with, but I couldn't resist taking the piss out of him for a few months every time I saw him. He took it all in good heart. He's a good lad and has done well for Chesterfield – when he's not been swinging his bat for his local cricket club!

On another occasion I had to act following an even more bizarre breach of discipline by a player. Anthony Gerrard, the cousin of Steven, had been signed from Carlisle by Sheridan but had suffered a difficult start to his Chesterfield career. Gerrard was a typical scouser, cheeky with his wit and I liked him and his sense of humour was typical Liverpudlian. The fans didn't take to him, thought he was lazy, overweight and not good enough. So consequently he received lots of abuse, especially on his own Twitter feed.

One weekend he went into meltdown and had running argument with some fans on the social media site. It came to a head when the exchanges led to what was in effect an arrangement for him and a fan to meet to "sort it all out" in an unconventional way. Unfortunately, the fan turned up in the car park of the stadium the following Monday in his car and waited for Gerrard, who wasn't around. However, the supporter took a photograph from his car outside the stadium to prove he was there waiting for him, together with a comment about Gerrard not turning up for the showdown. Twitter went into meltdown, with the club bearing the brunt once again over the fact we were employing Gerrard, when he was being like that with fans. Once again, I had to commence an investigation and interview him.

Anthony admitted what had happened, but said it was all done in jest and that he never expected it to escalate like it did. But it shows just how things can get out of hand with disgruntled supporters and the dangers of social media. In a typical Scouse way, Anthony didn't want to wait for the outcome and sought to "do a deal" on the penalty he would receive, so we agreed there and then that a two week fine would be imposed. Then there was the problem of the supporter, who we also felt we had to deal with. We couldn't have fans turning up wanting to have a scrap with the players! We felt that we needed to send a message out, so under the applicable tariffs for supporter misconduct, I issued the supporter with a three-year ban. Once again this caused uproar. I was initially supported by Carson. I was away on holiday the following week and learned on my return that he'd taken it upon himself to meet the supporter and revoke the ban, once again undermining my position!

Sometimes supporters can't see the wood for the trees. They continually moaned and were downright nasty at times to Anthony Gerrard but what they didn't realise at the time was that Anthony was working closely with me to get Glasgow Rangers to play Chesterfield in a pre season friendly the following year. Chesterfield supporters used to go on and on and on about this ridiculously romantic football tale about how in 1980 they beat Rangers in the not so credible "Anglo-Scottish Cup" as if it was some sort of pre-cursor to the Champions League and how they would love to play them again in some sort of anniversary game. Anthony was best placed to help that happen as his cousin, former Liverpool midfielder, Steven, who he was very close to was the then manager of Rangers. Me and Anthony discussed this possibility on several occasions with Anthony acting as the go between to try to make it happen. Unfortunately, both of us left the club before anything could be finalized so perhaps given the vindictive attitude of some of the supporters towards him it was something of a pay back when it didn't progress. If Gerrard had stayed, and the game had come off, then the same supporters would have been singing his praises for helping make it happen!

Another crisis at Chesterfield was 'Dugout-gate', only this was all of my own doing! Sheridan had decided that he preferred to have some dugout shelters in the technical area as opposed to the open area that was in place, and the only way we could fund this given the financial position of the club was by sponsorship. The commercial department did an excellent job in raising £30,000 from a sponsor to allow them to be constructed. It took all summer for them to be made and they were not installed until two days before the 2019/20 season started. That was a major mistake because once installed it became apparent that whilst vision was not directly affected, they were very imposing and caused issues with the fans who had sat behind the technical area for many years. Not only that, but we had also not informed them of their installation until the day of the first game, when they received a notice attached to their seat advising them if they wanted to move seats because of the shelters, the club would facilitate this. It was wrong to do it that way and very amateurish, but as the pressure built up to preparing for the start of the season it was an issue that wrongly got overlooked. Having said that, I had been telling the ticket office manager for some weeks to contact season ticket holders in that area about the possible problems but given her heavy workload the ticket office staff had not got round to doing it. That was a major mistake, but I take full responsibility for it. I should have managed the process better.

On the following Monday morning after the first home game of the season we were inundated with complaints from the people who sat behind the dugout, many of them since the stadium had opened ten years earlier. They were seething and rightly so. However, I made it my business to see every single person who complained – and sat down with them to talk it through. There was a never-ending line of people waiting to see me over the next couple of weeks, but aside from just two people, everyone went away satisfied with either the change of seats I arranged for them or upgrading them to the comfy seats at a small extra charge, meaning we raised more funds, even at a time of major complaints. I recall I even managed to sell an advertising board to one disgruntled customer! Overall I think I did well for the fans who were affected when dealing with it. Of course, the idiots on the internet message board didn't see it that way, even though it didn't affect most of them. I think the supporters who it did affect appreciated me taking the time to have personal meetings with anyone who wanted one. There were a couple who would have whinged even if I had given them seats for the rest of their life for free, but there will always be people like that. It seemed the main complaint was not about the cumbersome shelters but that they could no longer hear what was being said in the technical areas! Nevertheless, it was my fault, and the sponsors were not too pleased at the publicity it generated, but I put that down to the cosy relationship they had with the commercial staff as opposed to anything else. I felt that the commercial staff and the sponsor's representative were far too close and used the issue to stick the boot in. Carson really threw me under the bus with it though – and then reversed it over me. He wanted to put as much distance between himself and the problem as he possibly could. After all the issues and embarrassment he'd caused the club over the years due to some of his decisions, he had the gall to give me a kicking about it. In my mind it was the issue that started the downward path in our relationship. Mind you, I bet he was relived that someone else was taking the flak for once instead of him!

As mentioned earlier, the increase in season ticket prices went down like a lead balloon, but I managed to oversee a process that saw season ticket sales increase by about 250 on the previous year, taking the total to almost 3,000, which is good by any non-league club standards. This was done by using a decent marketing campaign. We were all very surprised at the club when sales increased, as we fully expected them to be well down on the previous year considering how badly the team had performed.

When John Sheridan returned to the club in January, 2019 results had generally improved and from a relegation spot we finished in a relatively comfortable mid-table position. It boded well for the following season, and we were quietly confident things would improve on the field in the new season. Unfortunately it didn't quite work out like that and results were poor. Nevertheless, on the back of the previous season's revival I decided that the season ticket campaign would focus on a theme of *"Shez is Back"* – hailing the return of one of the most successful managers in the club's recent history. We also offered the opportunity for supporters to be entered into a draw for twelve of them to win a question and answer session with John. In reality it wasn't a draw, we just picked twelve names from a list from various categories of tickets across a range of supporters of all ages and seat types but we made sure that none of these people had connections to anyone at the club, to avoid allegations of favouritism. When the day came to meet the manager we held it in the home dressing room with their name above their place in the room where the players would sit on match day. They were also provided with a "goodie bag" of Chesterfield FC memorabilia and got the chance to ask John anything they wanted. It went down really well and the fans who attended bought into it. It was a good exercise, and I would recommend other lower league clubs doing the same thing as an incentive to get supporters to buy season tickets, which are a life saver to lower league clubs.

We had a good laugh in that season ticket campaign at Sheridan's expense. When we were producing the season ticket application booklet we had a number of front page designs to choose from. One of them was horrendous. It was John's face superimposed onto the Lord Kitchener "Your Country Needs You" poster, changing the word "Country" to "Club" with Shez pointing outwards. We were in fits of laughter about the crass design, but we didn't tell Shez about it. I showed it to Snods and told him to keep a straight face when I let Shez have a look at it. I walked into his office and casually showed him the design, saying how great we all thought it was and that we intended to use it in the season ticket campaign. Snods was in on the joke and played a good part praising the designers. I could see by Sheridan's face he wasn't amused, before we all fell about laughing. He was using every expletive you could think of at us! Shez also gave us some real ammunition the day he took possession of his brand new company car, a top of the range Kia Sportage. I was at home that evening when I got a call from him querying the insurance details for the car. When I asked him why, he had to confess that he'd been at the local chip shop getting his tea, when he looked outside and saw his car disappearing down the street driverless and careering towards an unsuspecting road sign. It turned out he had left the handbrake off. He had to suffer much rib tickling about it throughout my time at the club and we never let him forget it. He did see the funny side though, until it came to him footing the bill for the damage!

Going back to the Martin Allen period though, Martin had designated 'Sailing' by Rod Stewart as the run out song for the players on match day. It wasn't exactly a piece of music to get you up for the fight with it being a slow ballad. It wasn't in the league of 'You'll Never Walk Alone' at Anfield, or 'I'm Forever Blowing Bubbles' at West Ham, 'Blue Moon' at Manchester City or even 'Robin Hood' at near neighbours Nottingham Forest. When Allen left we did away with that song and I saw it as a chance for a spot of self-indulgence and designated a live version of 'Wages Day' by my favourite band Deacon Blue to be the run out song for the team. One day one of the players asked what the song was and I told him the title. "Why this?" he asked. I replied quickly, "Because every time you go out on that fucking pitch it's wages day". He didn't need to ask again.

There was always a crisis at Chesterfield FC. Just when you thought things were turning, along came another fire to fight.

One day I was sat in my office when the lady who administered the club's lottery scheme came in to see me looking very worried. It transpired she'd uncovered a major problem with the "Spire Lotto", which was a weekly draw for cash prizes. Supporters paid a pound a week to be entered into it and the entry fees were collected by Lotto Agents or by direct debit from the bank.

She had discovered that some people who had been paying into the draw over a number of months or even years by direct debit had actually not been entered into the draw. I was stunned at the revelation. I immediately instructed her to do a full analysis of the system to discover how many it affected and arrange reimbursements. From the enquiries we made, it seemed that the problem had arisen when members of the same family were paying into the draw, but only one member was being entered due to discrepancies with the Lotto reference number for the transactions on the bank account, which it seemed had been completed by the customer before sending it in. The lottery was run by a third party company and we discussed it with them but they were not overly interested as they were only responsible for the actual draw taking place. I had a number of concerns about it, these being;

1.   *How many people did it affect?*

2.   *How long had it been going on?*

3.   *What was the financial impact it would have in repayments?*

4.   *Had anyone missed out on a winning combination of numbers?*

5.   *Were any licensing rules being broken?*

6.   *The further impact it would have on the reputation of the club.*

I knew that if word leaked out about this, supporters would be up in arms about it, with claims of yet another scandal engulfing the club. In fact, as soon as the problem was identified we took immediate action to rectify the situation. I knew though that would not make any difference to the cynics. It was imperative we kept it quiet, so only a few people in the club were aware of it, including Ashley. No doubt he, like me, could see the issues that were likely to be raised if word got out. If it had, then I'm sure I would have been the one taking the hit from the supporters as opposed to him, even though this was a historical issue from before my time at the club.

Whilst the analysis of the draws and payments were being made, I contacted the local council licensing department and advised them of the problems and followed this up with a letter. It transpired that only a small number of people had been affected, but I instructed that full repayment of their contributions when they were not actively in the draw be repaid, together with a compensation payment as well as a payment of any prize money they would have won had their numbers been entered into the draw. Thankfully nobody had hit the jackpot and only small amounts needed reimbursing. The matter was fully resolved quickly and the licensing department of the council were happy with the action I had taken but once again it was just another example of another crisis.

It was clear that the financial situation of the club was dire and Carson was coming under intense pressure about it and Dave Allen asked me to do a report where savings could be made. He was looking to save about £1m so I looked at all areas of the club's operation. Some of the things I discovered were just beyond belief. The stewarding costs were astronomical at £19,000 per year just for the hospitality area, which I found could be easily reduced to £7,000. Money spent on entertaining the visiting away directors on match days was another eye-watering £55,000 per season, which I felt could easily be reduced to £2,500 by changing the hospitality arrangements. The club had just been carrying on as if money was no object, until the realisation of their non-league status hit home about eighteen months after it should have done. In total I identified where savings of about £600,000 could be made, only to be told by Carson that I was still £400,000 short of the target. In my report I had stripped back on absolutely everything I could and there was just no more room for manoeuvre. It had got to the point where Carson threw a real wobbly because John Sheridan had arranged a behind closed doors practice game against Huddersfield Town at the stadium, which would have cost £250 in pitch preparation costs. He was going mad about it and had a real meltdown. He was even threatening to stop the game from going ahead. I told him that was ridiculous and would say a lot about the club's support for the manager if he did such a stupid thing. Not only that, imagine the embarrassment it would have caused?

I was being ordered to make some people redundant, which is always a difficult situation, particularly when some people have done nothing to deserve it. One day I was told to make club secretary Nigel Smith redundant and give him his P45, yet they expected him to work his three month notice period. I was fuming about it and told Carson how bad a decision it was. Ashley wanted to incorporate some of Nigel's duties into my own role and whilst I was more than capable of doing that, I didn't think it was a feasible option given the intensity of a club secretary's role. I pointed out that it could lead to mistakes being made due to having the CEO and club secretary workload combined, especially with the club's turnover of players. I argued and argued that Nigel should be kept and really fought his corner but it was to no avail and when I went to see Nigel to give him his marching orders, it was one of the worst things I've ever had to do in the game. I was absolutely gutted, as he was, but I asked him to hang fire before he did anything as I would continue to fight his corner and try to get the decision overturned, which I eventually did, with Carson subsequently saying he had given it more consideration and felt I was right, it was a near miss for him. I'm glad though that we kept him and I was really appreciative that Ashley reconsidered it.

I have represented a number of people in the game when it comes to contravening the FA's strict rules on betting. These rules have changed over the years but several years ago the FA, rightly in my view, tightened them considerably placing a complete ban on any type of betting on football issues anywhere in the world by participants in the game under their jurisdiction. It was the decision to take and very simple to understand. You can't bet on football if you are involved in the game.

Imagine my surprise and embarrassment then when I got caught up in a betting issue whilst at Chesterfield. It showed just how easy it was to fall foul of the betting rules. I am like a lot of football fans who like to have a flutter on the football coupon when I'm not involved in the game. In all my time in football, I have never bet on any football issue when I have been under the jurisdiction of the FA, except on one occasion which was an almighty error by me.

On April 4, 2019, Grand National Day, like many people around the UK I had my annual bet on a horse via a betting account. Once I had completed the Grand National bet a "pop up" flashed up on the page offering increased odds on the FA Cup semi finals which were also taking place that weekend. Without even thinking and given the attractive odds, I placed a ten pound double on Brighton and Wolves to win their respective semi finals at great odds. As I pressed the "Place Bet" button, I suddenly realised that I was breaking the betting rules but it was too late to stop it. It was as if it all happened in slow motion. My finger was pressing the button as I realised I couldn't make the bet. I was immediately aghast at my foolishness even though it was done unconsciously, and I tried to cancel the bet. I was unable to on the system and so I telephoned the betting company and tried to cancel it again, but they were unable to cancel it after it had been placed. I was sick with worry, but fortunately the bet lost, and I forgot all about it. In hindsight, I should have telephoned the FA the following Monday and explained my mistake to them. That would have been the best thing to do.

Several months later, and completely out of the blue, I received a letter from the FA telling me I was under investigation for breaching the betting rules, listing several bets I was alleged to have placed whilst under their jurisdiction, including the semi final bet. The Governing Bodies' Compliance Department had been informed of the semi final bet by the betting company under the arrangement they have with betting companies – and the FA had then reviewed my account. They claimed that I had made a further eight "perm" bets whilst under their jurisdiction and working at Chesterfield, but this was completely wrong. The additional bets they referred to were when I was not working at Chesterfield or in football – and following proof that this was the case eventually they retracted the allegation recognising that I was not under their jurisdiction. However that still left me having to deal with the semi final bet.

It made me really ill. I was annoyed at myself for being so stupid, even though it had been done without thinking and then, on realising, I had immediately tried to cancel the bet. I was in a real state. I couldn't sleep with worry, and I even got visited by the Chesterfield FC club chaplain to talk to me to calm me down. The only people in the club who knew about it were John Croot, Nigel Smith and Carson. John arranged the chaplain's visit because he was so concerned and spoke to the FA on my behalf, explaining how ill it had made me without me knowing. It was a real friend looking out for another friend and I will always be grateful to John for that intervention.

Carson was different though – and tried to use it as a stick to beat me with. He was making veiled threats about my position, including one en-route back from a game at Bromley whilst my wife was in the car listening to it all. He was out of order doing that. If he wanted to flex his muscles he should have waited until we were one on one. It was insensitive and caused my wife some upset. I realised I had made a genuine mistake and had not made any profit, but I knew I had to take my punishment from the FA. I fully assisted them. I was open about it and they did not proceed any further with it, taking no action after recognising it was a genuine error on my part. They did though send me a letter reminding me of the rules, which was quite ironic seeing as I knew them inside out!

To be fair to the FA they dealt with it sensitively and with a great deal of dignity. However, within the letter they sent me they stated that they would be retaining all my information on file, including the information from when I was not under their jurisdiction. I challenged this, stating they had no authority to hold it as I was not a participant at that time, but they still refused to delete it. I decided to raise this with the Information Commissioners Office, who investigated it and found my complaint to be valid and ordered the FA to delete the information, as they were in breach of the law. This got me thinking that if the FA were holding information about me which they had no legal authority to do, then how many other people were they doing the same thing to, particularly in connection with betting investigations?

This was a terrible few weeks for me and I was thoroughly ashamed of myself, even though it was a minor and unintentional breach of the betting regulations but it just goes to show how easy it is to break them without thinking. You have to be alert to the dangers of rule breaking all of the time.

The parlous financial state of the club was always likely to put my job in danger. The club could easily make an immediate saving of £60,000 by chopping me, and it wasn't long before Carson sacrificed me. I'd always found it strange that the club didn't have a finance director who worked at the club who would have had a better handle on things. It should have happened, but Carson always kept the finances close to his chest and handled them himself. He should have farmed it out, as all it did was cause him stress which then led to him having meltdowns over trivial issues. He just wouldn't delegate and all he was doing was bringing more stress on himself. Had the club employed a finance director I believe it would have been in a much stronger position and Dave Allen wouldn't have had to invest so much of his money to keep it afloat.

By the end things were very strained between Carson and I. He was always ready to point the finger for the club's failings at others, when in reality he had overseen the whole shit show for several years. Naturally, with my days at Chesterfield numbered, I began to look around to see what other jobs were available in the game and applied for several, including the role of CEO at Huddersfield Town. I told nobody about this application other than my wife and my best friend, so was very surprised one Friday afternoon while driving home to get a call from Carson asking me if I had applied for a job at Huddersfield Town. I tried to deflect it, but it was obvious he knew something and he then disclosed that he'd been told by the incumbent CEO at Huddersfield, who was a friend of his, that I had applied for the job. He said "*There's no secrets in football*" – which is true, but I think it was a shitty trick to disclose that I had put in for a job. It was also a breach of confidentiality. There was no game that weekend and normally I would have heard from him several times over the weekend but this time there was radio silence. I said to my wife on the Sunday night that I'd be "chopped" the following morning – and as sure as night follows day, it happened.

The following morning, Monday, October 14, 2019, I was in John Sheridan's office when someone told me Carson wanted to see me. I knew straight away what was about to happen. As I got in, he didn't waste any time and told me that I was being made redundant with immediate effect, describing my dismissal as a 'cost cutting move'. I told him that it was a load of bollocks and to stop acting like the cunt he was and had been for some time, it was clearly because of the Huddersfield application. He just sat, arms folded, staring into space, answering in a monosyllabic fashion to my questions. He was very defensive, so I told him what I thought of the whole shit show. I switched into my unemotional mode and told him to deal with my solicitor, who would sort it directly with him in regard to any settlement I was due. Once again, the club was the enemy. I didn't owe them a thing and it was all about getting the best deal out of them. I didn't give two hoots about the financial state of the club at that point. It was just a mercenary attitude to take.

I made it clear to him that I didn't want any announcement about me leaving until I had told who I needed to tell and would make my own arrangements to leave the building, He assured me that nothing would be said without my authority and left the room for me to sort my things out. Imagine my surprise when ten minutes later I got a call from Liam Northcliffe, the *Derbyshire Times* reporter who covered Chesterfield, asking me about my departure from the club? I asked him how he knew about it and at first, he was reluctant to tell me saying, *"You know I can't tell you because I will get in trouble from the person if I do"*. I pointed out to Liam how helpful I had been to him during my time at the club and wanted confirmation that Carson had told him. He admitted that he'd called him a few minutes earlier but told me not to divulge this because he would not be happy about it. Carson was even trying to censor the local paper! It shows just what a snake he was at that moment. Within a few minutes of promising not to divulge details of my leaving, he had left the room and immediately tipped off the local newspaper. That says it all!

I'm still quite bitter about Carson and the way he acted in my departure from the club, because in my contract I had negotiated that if the club was taken over by new owners I would have to be retained by that party for a minimum of eighteen months, or alternatively be paid a nine month notice period in full within fourteen days of leaving. I knew Dave Allen wanted to sell the club right from the start of my time there, so I put this in as an insurance policy. I knew that the club's Community Trust were keen on taking it over, to the point that they had made at least one offer to take control. Not only that but, unbeknown to Carson, a Trust representative had been in constant contact with me for several months about the potential takeover and I knew that such a deal was the best way forward for the club, so I was happy to assist them with any information they needed to move it forward. I was keen for the Trust to take over the club. The fact that I was "made redundant" just a few months before the takeover eventually took place leaves a bitter taste, because I reckon it cannot be ruled out that it was done to stop me enforcing the terms of the employment contract I had negotiated. Not only that but when the total of the payoff I received is calculated, then it would only have cost the club less than two thousand pounds more to retain my services until the end of the season, when I fully expected to be let go. In my view it was a dirty trick on Carson's part.

As for the Huddersfield job; I was selected and went along but was not successful, but it left me wondering if that was because of any "off the record" conversation between Carson and his so called buddy about who the successful applicant was going to be?

Working at Chesterfield was another experience of working within a club full of conflict just as I had experience at Leeds United. During my time there I had introduced new systems and things like staff appraisals, a temporary match day bar with promotional offers on beer and merchandise to encourage fans in, regular staff meetings trying to get everyone involved but in reality it was a toxic environment which in my view was caused by the presence of Ashley. He should have stepped away from the club in full because he was never going to be accepted by the fans but his vanity enjoyed the kudos and limelight too much for him to be able to do that. Had he used common sense and stayed away and perhaps just turned up to the odd game, the club could have got the fans back onside but that only happened once the credible Community Trust took over and now the club is flourishing once again. I for one am very pleased about that as are the Chesterfield keyboard warriors!

12 - *A SLAP IN THE FACE*

IN MY OPINION ONE OF THE most ridiculous charges the FA ever issued was the one following a spat between Wayne Rooney and Bolton defender Tal Ben Haim. There had been a coming together between the pair during a 2004 Boxing Day fixture at Manchester United. It never had a chance of succeeding but my old adversary, David Lampitt from the Compliance Department, obviously thought it did. As it turned, out not only was it a "slap in the face" for the Israeli international, Ben Haim, but also one for Lampitt and the FA as well following my representation of the player.

In the 45th minute of the game Ben Haim had challenged Rooney for the ball and the United player theatrically fell to the floor in an attempt to win a free kick. Ben Haim claimed, and the video supported him, that he never made contact with Rooney and the referee, Dermot Gallagher, obviously agreed as he waved play on. Rooney bounced back onto his feet and in a mad moment raised his hand and pushed it into Ben Haim's face forcefully. The Bolton player was off balance and fell to the floor holding his face. It seemed that the only people in the stadium who didn't see Rooney's actions were the four match officials! Rooney was later suspended for three games under the FA retrospective punishments system, because the referee had not seen the incident.

Needless to say the media made a big thing of it and as usual the FA reacted. Just three days later Lampitt had signed a letter to the Bolton player charging him with misconduct. In an effort to prove this ridiculous charge, he relied on a video of the incident together with a number of reports that the FA had chased from the officials. The charge letter stated;

> *"The video shows the contact made between Mr Rooney*

and you, and your reaction to this contact. The Football Association alleges that you exaggerated the impact and/ or effect of the contact made between Mr Rooney's hand and your face and in doing so, your conduct was improper".

It was a laughable situation. Here you had an FA jobsworth trying to claim he could tell from watching a video that a player had overreacted to an act of violent conduct which had been committed against him. I knew straight away that the FA would have absolutely no chance of proving the charge. The defence was going to be a very simple one – and it appeared that the FA had not even considered it. My immediate thought was that the only person who could say what the effect of the contact from an act of violent conduct was the recipient of that contact. Nobody else can say how it felt, with what force he felt it or whether the reaction to it was over the top. For example, if I was to slap two different people in the face with the same amount of force, the likelihood is that the effect of my contact with them would be different with each person. Some people may be able to withstand it, some may not. Some have a higher pain threshold than others. It's just something that you cannot guess at. It was a very simple defence to run.

The FA also relied upon several reports from the officials, which said absolutely nothing because nobody claimed to have seen the full incident between the players. In fact, Gallagher pulled the rug from under Lampitt's case when, in answer to a query from the FA man about Ben Haim's reaction, the officials replied with;

"Regarding the Ben Haim incident. If, as subsequently proven by yourselves at the FA, Wayne Rooney was guilty of violent conduct and subsequently suspended for three matches as a referee on the day making that decision, I would be hard justified to take any action against the other player"

That put a huge hole in the FA's case against Ben Haim

before it had even started! Even the Head of Referees for the Premier League, Keith Hackett, got in on the act by lobbying Lampitt by email about his view of Ben Haim's "over reaction" in an effort to bolster the FA case.

I went straight into action to challenge the FA's claim by writing to them asking:

> *"What evidence do you rely upon to conclude that the effect of the contact made by Mr Rooney on our client caused an exaggerated reaction?"*

Lampitt responded by simply saying they intended to rely on the evidence indicated in their charge letter. He was just being awkward in my view and couldn't substantiate the charge. I went straight back at him, pointing out the lack of investigation by the FA and arguing:

> *"We fully understand that the FA intends to rely upon the evidence outlined in your letter. However, we would point out that in our opinion no evidence has been served that concludes that contact made by Mr Rooney on our client had an effect which caused an exaggerated reaction. Neither, it appears, have any enquiries been made to show that."*

In the meantime the FA had got to work on briefing the newspapers about coming down hard on players who engaged in simulation and on New Year's Day, 2005 the *Daily Mail* ran an article with quotes from an anonymous *'FA senior source',* using the Ben Haim case as the watershed moment for dealing with such incidents. According to the article which had the headline, **"WAR ON CHEATS – FA WILL SEIZE ON ROONEY AFFAIR TO RID GAME OF DIVING SCOURGE"** the *'senior source'* said *"This is the first case of its type. The FA hope that it serves as a warning to players".* The reality was, though, that they were trying to compare Ben Haim's actions at being hit in the face with a simulation of diving, which was wrong and unfair. I immediately wrote to Jonathan Hall, the FA's Director of Governance, complaining the article had been briefed by the FA, was prejudicial to Ben Haim's case and that it could not be ruled out that the *"inappropriate comments and suggestions"* placed any Disciplinary Commission under pressure to find the case proven. Of course, in true FA fashion, Hall rejected my claim. When it comes to defending their position in farcical situations, it makes me wonder if they gave lessons to Boris Johnson's Conservative Government?

In the meantime the FA were getting tetchy about our reluctance to provide the full details of the defence that we were going to use and the evidence we intended to rely upon. Lampitt was keen to get his hands on it, but the rules at that time were specific that as long as we had served our evidence at least seven days in advance of any hearing, then we had conformed with the rules. That being the case, I always waited until the last possible minute to serve any evidence. In this particular case Lampitt wanted to flex his muscles, because he wrote to me with a warning:

> *"I would also make you aware that obstruction of the disciplinary process may constitute misconduct and may result in formal disciplinary action".*

He was trying to tell the guy who had done the job for five years before him what the rules were. Talk about being full of your own importance! Of course, I just ignored him and carried on, regardless of his veiled threats.

Then the FA, in their desperation to prove the charge, stupidly decided to rely upon evidence from the 2002 World Cup when Brazilian superstar Rivaldo was fined for feigning injury in a game against Turkey. There was one big problem with that. Rivaldo had admitted that he had feigned the injury when a ball was kicked against his leg, and he fell to the floor holding his face. The divide was so great between the Rivaldo case and the Ben Haim case that it showed just how desperate the FA were becoming in their quest to prove their case. As it turned out, the panel that eventually deliberated on the case thought the same.

The disciplinary hearing against Ben Haim took place on Wednesday February 16, 2005 at Birmingham City FC. The player, together with manager Sam Allardyce, was in attendance with me. We had served several documents on the FA which we intended to rely upon, the most important being his own witness statement, as well as some supporting medical evidence. When describing the incident with Rooney, Ben Haim had said in his witness statement:

I recall that Wayne Rooney made a run with the ball towards and across the front of me, just in front of the penalty area. As he reached me, he momentarily lost control of the ball. I did not make any contact with him; however, he fell to the floor in a deliberate attempt to fool the referee into awarding a free kick in favour of his team. As he fell to the floor I instinctively held both hands in the air so that the referee could see that I was not touching him. The referee was close to the incident and indicated that play should continue.

As Wayne Rooney started to get back onto his feet I shouted to him, "I DON'T TOUCH YOU, I DON'T TOUCH YOU". As Rooney stood up, he shouted back to me, "FUCK OFF". At this point, and without any provocation from myself, he raised his hand and forcefully pushed it into the centre of my face, making full contact with my nose. The push was forceful enough for me to be very slightly off balance and my left hand and arm was extended to try to momentarily stop myself from falling. However, I fell straight to the floor.

Whilst on the floor I held my hand to my face, and I was in fact checking that my nose had not started to bleed. I did this on a number of occasions. I held my hand to my nose, as that was causing me some discomfort as a direct result of Wayne Rooney pushing his hand in my face. The referee and a number of other players came to the area where the incident had happened. I do not think that Wayne Rooney came back. After a short while, I do not recall exactly how long, I was helped to my feet by a colleague.

I recall that whilst I was laid on the floor the referee did not at any time tell me to get to my feet. I recall Roy Keane running over and he could see that I was checking whether my nose was bleeding. I remember him saying to me "THERE'S NO BLOOD".

The FA's charge alleges that I exaggerated the impact and effect made by Rooney's hand. This is not true. As a result of Wayne Rooney's actions, I felt and saw his hand make contact with my face with a degree of force. Discomfort was caused as a result of that contact.

Ben Haim gave his evidence in a very confident and truthful manner to the panel, who could not have failed to have been impressed by him. We also then called Dermot Gallagher to give evidence on our behalf. The FA had resisted us getting Gallagher to attend, but we pushed and pushed saying his evidence would be crucial. It was obvious why they didn't want him there. He had already torpedoed their case with his written report submitted a few days after the incident, so they knew him being there in the flesh would be the death knell on the case. Dermot didn't disappoint and in questioning we got out of him what we wanted to about him not acting against a player who had been subjected to violent conduct by an opposition player.

I then made my representations, basing it strongly on the strength of the oral evidence from the player, the failures of the officials, including the admission from Gallagher that he would not have sanctioned Ben Haim. I then went into great detail about how the only person who could state the effect of any contact was the person who had received it, and for the FA to try to prove otherwise was folly. It was unrealistic to expect a disciplinary panel to find in their favour. The panel retired to

30 Dec 04 09:46   p. 1

Please quote in all correspondence
Our Ref: FO/04/0503

29 December 2004

Mr Tal Ben Haim
Bolton Wanderers FC
Reebok Stadium
Burnden Way
Lostock
Bolton BL6 6JW

By Post and Fax No 01204 873918/ 01257 226225

Dear Sir

Direct Tel: 020 7745 4521
Direct Fax: 020 7745 5521

Manchester United FC v Bolton Wanderers FC
FA Premier League
26 December 2004

You are hereby charged with misconduct for a breach of FA Rule E3 in respect of the above fixture.

The Football Association intends to rely on the enclosed reports from the Assistant Referee, Mr. Atkins; the Fourth Official, Mr. Wiley; the Match Assessor, Mr. Rejer; an e-mail from the General Manager of the PGMOL, Mr. Hackett, and a video clip of the incident in question.

— says without proof

The video clip can be accessed and viewed at http://www.TheFA.com/disciplinary/BoltonWanderers using the Club's username and password. The video shows the contact made between Mr. Rooney and you, and your reaction to this contact. The Football Association alleges that you exaggerated the impact and/or effect of the contact made between Mr. Rooney's hand and your face and in so doing, your conduct was improper.

The Football Association has also sought the view of the Match Referee, Mr. Gallagher, who has confirmed that he did not see the incident in question. Mr. Gallagher will be e-mailing The Association tonight and we will forward his correspondence as soon as we have it.

You are required to submit the enclosed Reply Form A by 20 January 2005. This should indicate whether you wish to admit or deny the charge and whether you request a personal hearing. In the event that you request a personal hearing and wish to be represented, the identity of your representative must be indicated on the reply form.

If you request a personal hearing please enclose a hearing fee of £100. Failure to provide the hearing fee within the time limit may result in your request for a personal hearing to be denied.

You must provide The Football Association's Compliance Department with your submissions comprising copies of all evidence and documents upon which you intend to rely in support of your plea including the details and statements of any witnesses you intend to rely upon.

If the evidence and documents are not submitted, they may not be considered by the Disciplinary Commission.

You should note that failure to reply to the charge in the stipulated time will result in your case being dealt with on the evidence of the enclosed material and any further evidence The Football Association seeks to bring in support of its charge.

Please find enclosed a Reply Form (A), which you should fully complete and return with your answer to the charge by the deadline specified above.

In the meantime, please acknowledge safe receipt of this letter by immediate return either on the contact numbers specified above or e-mail to Disciplinary@TheFA.com.

Yours faithfully

Senior Compliance Officer

Encl.

cc: Simon Marland, Club Secretary, Bolton Wanderers FC
       Alan Wilkes, Disciplinary Manager, The FA

A typical charge letter from the FA, this one accusing Ben Haim of Bolton of diving which we successfully defended.

consider their decision, but were not thinking very long about it because they quickly concluded that the charge against Tal Ben Haim was not proved.

It was yet another example of the FA bringing charges they had no real chance of proving. They were just reacting to newspaper stories and being influenced. Once again it was an embarrassment to the governing body, brought about by what appeared to be Lampitt's insistence that the charge be pursued. As in cases before and since, when they realised it was unlikely that the charge would be proved, they should have stopped wasting everyone's time and just pull the plug on them.

I dealt with a couple of other cases where there could be no question that very significant contact was made between the people involved, which had very serious consequences for all those involved. On New Year's Day, 2005 Peterborough United were playing an away game at Bristol City when a very serious altercation took place in the tunnel at half time between Bristol defender Tony Butler and Peterborough striker Clive Platt. During the fracas, Butler received serious mouth injuries, with eight teeth being damaged and lots of blood being spilled, while Platt received a hand wound because of the force of the punch he meted out.

The events in the tunnel were the culmination of something that had started on the pitch in the first half, with Platt alleging that Butler had used excessive force against him on several occasions. Platt later claimed that Butler had used his elbow to make contact with his throat in a challenge for the ball on one occasion, and on another had swung a punch at him which failed to make contact and had not been seen by the match officials. Things were obviously festering and as the half time whistle went both players were first into the tunnel with Butler just ahead of Platt.

In his initial statement to the FA, Butler said:

"I was walking back up the tunnel towards the dressing

room at half time. I was walking in front of the Peterborough United player Clive Platt as we entered the canvas tunnel, he passed me and turned and struck me in the mouth, which made me stagger back".

That was the simple version of what had occurred, and Butler was backed up by several other people who were in the tunnel.

Once again though, the FA responded to a newspaper report as opposed to waiting for any match official reports. As you can see, there is a real pattern emerging here in the way the FA rely upon sensational media headlines, sometimes to their detriment. On this occasion, Tark Shamel from the Compliance Department, cited a report in *The Sun* newspaper from January 3, stating that Butler had needed an operation to repair the damage to his teeth and Platt had three stitches in his injured hand. It was ironic that Shamel was using the newspaper article as a source for starting the investigation, especially after a FA spokesman had said to the newspaper:

"We are aware of an incident in the tunnel and will await the referee's report before deciding what course of action to take. The report is always the first port of call and if, as it seems, an extra-ordinary incident did occur then the matter will be investigated further".

If the referees report was the *"first port of call"* then why was the Compliance Department relying upon sensational newspaper stories to seek an explanation from Platt? It just shows how poor the communication was between departments at the FA.

We responded confirming an incident had occurred, but then followed this up with another letter requesting sight of any official reports about the incident, including any statements from witnesses. However the FA refused to hand these over for reasons best known to themselves and the first time we saw them was when Platt was charged with violent conduct on January 20. It seemed unfair that the first time the player had seen the official allegation and reports was when he received his charge, when the fair thing to do would have been to ask him to comment on the official reports rather than the newspaper headlines. Once again it shows a disregard for fairness at that time.

In the meantime a real row was brewing because it emerged that the FA had obtained a copy of Platt's private medical records about his hand injury when he was initially treated at the Bristol City stadium, which had been secured without his consent. We challenged this with the FA, to ascertain how they had got into their possession. Somebody wasn't telling the truth. In response to our letter to the FA asking for an explanation Director of Governance, Jonathan Hall replied on February 9 stating, "*Both the reports that you have mentioned were sent to us unsolicited by Bristol City FC*". But in a letter from the CEO of Bristol City, Colin Sexstone, he contradicted the FA's explanation by saying, "*I am writing to confirm that Bristol City only released the medical documents referring to Clive Platt in response to a request from the FA*". He followed this up with a further letter a few days later confirming that the club secretary had faxed the reports to the FA at their request. Platt had not given any permission for the medical reports to be released, and the FA had not even had the courtesy to ask him for them. It was yet another example of them just doing as they pleased, but this time with highly confidential material.

Platt made a detailed witness statement and was supported by several people connected to Peterborough United, including the then manager, Barry Fry. Platt described how, as the two players left the field at half time, Butler had turned around and winked at him before passing a comment. As they entered the tunnel the Peterborough striker claimed that Butler had then turned around and "*dipped his head and in the same movement brought it upwards in a head butt action, making a deliberate attempt to head butt me*". He went on to say that this caused immediate and painful contact to his mouth which caused a cut to the inside of his lip. Platt continued;

> "*In an instinctive defensive movement as his head made*

contact with me, I struck out at Tony with a clenched fist. This was in an "uppercut" movement. I made contact with him however at this point I did not realise where in his body I had made contact".

Given the force of the blow Platt sustained a cut to his finger, which was presumed to have been made when it made contact with Butler's teeth, and he required a minor operation the following day to repair some tendon damage. It must have been some punch!

On receipt of Platt's statement, the FA then had a second bite of the cherry and obtained further statements from Butler and others denying Platt's version of events. Whilst Platt admitted the charge it was felt that the circumstances of the case needed what is called a "*Newton Hearing*" – which is a legal term where an allegation is admitted, but there is a difference of opinion as to what occurred. That being the case, a short hearing is held with witnesses to give evidence, to allow the disciplinary panel to reach a decision on the facts of the case.

The hearing was held in a Birmingham city centre hotel on May 19, 2005, by which time Platt had transferred to Milton Keynes Dons FC. Butler reluctantly attended the hearing to give evidence against Platt. He had made it known he did not wish to make a complaint about the incident, but the FA had pursued it. It was a difficult situation because the room we were using was so small that both these players were practically sat on top of each other and you could you could cut the atmosphere with a knife. I successfully argued that Platt had reacted to a perceived act by Butler, with the Disciplinary Panel concluding;

> *"Having admitted an act of violent conduct against Mr T Butler – a player of Bristol City FC – at half time – unseen by all of the Match Officials – the Members (of the Disciplinary Panel) decided that the act which caused the injury to Mr Butler was instinctive and a reaction to a perceived act by his opponent"*

Platt was suspended for four games and fined £500, which in my view was a good result. Had that happened in today's climate, taking into account the injuries Butler sustained, then I think the ban would have been in months as opposed to games.

Garry Hill is something of a legend in non league football. His name may not mean a lot to those who follow teams in the Premier League or EFL, but around the semi professional circuit he is very well known, having managed at a host of clubs with an impressive record. On September 8, 2007, whilst managing the now defunct Rushden & Diamonds FC, he got himself in some bother. Garry is no shrinking violet and is a loud, yet good humoured individual who is passionate about the game. The match that day, away at Salisbury City, was a little feisty to say the least. It included a mass brawl in front of the technical area just before the final whistle that involved over twenty players and officials from both teams. It also transpired that Garry had allegedly been subjected to abuse and derogatory comments from Salisbury assistant manager and former Southampton player, Tommy Widdrington, which had led Garry to raise the matter with the fourth official.

In the final minute of the game Salisbury scored an equaliser, which was the cue for Widdrington to run through the Rushden technical area towards the end of the stadium where the goal had been scored to celebrate with his players. As he did so, Garry alleged that Widdrington had deliberately bumped into him.

A short time later the final whistle sounded and handshakes were exchanged between the occupants of the technical area, but it seemed that Hill and Widdrington snubbed each. Hill explained that he had then gone up to the director's box a few steps away from him to shake hands with another Salisbury official, before returning to the pitch side and making his way towards the officials, who were walking off the field. As he did so he was followed by Widdrington. It was at this point it all went terribly wrong for Garry, with the whole incident taking place on camera. The match official's report summed it up perfectly when he stated:

> *"I saw Rushden Manager Garry Hill and Salisbury City FC Player Coach Tommy Widdrington walking towards us. I therefore had a clear and unobstructed view and I witnessed Garry Hill violently headbutt Tommy Widdrington in the face. The two were immediately separated by stewards and security officers. It was evident that Tommy Widdrington had sustained an injury to his nose and had blood streaming down his face".*

The head butt was something you'd see at chucking out time in a town centre on a Saturday night. It was vicious and done with a high degree of force, leaving Widdrington with a broken nose. It was there for all to see on video. The inevitable charge of violent conduct arrived within a matter of days and Garry was straight on the phone to me asking me to help him out. He had no option but to admit the charge, but to make matters worse Wiltshire Police got involved which eventually led to a criminal assault charge being brought against Hill when he was fined £1,500 by the local Magistrates Court.

A disciplinary hearing was set up a few months later for Garry, who made a detailed witness statement about what had occurred. He claimed that Widdrington was continuing to abuse him as they approached the match officials and the video clearly showed Garry telling Widdrington to go away. According to Garry, it was at the point that Widdrington made a remark to him which he viewed as inappropriate and in a momentarily loss of self discipline he head butted him, immediately regretting his actions. Widdrington had got a lot more than he'd bargained for and now Garry had too, because he received a two week fine from his club on top of the court fine and the penalty from the FA.

Whilst researching the case I came across a similar incident in the National League involving Kidderminster Harriers' boss Mark Yates, who had head butted Exeter City player Lee Elam some months earlier. Yates was fined £350 and received a four game touchline suspension. I was hoping that I could secure something similar in terms of penalty for Garry - but I was mistaken.

The disciplinary panel hearing the case didn't hold back in their judgement of Garry's actions. The video sunk him without trace, such was the impact it had on proceedings. They were damning of Garry's behaviour and viewed it so seriously that they issued an immediate suspension *"from all football and football management activities for a period of fourteen days"*, meaning Hill could not even go to the club to do his job. That wasn't all though, as they went even further and gave him a ten-game touchline ban commencing as soon as the fourteen-day suspension had been completed, although five of those games were suspended for a period of one year. Just to rub salt into the wound, they topped it off with a fine of £500. Given the seriousness of the incident, it was no more than we could have expected and probably the right type of punishment.

Normally fights between players and managers are over in a matter of seconds and are nothing more than momentary losses of discipline which are brought under control quickly with no real harm done. The referee deals with it, or in the odd case the FA will issue a charge and a standard three-game ban is given out. But in the cases of Clive Platt and Garry Hill these were extreme cases which thankfully are few and far between. As mentioned earlier, sometimes the evidence is so overwhelming that a player or a manager has no option but to admit the charge issued against them - and in these two cases that was absolutely the correct thing to do. It also meant that by admitting the charge immediately, the penalty is more lenient than it could have been.

Fans love to see a punch up between players but the aftermath of this type of "match day entertainment" often has very serious implications, as these two cases show. Put that into comparison though with the Ben Haim case, where the FA went to the other extreme, and you can see why their case against him was pure folly and was destined to end in failure.

I viewed the Ben Haim case as one of the most interesting I had dealt with. It was something different from the normal stuff that was referred to me. Whilst the rules relating to simulation in the game have now changed, correctly in my view, I've never heard of a player being charged with the same thing ever since. It was another lesson learned the embarrassing way for the FA.

13 - SATURDAY AFTERNOON'S ALRIGHT FOR FIGHTING

IN MY VIEW THE MOST difficult charges to defend under football rules are the ones referred to by the media as "mass confrontation", when there is a coming together of both teams following an incident which ignites emotions on the field. The rules which the FA use are so wide ranging and cover such a vast spectrum of issues and such a multitude of sins that it becomes an easy hit for the governing body. Someone like me, attempting to defend someone, is on the back foot from the off.

The FA rule relating to "mass confrontation" actually says that clubs should ensure that its players or officials:

> *Conduct themselves in an orderly fashion and refrain from any one or a combination of the following; improper conduct, violent, threatening, abusive, indecent, insulting or provocative words or behaviour.*

So, as you can see, even the slightest reaction from several players allows the FA to issue a charge, safe in the knowledge that in all likelihood it will be proved. Even a player acting as a "peacemaker" is viewed as acting improperly. The issuing of a charge of this type is akin to a mobile speed camera. It's just a source of easy revenue for the relevant authority. It's no wonder the FA are so quick off the mark to charge a club in these circumstances! Players' emotions in the heat of battle only need a little spark to ignite the flames, but the FA don't seem to consider emotions in football because this type of charge is so wide ranging and difficult to defend, I normally advise clubs to take it on the chin, pay the standard fine and move on.

Over the years I have been involved in representing many clubs in cases of this type, but in all my years of doing so, no case came close to touching a game involving Peterborough United and Notts County which *The Sun* labelled the *"Most Violent*

Match - Ever'!

They certainly weren't wrong.

The match took place at Peterborough's London Road stadium on September 20, 2010, and saw two mass brawls and the same number of red cards and became known as the *'Battle of London Road'*. One player involved was quoted as saying after it had all finished that:

> *"It was the worst violence I've ever seen on a football pitch. There were no handbags, only right hooks. Nobody was holding back. Proper punches were thrown. When the final whistle went, it was almost like the bell to signal the start of round two. Even players that had been sitting in the stands came on the pitch to join in."*

The FA issued charges to both clubs very quickly, while Ben McKenzie, the Head of Sports Science at Peterborough United, was also charged because of his alleged behaviour during the brawls.

I was asked to represent Peterborough but the interesting thing was that Notts County were represented by a former FA colleague of mine, Mark Knowles. Mark and I had worked very closely together for several years in the Compliance Department, so we were able to combine our abilities and knowledge to use the situation to our advantage. We worked in cahoots with each other, to get the best outcome for both our clients. Quite simply, we had decided to sing from the same hymn sheet and use the same criticisms of the FA process. Our thoughts were that if two people representing different clients were using the same criticism of the FA, then it would make more of an impact with the disciplinary panel than if just one person was saying it.

There were two charges of mass confrontation made against each club, whilst McKenzie, along with a Notts County official, Mark Draper, were also charged with violent conduct.

The first brawl took place on 64 minutes after Posh's Grant McCann had been sent off for scything down Alan Judge. The second brawl took place on the touchline after the final whistle and involved almost everyone connected to both teams. It was absolute carnage, like a scene out of *Green Street*. It was a no-brainer in terms of the club charges, and both of them admitted them and were fined a total of £15,000. But the case against McKenzie was a different kettle of fish.

The match officials all claimed they'd seen McKenzie attempting, on numerous occasions, to *'strike an opponent in a violent manner'*. Given the fact there were over thirty people involved in the huge scrap, we found it strange and difficult to comprehend in all the mayhem how one person had been singled out. McKenzie denied the charge and in his statement told how one of the Posh players, Ryan Bennett, had been punched and knocked to the ground. McKenzie went straight to the player's aid and then found himself getting pushed about. Photographs relied upon by the FA, along with a video, simply didn't back up the accounts given by the officials in relation to McKenzie's conduct. McKenzie was also supported by another Posh player who described in detail how McKenzie was not involved in any violence and despite the FA's best efforts, the disciplinary panel overwhelmingly found that the charge could not be proved against Ben, so he was subsequently cleared.

Given the circumstances, and while we understood they had to rely on the evidence of the officials, it was clear from the photographic and video evidence that at no time had he acted in a violent manner. Once again it was a case of the FA not doing their job properly and just issuing a charge without looking beyond the match officials reports. Life would be so much easier for them in terms of avoiding unnecessary discipline cases if they just took a step back and did a little more pro-active investigation, rather than simply reacting to everything that lands on their desks.

On the subject of pro-active investigations, I got involved in one on behalf of the FA back in 2000 concerning Arsene Wenger and Thierry Henry that turned into an absolute farce. In the close season of that year the FA did yet another disciplinary "crack down" launch and Wenger was the first victim. On the opening day of the 2000/01 season Arsenal visited the Stadium of Light, where they were beaten 1-0 by Sunderland in a fiery game which saw midfielder Patrick Vieira sent off in the 90th minute for throwing an elbow at Sunderland's Darren Williams.

As the teams made their way down the tunnel following the final whistle it seemed that a verbal altercation of some kind took place between Williams and Henry prompting Wenger to intervene. This in turn led to the fourth official, Paul Taylor, getting involved and he reported that Wenger had made physical contact with him in the dispute.

A few days later I was sent to Sunderland to investigate the incident and spoke with Williams in the office of Black Cats manager Peter Reid. It was clear that Reid had no time for Wenger and was more than happy to assist with the inquiry. Williams explained to me, in the presence of Reid, what had happened in the tunnel and before I left Reid said if he could trace anyone else who had witnessed the events then he would get them to contact me. This is where the fun and games began. As I drove home my phone rang and it was Adrian Heath, the Sunderland assistant boss, who told me he was ringing about the tunnel incident. He relayed what had occurred, which was in line with what I already knew from Williams and we ended the call. A short time later the phone rang again. This time it was the Sunderland kit man who also told me his version of events, which just happened to be precisely the same as every other account I had heard from Sunderland. Once again the call ended, but only a few minutes later the phone rang again and this time it was a club official, who claimed to have been in the tunnel and saw everything, which just by sheer coincidence, was verbatim to what everyone else had said! By this time I'm driving along thinking to myself, *"what a load of bollocks this is"*. It was clear they'd all got their heads together, so I didn't pursue that angle of the investigation, but I found it highly amusing that suddenly all these witnesses appeared giving exactly the same version of events, even though nobody had previously mentioned them being there. In the end we just relied upon the official's report to bring a charge against Wenger.

He went before a disciplinary panel sometime later and was a victim of the FA clampdown after being fined a month's wages and given an eye-watering 12-game touchline ban, which was completely over the top and unfair. Wenger appealed against the verdict which was subsequently – and rightfully – overturned. The Frenchman ended up with a warning and a fine of £10,000, but I dread to think what might have happened if all the so-called witnesses had lined up to give their exact same version of events!

One rivalry that goes under the radar a little bit is the East Midlands clash between Derby County and Nottingham Forest. The supporters hate each other. In August 2009 Forest beat their rivals 3-2 in a pulsating clash at the City Ground, when the animosity between the teams carried on well after the final whistle. Things had started before the game even kicked-off, when it was claimed that Derby's Robbie Savage had been winding up the home fans. Some of them wrote to the club afterwards to claim the midfielder had been "*thrusting his backside deliberately*" towards them while warming up. It had really got to some of the Forest fans, so I think Robbie would have thought to himself "job done!" But this was nothing compared to what happened at the end of the game!

Nathan Tyson was to blame. For some reason – and only he knows why – the Forest striker decided it would be a sensible idea after the game to pick up a corner flag bearing the Forest emblem, hold it above his head in celebration and run across the width of the penalty area directly in front of the 4,300 travelling Derby fans stood in the Bridgford End. It was the cue for absolute bedlam. Within seconds Tyson found himself surrounded by furious opposition players from a team which included the likes of Savage, Lee Bowyer and Paul Dickov.

As we all know, these three were no shrinking violets. Tyson's behaviour created a serious crowd issue as well, with the Derby fans surging towards the pitch in anger.

Stewards struggled to calm things down as rival players and fans were involved in an angry confrontation. Referee Martin Atkinson was left with no choice but to report Tyson and both clubs to the FA and before the end of the week charges were issued against the protagonists. Both clubs were charged with failing to conduct themselves in an orderly fashion, while Tyson was charged with improper conduct. The whole case wasn't helped by the fact the local police commander submitted a report to the FA, stating that as a result of Tyson's actions:

> *"it increased the level of disorder inside the ground that led to supporters being exposed to greater risk of injury and lower levels of safety."*

It didn't make good reading, especially as he also reported that seats were thrown onto the pitch at the time of the brawl, while a 12-year-old girl was taken to hospital with abdominal injuries as a direct result of the crowd surge caused by the altercation on the pitch.

I soon had Forest on the phone, wanting my services. The chief executive at the time, Mark Arthur, was insistent the club wanted to deny the charge, although Tyson had no option but to admit his. Forest were adamant they wanted to challenge it, so I had to go with what my client wanted. The hearing was held in October at Leicester City's stadium and, despite the points put forward on behalf of the club, it made zero difference. Forest were fined £25,000, of which £10,000 was suspended. Arthur was very annoyed and stormed out of the meeting with a face like a smacked arse. Tyson, meanwhile, was fined £5,000 and given a suspended two-match ban. One thing I've learned over the years is that irrespective of how good or bad the outcome of a case is, you have to remain dignified, calm and not let your emotions get the better of you. You have plenty of time to celebrate a win or criticise a defeat away from the tribunal room and I always tell me clients just to take the FA's decision in your stride and not react, then deal with the aftermath later.

For many years I represented Queens Park Rangers – and they certainly got their money's worth out of me, they were one of my regular clients. I have a real soft spot for the club. I've always said that if I lived in London they would be my team. When I was working at the FA I used to jump onto the Central Line down to Shepherds Bush regularly to watch them. Rather than utilise the comfort of the directors box, I used to sit in the stands among the fans. There's something about their club's name that gives an air of football romance about it, as well as their distinctive blue and white hooped shirts, while the tightness of their Loftus Road ground that causes the crowd noise to reverberate.

During my time there they were involved in several mass brawls as well as having individuals getting themselves into bother as well. In December 2005 I was asked to represent them in relation to a brawl they'd been involved in with Stoke City. Ironically, 14 months earlier, I'd represented Stoke City in a case involving them having following a fracas with, you guessed it, QPR! Around this time there seemed to be a bit of needle between the clubs. The game in 2005 had taken place at the Britannia Stadium, which Rangers won 2-1, but the game isn't remembered for the result, so much as the action following the full time whistle. Referee Andre Marriner's report to the FA read as follows:

> *"At the end of the match, my attention was drawn to an incident in the goal that had been defended by the visiting team (QPR) during the second half. I witnessed a supporter grappling with the visiting goalkeeper in the goal, resulting in them being entangled in the netting. As other players became aware of what was going on, members of both teams rushed into the vicinity of the incident."*

It later transpired that in conversations between the police and match officials after the game, allegations had been made by Stoke supporters that QPR goalkeeper Simon Royce had made hand gestures towards them. This caused things to escalate and a Stoke supporter breached the pitch side wall and attacked Royce. In the melee that followed, centre half Ian Evatt had gone to the assistance of his keeper and dragged the supporter off him, but he was then attacked himself from behind and wrestled to the floor and punched. If anyone has ever seen the physique of Evatt they'd realise it was a very brave supporter who dared do that! It seemed that everybody from both teams got involved trying to ensure the safety of the goalie, as opposed to getting involved in any fights between themselves. Understandably, the FA started their own investigation and then, unbelievably, decided to charge QPR with failing to control their players. The charge specifically said;

> *"It is alleged that during the incident that followed the final whistle, QPR FC failed to ensure that its players conducted themselves in an orderly fashion and refrained from threatening and/or provocative behaviour."*

We thought it baffling that QPR had been charged, when all they were trying to do was stop one of their players from being assaulted by a fan. And yet the FA took no action against Stoke, whose own players had been trying to do the same thing. Even more baffling was the fact no action was taken against Stoke despite one of their own supporters having got onto the pitch to assault a rival player. Things got even more ridiculous following a report submitted by Staffordshire Police, who took it upon themselves to interview three QPR players under caution for their conduct, before deciding no action would be taken against them. It seemed to me that it was a classic case of the local police getting involved in one aspect of the incident and focusing all their attention on the visiting club but having no interest in looking into the role of their local club Stoke City. Make of that what you will.

Given the circumstances, this was one case in which I felt there was a chance of defending the actions of the QPR players, particularly as the FA's thinking and approach seemed skewed. It made me think that once again the FA were targeting my clients.

Following discussions with QPR senior staff we had initially decided to deny the charge. We were very unhappy that Stoke had escaped punishment when it was their supporter who had caused the incident to escalate in the way that it had and the fact that he had managed to get past the pitch side stewards. On reflection, however, I felt that there was a *"deal to be done"*, given the circumstances. As I've said earlier, these charges cover a multitude of sins, so they are easy for the FA to prove, but I'm still mystified after all these years as to why no action was taken against Stoke.

I chose my timing to perfection, approaching the FA immediately before the disciplinary hearing started to see if a compromise could be found. We reached an agreement that if the club admitted a less serious element of the charge, the FA would indicate what the punishment would be. I can't ever recall this being done before and I've not heard of it being done since, so it was probably a one-off for them. It was indicated to me that the charge would attract a fine of £5,000 which, given QPR's record, was a very attractive proposition. I asked that the meeting be paused for a short while so I could telephone Rangers chairman Giannia Paladini to talk it though with him. Following my advice, he was happy to accept the fine, but towards the end of our conversation he asked me to pass a message on to the FA once the hearing had been concluded, which I told him I would be more than happy to do.

I returned to the disciplinary hearing, and we went through the motions of conducting the tribunal, knowing full well what the outcome would be. The £5,000 fine was then issued. As we sat there packing our papers away, I addressed the Commission again and told them I had a message to pass onto them from Mr Paladini. They looked at me inquisitively, and with a deadpan look on my face, relayed the message saying, ***"I've been told by Mr Paladini to tell the FA 'to go fuck itself'"***. Everybody just cracked up! They took it in good heart and I'm sure they knew exactly why he had said it!

QPR were becoming good customers and it wasn't too long before I found myself back in their corner once again. In February 2007 Rangers played a friendly against the Chinese under-22 Olympic Team at the training ground. It certainly wasn't a 'friendly' game though, because the events of that afternoon went on to become a worldwide story. The Chinese side had also played Chelsea a few days earlier and word had spread that the game had become a little bit feisty but this game reached a different level altogether!

Dermot Gallagher had been asked to referee the match and he had no option but to report that in the 78th minute he witnessed a Chinese player trying to jump onto the back of a QPR player. Not knowing why it was happening, Dermot blew his whistle to stop the game, but the Chinese delegation on the sidelines saw this as their cue to invade the pitch and engage in a mass brawl. Substitutes, unused players and coaching staff, totalling over 30 people, ran onto the playing area and began fighting with QPR players. It was all caught on video by a Chinese TV channel covering the game. The pitch started to resemble a scene from a Bruce Lee film! The Chinese players were kung-fu kicking their opponents, forcing the QPR players to flee to the home dressing room for their own safety. It was surreal to watch on the video footage how violent it became, and it didn't take long for the film footage to hit television screens around the world.

The FA felt that they had no option but to issue a mass confrontation charge of the highest level against QPR but were unable to sanction the Chinese team as they were not under their jurisdiction. I think the FA just realised how bad a light it put the English game in given the coverage, so I knew they would come down hard on Rangers.

With the permission of the FA I wrote to Gallagher asking him to clarify a number of points relating to his official match report. He responded, saying that during the whole of the game none of the Chinese players spoke to him in English and said that *"many of the Chinese who invaded the pitch, dressed in long navy coats, adopted Bruce Lee-style aggression towards their opponents."* Dermot was very supportive of QPR and made it clear it had been the Chinese team that had fuelled the fight. I knew, despite the referee supporting Rangers, that this was a case in which 'damage limitation' was the best policy and I obtained numerous statements from QPR players and staff, who gave me their detailed version of events.

There was a very sinister side to it all, though, because on February 8, 2007, which had been the day before the game, QPR had received an anonymous email message which read;

> *"Fuck you QPR, your players really fuck in the match against Team China. This is a warning message, please forward this to your No. 8 and No. 6. We will stop their soccer life in the recently two weeks. We just want their hand or leg, but not their life, so they can continue their fucking life, but no more football. They will be fucked off soon."*

The email was signed off by a group calling themselves *'London China XT'*, but investigations into its origin by the club and police drew a blank. It seemed it was just a crank email trying to put the frighteners on the Loftus Road club.

The hearing took place at Soho Square the following June and the Commission came down hard on QPR, fining them £40,000, with £20,000 of it suspended. We thought this was harsh, given what had happened. It felt like QPR had walked into some sort of ambush. My own theory is that the Chinese team were not used to the physicality of the English game at that time and reacted to it when in fact QPR, like Chelsea, had just played their normal game. The bottom line though was that the Chinese team got away with it, despite the incident making national headlines back in China.

On the subject of players getting kicked, whilst working at the FA as Compliance Officer, I was involved in one of the most infamous cases in football back in 1999. Most people will remember it well, because the offence was committed by West Ham striker John Hartson against one of his own team-mates, Eyal Berkovic. I'd only been at the FA a month and it was the first time I'd found myself acting as a prosecutor for them. Hartson had lashed out at Berkovic during a training session and kicked the Israeli in the head. The incident had been captured on video and Hartson was bang to rights.

Hartson had been reacting to a challenge on him from Berkovic earlier in the session, but following the issuing of a charge against him, he had no option but to admit the rule breach. I clearly remember, when the hearing started, how I opened up the case by showing a video of the attack and made it clear to the Commission that a *"picture painted a thousand words, or in this case a video painted a thousand words"*. There wasn't a lot more for me to do.

Hartson attended the hearing to put his points across, and produced a sympathetic letter from Berkovic insisting the players had made their peace but the FA felt that it was such a serious matter they had to make an example of him, fining him £20,000 as well as banning him for three games. If the same thing happened today between players, the penalties would much stronger, such has the game moved on in terms of its sanctions for dealing with serious incidents.

Another player I represented who had lost his temper to find himself in the dock was Cardiff City's Simon Walton. During a game against his former club Leeds in February, 2007, the defender had been sent off in the 85th minute by referee Mark Clattenburg for a second booking. It later turned out to be the wrong decision to send him off, because in the referee's assessor's report, which I obtained a copy of, he failed to support

Clattenburg in terms of the action he'd taken against the player. Not only that, but the assessor gave a withering assessment of the Geordie official, criticising him by saying that he should be careful that:

> *"You do not give the wrong impression of yourself by inappropriate hand gestures, which could be perceived as arrogant and possibly inflammatory."*

I have to say that in today's game, lots of referees are guilty of this. They love to be dramatic with all their hand gestures. Maybe Clattenburg was just a pioneer in this dramatic use of hand signals? Clattenburg went on to report that Walton had refused to leave the field immediately, and had adopted an aggressive attitude, before stewards stepped onto the field to lead him off, before describing what followed:

> *"He (Walton) then proceeded, as he left the field of play, to kick the substitution board several times, resulting in the board being damaged, then aggressively was taken down the tunnel by stewards."*

Unfortunately for Clattenburg, Cardiff provided me with a video from a different angle to the one which he had. The video, taken from a vantage point almost directly opposite the tunnel area, was obtained from the Ninian Park stadium and actually showed Walton walking down the tunnel in a calm manner, followed by a member of the coaching staff, as opposed to him being dragged kicking and screaming down it by a steward, as the referee had claimed. But before making his way down the tunnel, contrary to what Clattenburg had said, Walton had never kicked the electronic substitutes board. It was a false accusation. What he actually did was kick a bag containing footballs in frustration just the once and it had been the movement of the bag of balls that had caused the board to fall over and get damaged.

It's fair to say Walton was seething about what Clattenburg had said about him, and was very strong in his condemnation of him in his witness statement. He didn't hold back by saying,

"This is a total fabrication of what occurred. The content of the referee's report is wrong and not supported by the events which occurred on the field."

Walton was supported by Cardiff chairman Peter Ridsdale, who had been sitting in the directors box overlooking the tunnel and confirmed Walton had kicked the bag of balls causing the sign to fall over, and that the player had walked down the tunnel in a calm manner. In the final paragraph of Ridsdale's statement, he reiterated what Walton had said in his statement and said,:

> *"In my opinion the report submitted by Mr Clattenburg is misleading and wrong and I fully support the stance of the player on this occasion."*

It didn't make a lot of difference because Walton was charged with improper conduct by the FA of Wales (FAW). Sitting in front of a Disciplinary Panel from the FAW was an entirely different experience to that of the English FA. It seemed as if you were going back in time, because their view was that the referee could not be criticised. They were used to dealing with small League of Wales clubs, so when one of the bigger fish had to appear before them, like Cardiff or Swansea, it was a big event in the football calendar for them. They went power crazy! You would find that members of the referee's committees would on occasions sit on the disciplinary panels, so you were at a disadvantage all the time. The system has now changed for the better in Wales, but back then it was difficult to make any progress. I didn't think they were as able or competent as the English FA when it came to dealing with disciplinary cases.

The hearing was held at the FAW headquarters in Cardiff, which is a nondescript, bland looking building tucked away in the corner of an office park on the outskirts of the capital, unlike the prestigious location of the English FA, who are based at Wembley Stadium. When Clattenburg got into the witness chair he immediately changed his story once the video of the incident relied upon by the FAW had been shown to the panel. When asked by Claire Thomas, the FAW prosecutor, why he had said he had seen Walton kick the substitutes board "several times" Clattenburg replied, *"On the match day I saw two kicks, but now seeing the video I realise it was only one"*.

It made him look stupid. How can someone say they have witnessed one thing and then when shown evidence to the contrary change their evidence to fit the scenario, yet be allowed to get away with it? Well, the FAW let Clattenburg do that. When it came to my turn to cross examine the Geordie official I went straight for the jugular, asking him if he viewed all the incidents in his report to be correct? Once again he had to concede that his report was wrong. Despite all the inconsistencies however, the FAW found the case proved against Walton and fined him a week's wages. It wasn't a surprise, as I knew whenever I sat before the FAW Disciplinary Panels I was in a kangaroo court. It was bad enough at the English FA but going into the dragon's den at the FAW was ten times worse.

Astonishingly, though, in their written reasons for reaching the guilty verdict, the FAW accepted that the video did not show Walton acting aggressively as he walked down the tunnel, which was once again contrary to the evidence given by Clattenburg. You couldn't make it up. However we didn't take it lying down because, in our opinion, the evidence submitted by Clattenburg was so inconclusive and misleading that we complained to his General Manager Keith Hackett about him. The video we had obtained clearly showed Walton kicking the bag of balls, as opposed to the referee's substitute board, while also confirming that he walked down the tunnel in a calm manner escorted by a member of the Cardiff bench, as opposed to burly stewards dragging him kicking and screaming. Not for the first time, I went on the attack against Clattenburg and with the support of Cardiff, said to Hackett;

> *"I am saddened that a match official has, in our opinion, misled a commission in this way. The video (which we had obtained) clearly shows that Mr Clattenburg was*

not in the position that he consistently said that he was, and therefore could not see into the tunnel. Furthermore, despite evidence being shown to the contrary, his report was wrong and misleading"

As usual, despite the video showing a different series of events to what Clattenburg had claimed he'd seen, the Professional Game Match Officials Organisation (PGMO), which employs referees, unsurprisingly supported Clattenburg with Graham Noakes, the then secretary to the PGMO, writing back to me saying;

"I am disappointed that you believe the match official has misled a commission. The PGMO believes that Mr Clattenburg would have given his evidence honestly. I regret that you have felt it necessary to question the integrity of Mr Clattenburg when giving his evidence, but can assure you that match officials are reminded of the need for accurate reporting on a regular basis."

It came as no surprise to see a protective wall being thrown around a referee yet again. We had made our point, but not before I also wrote to David Collins, the then Secretary General of the FAW, complaining about their procedures and attitudes by saying;

"In all honesty I am appalled at the lack of efficiency and antiquated systems being applied by the FAW. It is quite frankly a disgraceful attitude to adopt towards participants in the game. With all due respect, Mr Walton and Cardiff City have been dealt with unfairly throughout this matter."

Players play with emotion. They are a group of closely bonded young men or women who look out for each other. That inevitably leads to each of them protecting others, so when one of their group is threatened inevitably tempers rise and the inevitable mass confrontation scenario occurs.

Of course, there should be a strong element of ensuring

behaviour by players is acceptable, but the mentality of the players at that moment has to be taken into account. Managers can tell players until they are blue in the face to keep calm in that final message before they leave the dressing room, but the reality is it won't make a lot of difference. The problem is that those making the decisions to issue mass confrontation charges have never played the game at a professional level. They, and I include myself in this analogy, don't understand the thought processes a player experiences. It's only since I left the FA and have spoken on many occasions to players and managers about these very problems, that I have grasped the reality of the situation and understood the subject better. One of the last things a manager will say to a team of players when they leave the dressing room is *"Don't leave anything out there on then pitch when you come back in at full time"*. There is no doubt players follow those instructions to the limit – and unfortunately that's when I get the call the bail them out.

Mass Confrontations will always be part of the game. Perversely, it's something that fans like to see. It's tribal and shows that players care about each other and their club. Sadly, it's not as simple as that, as clubs have found to their detriment over many years, because paying huge fines out still doesn't make an iota of difference.

14 - *THE FINAL WHISTLE*

OVER THE YEARS I've dealt with many different types of cases, representing over 70 clubs from the professional leagues, from the likes of Manchester United and Liverpool right down to Macclesfield Town in the lower echelons of the football pyramid. Every case is different and to be honest nothing in football disciplinary matters surprises me anymore. Just when you think you have represented a client where you think it can't get any worse or more ridiculous, along comes another case to surpass that. And just like life itself, it's been one heck of a rollercoaster with some huge highs, very serious lows and some very funny moments along the journey.

Outside the city of Newport, few give a stuff about the Welsh club but, regrettably as it turned out, I ended up taking a job there in 2015 and it resulted in me discovering the unthinkable – that there was bigger arsehole in football than Massimo Cellino! His name was Graham Westley. Put it this way, at least Massimo had a sense of humour.

They appointed me club secretary but within 48-hours I realised I'd made a huge mistake. The club, who were adrift at the bottom of League Two at the time and facing relegation into the National League, didn't even have any proper offices. In fact, it was such a ramshackle set up in the corner of the stadium that they shared with the local rugby team that they didn't even have central heating. The office areas looked like they'd not had a lick of paint since the day the Rodney Parade stadium opened in 1877. The damned place was so cold that come the middle of October I was just relieved I'd packed my overcoat and woolly hat for the long trip to Wales. You were having to work wearing your winter thermals and a big jacket just to keep warm. I had to wear fingerless gloves, just to type on the laptop!

The place was just so amateur, it was unbelievable. Because

supporters had the controlling interest in the club and ran the show, it meant fans believed they could just walk into the building at anytime. There was no reception area, or receptionist and unfortunately my so-called 'office' was the first that they would come to, so you struggled to get anything done. And the pitch, which was used every other week by the rugby team, was so bad it looked like a ploughed field. I remember one night there was a game on and there were standing puddles of water on the pitch amongst the deep ruts. The ball was just dropping like a stone and sticking in the mud. The match shouldn't have taken place, but when the referee did a pitch inspection alongside the match assessor, I asked the assessor, *"are you sure we're playing?"*, convinced that the pitch would be deemed unplayable. His response summed things up when he replied, *"I've said to the referee, if you think I'm driving back home to sit in front of the TV with the wife watching Eastenders, you've got another thing coming"*. It was game on then!

It felt like comedy hour all the time. The club was so dysfunctional it even had two different chairmen, along with committees for this and committees for that. So it felt quite appropriate that a short-arse like Westley was the manager of the team!

As usual I had made my own enquiries and heard lots of stories about him before arriving in Newport and he didn't disappoint. Sometime after I'd left the club, somebody suggested to me that Westley might have had it in for me from the start because, apparently, I'd prosecuted him once during my time at the FA. I can't recall this, which shows how insignificant it must have been. Insignificant is how I'd also describe Westley, if I'm being honest.

We didn't get on from the start. He was just another Martin Allen, full of his own importance. He had some weird and wonderful ways of doing things. He was what's known as an 'old school manager'. It appeared that he liked to think he ruled by fear and suffered no fools. He loved having the power. Here he was at a club at the bottom of the league, with players who were playing for a pittance in footballing terms, but thought it was appropriate to arrive at training in his Bentley and park it straight outside the doors to the 'training ground' – which was in effect a local sports centre with a football pitch. It used to piss the players off so much.

I recall one night Newport played Wycombe Wanderers at Rodney Parade. Wycombe were like a modern-day version of the Wimbledon 'Crazy Gang' team of the 80s and 90s. They had a ghetto blaster booming out music in their dressing room, which really pissed off Westley to some tune, if you'll pardon the pun! His mood was even darker when Wycombe scored a deserved last minute winner, then returned to their dressing room in good spirits and immediately switched the music back on courtesy of a plug point in the tunnel. The ones in the away dressing room didn't work! As he came off the pitch and into the tunnel with a face like thunder, Westley began demanding someone pull the ghetto blaster's plug out of the wall, but shit himself when he realised the person in charge of it was Wycombe legend and man-mountain Adebayo Akinfenwa! Needless to say, the music carried on. I have to admit, it did give me a rare moment of amusement in my time there.

There was also the time Newport played away at Blackpool and lost 3-0. It had been decided late in the day that the team would do an overnighter before the game and I'd been asked to book the team hotel through the booking agents the club used. However because it had been left so late before making the decision to stay overnight, accommodation was in short supply. This was because it was the first weekend of the Christmas party season, which Westley had not accounted for when he requested that the team be allowed the hotel stay. As is normal, when a team stays away you usually get three options where to go and then pick the most suitable. I gave Westley his three options, which were in Manchester, Blackpool itself or Preston. Preston was deemed the most suitable location, considering the time it would have taken to get to the Blackpool stadium on the day of the game. But I was left mystified by his response when giving him the Preston option because, bearing in mind he used to be manager of Preston North End, he initially declined the opportunity saying, *"there's some not so very nice people in Preston."* It made me wonder if there was some history or baggage attached to him from his time there some years previously.

Because the choice of accommodation was limited, the team headed to Preston anyway, only to discover a massive Christmas party in full swing at the hotel. The team ended up being spread out in different rooms around the place and Westley had a room near reception, which "disturbed" his sleep. His beef was that people were using the ice machine in the corridor near to his room! I'd been warned by several people that one of his traits was sending texts to people in the middle of the night, and this is what he did with me, complaining about the ice machine into the early hours while I was laid in bed. What the fuck did he want me to do about it back in Barnsley? I just ignored him. Anyone with an ounce of nous would have gone to the reception desk and ask to be moved. But it provided an example of just what I was up against.

County lost the game and his texts went into overdrive again less than 24 hours after the result claiming I'd been less than professional when it came to making all the travel arrangements. Given the time frame I'd had to work in and the fact it was close to Christmas, I thought I'd done well to find them anywhere at all. I just replied curtly saying I'd speak to him the following day when I was back in Newport. But he'd touched a nerve, questioning my professionalism, especially as given the conditions I was working under I felt like we were trying to make a silk purse out of a sow's ear.

The following morning I went straight to the training ground ready for him. I bounced into his office as he sat at his desk. Given his lack of height, I towered above him and told him straight and in no uncertain terms:

"You might be able to bully your players, but you won't bully me, and next time, it won't be one to one inside this office, I'll come onto the training pitch and tell you straight before your players and make you look the cunt that you are."

Westley got up from his chair bristling, in an attempt to intimidate me, so I hit him with another verbal blast. "*If you want to look me in the eye mate, you need to get on your orange box.*" Then I turned round and walked out. I'd already had enough of yet another shit show of a football club!

In truth I'd had enough within two months and it was mutually decided there should be a parting of the ways. Westley had obviously said to whichever chairman would listen it's either him or me, but that didn't bother me one bit. I fucking hated working with him anyway and I wasn't disappointed to be leaving. The final insult was when they tried to avoid paying me any compensation. Once again, I set solicitors onto them and Newport soon rolled over, such was the lack of experience at board level when it came to dealing with such matters.

Westley should have been sacked much earlier than he was. The team was going nowhere under him and everyone in the dressing room, from the players to the kit man, moaned about him. A month after I'd left, the board of supporters finally saw the light and got rid of him. Mike Flynn replaced him and led them to safety, before engineering a period of decent success.

Accrington Stanley is a famous name in the history of English football. In 1962 they went bust but rose from their own ashes to return to the Football League in the mid noughties. It became one of the truly heart-warming stories in football. It took 44 years for a newly formed club to get back into the league, having worked their way through all the divisions to get there.

But looking back at the time I represented them in 2007,

it was no fairy tale. It looked like they were walking into a nightmare scenario, with the real possibility of them being relegated from the league almost as soon as they got back there. The owner and chairman was a man called Eric Whalley and he was quite a character. He had also played for and managed the club. Eric was Accrington born and bred. He spoke with a strong Lancashire accent and had a deadpan sense of humour. He was the perfect foil for Scouse manager John Coleman.

The club's problem was that they'd fielded unregistered young players in two league fixtures against Mansfield and Wycombe, one of which they'd won to gain three points. The Football League had charged the club and it was likely the points they'd won would be stripped from their total. This scenario would have likely led to them being relegated from League Two. Eric rang me to see if I could help. The prospect of losing the points and his club's league status scared him stiff. Getting relegated again would have been a massive blow to the town and its people. Eric lived and breathed the place, but he had no choice but to admit the charges. We decided on a strategy to play on the emotional side of the club's story, as well as being heavily critical of the league's registration system, which in this case was at fault to a certain degree. Club officials had made numerous attempts to ensure that the rules were being complied with regarding the registration of the players involved – and were under the impression that the league had sanctioned them.

I also had an ace up my sleeve, although I never thought it would work in a million years! I decided to criticise the way in which the league presented their case. They were keen to get the maximum penalty against Accrington by having the points deducted, but I had other ideas. The league claimed that it could not be discounted that the players in question would have had a clear impact on the outcome of these two matches. I thought on my feet in the hearing as the league put this point across, I wondered why the league had not obtained evidence from scouts who had been at the games, who could speak about the impact these players might have had?

The league never saw that argument coming. They were somewhat taken aback and tried to counter it by saying it was an unrealistic argument to put forward. By not obtaining any scout reports, I claimed it undermined the league's assertions. It was a massive try on by me and I couldn't believe it when the panel seemed to accept the submission. I just didn't expect them to swallow it, but somehow they did. I was just winging it with those points, but it paid off. As a result, Accrington avoided a points deduction and were only fined £12,000. It didn't go down well with the other clubs battling Accrington in the relegation fight and they made their disgust clear, but Accrington had just got their best result of the season!

I'd saved Accrington's skin, but this must have gone over Eric's head. He was notoriously thrifty to the point of being comical with it, but he was such a nice fellow you couldn't fall out with him when trying to squeeze money out of him. As usual, getting my bill paid was like getting blood out of a stone! It took forever!

As I have said, I have encountered many funny things over the years. On one occasion a foreign goalkeeper playing at Havant & Waterlooville, of all places, blew one of my secret codes when dealing with interviews by the FA. The goalkeeper in question had a poor command of the English language, but the FA needed to interview him about an issue they had with him. The south coast club asked me to assist and sit in on the interview, so I travelled down there and met with him immediately before the interview took place in the boardroom area of the stadium.

I gave him clear instructions – or so I thought. Whenever I attended an interview with a client, I would always take two pens into the meeting with me; one black biro and one red one. I would make notes of what was being said with the black biro, but gave clear instructions to the client that, if at any time I picked up the red pen and started writing with it, this was the code for him to ask for the interview to be paused as something had come up which I needed to speak to him about and advise him on. It was a very simple thing to do, and I slowly went through this procedure with the goalkeeper in question. He said he understood, so we told the FA we were ready to start. The FA interviewer came into the room and was preparing things, when in his presence the goalkeeper then turned to me and said, "*Mr Bean, tell me again which colour pen is it that you write with if you need me to stop this meeting?*". I just stared at him in deathly silence, shaking my head, whilst the FA interviewer's face displayed a big grin and said, "*Thanks for that*". I could have screamed.

There was the occasion when I worked at the FA that I was invited to a Liverpool home game against Middlesbrough and sat in the Directors Box. As is the tradition at Anfield the crowd sang the club anthem, 'You'll Never Walk Alone' I recall thinking to myself, "Fucking Hell, who ever the bloke is who is sat behind me can sing a bit". I couldn't resist a sneaky look to see who the mystery singer was whose melodic voice was pitch perfect as we sat down only to see it was 'Lady in Red' singer, Chris de Burgh. I don't think he would have wanted to check who I was with my dreadful singing tones!

Then there was the time when Derby County asked me to sit in on a series of interviews as they underwent a standard FA transfer audit involving Robbie Savage's move to Pride Park. I had to sit in with both the chairman Adam Pearson and Savage himself. When it came to Robbie's turn, before we started he said he would nudge my foot with his foot if he needed to ask me anything when the FA people were questioning him. I didn't realise that it was going to feel like playing in a match with him. Almost as soon as the questions started Robbie's nerves got the better of him, even though he had not said anything wrong, and I felt him start kicking me on the shin which continued throughout the meeting. By the time he had finished my shin was sore and bruised!

I also got involved with a case in which I thought I was going to be representing two of the world's greatest players,

Messrs Thierry Henry and Lionel Messi, until it was explained to me that was not quite the case. In May 2004 Swindon Town Reserves played a game against their Bristol Rovers counterparts. A French based trialist was supposed to be playing in the game for Swindon, but the venue of the game was switched at the last minute from Swindon's County Ground to the training ground but nobody told the trialist. Therefore, having submitted the team sheet with a youth player's name who they intended to use instead, until the French trialist arrived at the ground 10 minutes before kick-off and hastily got changed, only to find himself dropped just as the teams ran out to play. Unfortunately, nobody mentioned the swap and the trialist got booked when he went on. When asked for his name he gave it as "Thierry Messi". As it didn't appear on the team sheet, Swindon felt the force of the FA's Registration Department and ended up facing two charges of misconduct and got a hefty fine.

Once, whilst at the FA and on a visit to AC Milan to interview the then president of the club over a transfer I was investigating, I found the tables turned on me. I turned up cock sure of myself and the things that I needed to put to him, but the Italian giants had other ideas! I was led into his office to find a single chair in the centre of the room, with me facing the president and his right-hand men all staring intently back at me. It was like a scene from a *The Godfather*, and I was made to feel distinctly uncomfortable. I couldn't get out of the place quick enough, which meant a whirlwind viewing of their magnificent trophy room that I undertook in about five minutes!

Dean Windass is one hell of a character and in 2004 I found myself being asked to assist him. He was playing for Bradford City against Luton and got involved in a dust-up with referee Joe Ross at the end of a game. At the final whistle Ross reported that Windass had approached him and said "*In all the years I have been playing you are the worst referee I have ever seen*". It must have been some performance from the match official considering Windass played in over 600 games! We went along to a disciplinary hearing in Birmingham and spent the entire afternoon fighting his corner. However, Deano's mind was on other things rather than the hearing, he needed to get home to feed the dog so the hearing took second precedence!

How many times have you heard the phrase, 'From Manchester United to Macclesfield Town' when talking about the huge difference in the status of clubs? It's fitting then that I started my story with Manchester United and end it with Macclesfield Town. I dealt with many cases on behalf of 'The Silkmen' until their expulsion from football in their former entity, but none as serious as the investigation into the financing of the new East Stand at their quaint Moss Rose stadium.

In 2005 they found themselves the subject of a very serious investigation from the FA after it was alleged that they had dishonestly obtained £195,000 in grants from the Football Foundation to help finance the new stand. In fairness to the FA, it was a very thorough investigation, with a file of papers running into hundreds of pages which took some getting through and understanding, given the complexities of the case. In a nutshell, what Macclesfield had done was supply bogus invoices which suggested they had paid their share of the construction costs up front, when in fact no payment had been made. This meant that the Football Foundation bore the whole cost of the stand, as opposed to the 80 per cent maximum they were entitled to. As well as the charges relating to the bogus invoices, the club faced a charge relating to the sponsorship of the stand itself, which was found not to be a true sponsorship deal, but more of a discounted price against the cost of building the stand. It was real heavy going having to trawl through pages of financial records, but the reality of the situation was that they were bang to rights, even though it was a former owner's regime which had committed the crimes.

The Disciplinary Panel didn't mess about with Macclesfield,

fining them £62,000 and ordering them to pay the £195,000 back to the Football Foundation, which was devastating for a club who, even at that time, were only just surviving. But it brings home the huge difference in the finances in the game, considering what Manchester United can afford to do in comparison to the likes of Macclesfield Town. I'm not trying to condone the actions of Macclesfield in any way, it was wrong what they did whoever the owners were, but it seems today that the chasm between the highest echelons of football and the bottom is so vast that there should be a greater distribution of finance filtering down the football pyramid.

There are many cases I've not mentioned in this book simply because there was just not the space to fit them all in. It doesn't mean they were any less important to me because I tried to do the very best for each client. I'd like to think that my clients could see that I was a real fighter for them in their times of difficulty. One thing I have learned, though, is that clubs run scared from the FA and rather than challenge them direct, prefer a '*go between*' like myself to do the dirty work and take them on, because doing it that way it doesn't feel like it's coming directly from the club itself. In effect you become the protective barrier between the governing body and the club.

When I started writing this book, I wanted to get my personality across. I hope that I have done that. I would also hope the reader sees me for who I am – a straight talking lad from Barnsley who made good for some part of his life. I have made many mistakes, some of which I bitterly regret and some which I have learned from. I am far from perfect, but my imperfections make me who I am.

The football industry is glamorous by those on the outside but behind the scenes it's a dog-eat-dog world, full of shark-infested waters, where an omertà or code of silence exists in some areas in which those who seek to abide by their own honest standards and principles are very rarely rewarded. On many occasions nepotism comes to the fore and jobs go to a friend of a friend, instead of the best person for the role.

I've had many ups and downs over the last twenty years or so. Some thrilling highs and some very dark lows, when mentally I've visited places no person should ever have to. I've done things that, had I remained that steadfast detective, I would never have experienced. Many people ask me if I could turn the clock back to the day I entered the football industry would I do it all again, and my answer is always the same…

Not a chance.

If I knew then what I know now, I would never have entered the world of professional football. I would have remained doing what I did best, working as a detective, doing a public duty, and putting bad people in prison. Countless times over the years I've reflected on my decision to leave the police service and wished I was back in the CID office at Barnsley Police Station. My late mother's words still ring true with me, *"Football jobs are no good lad"*. After years of denial, I must accept they were right.

So that's my story. How a tenner subscription led all the way to the door of the greatest football manager of all time.

EXTRA TIME

THIS BOOK HAS BEEN a long time coming. I've wanted to do it for quite some time but had to wait until the right moment.

Writing the book has been something of a release from the most harrowing period of my life, following the passing of both my parents within a short time of each other. Throughout my life I was brought up in the right way by a doting, beloved mother full of love, striving to do the best she could for me and making sacrifice after sacrifice. I hope my honesty within my story reflects her own values. I hope that some people can see the fighter in me that the likes of Sir Alex Ferguson alluded to in that first meeting that we had. I hope that the *"stand up for yourself and your rights and fight"* ingrained deep within my soul has shown itself.

However my journey and my story would not have been possible without the involvement and support of many people. There are too many to mention, so my apologies to anyone I have missed out. Firstly, my darling wife, Julie, and my sons, Jonathan and Matthew together with my in-laws Janet and Alan who spent many an hour looking after my young kids while I was working all over the country. They have given me so much support over the years, while putting up with a lot. They have been there when they were most needed.

My good friend, journalist Jeremy Cross, who I met during my early weeks at the FA, and who has helped me write this book. Ever since that first meeting we have been good friends and shared many stories, some that could be published, others that could go nowhere near being in print. But we've had lots of laughs together over the last twenty years. I don't think he's forgiven me yet for showing him a text from my son when we bumped into each other at a game which said,*"Rafa is dead"*, believing it to be the Liverpool manager, when in fact it was my son's pet mouse!

David Walker, former Sports Editor of the *Sunday Mirror*, has been a huge help to me over the years and guided me through some minefields within the sport, for which I will always be grateful, as has lawyer Richard Cramer from Front Row Legal based in Leeds.

Ben Kamara, (son of Chris) who worked for me for several years and without whose input and outstanding research, as well as his IT ability(!), we wouldn't have got the results that we did together. I am yet to meet anybody else who can sleep as deep and as long on a plane journey than Ben!

People who I will be forever grateful to for their friendship and help. The man who is my best friend, father figure and the best detective I ever worked with, and true confidante, otherwise known as "*The Chief of Detectives*" (even though he never attained any rank other than Constable) Don Murphy, along with his wife Gill. Only they know what they have done for me, and how they pulled me from some dark places. I will always remember this. As have my good friends Keith Brown and Dave "Glymo" Glymond. You were there when I needed you – and I won't ever forget that. Neither will I forget the unyielding support I received from a lady called Janet Rowley when I worked for a short time at the Yorkshire Ambulance Service. She was so patient with me during a very difficult period of my life. I'm sure Janet will be surprised to see her name in lights here, but I never got the chance to thank her for her patience, guidance and friendship.

I can't sign off without placing my gratitude on record to the likes of John Croot from Chesterfield FC, Neil Redfearn and Lucy Ward from our time at Leeds United together – we didn't half have some laughs at the expense of the Mad Italian, and most of all you, the reader for allowing me the privilege of sharing my experiences.

In football everyone has a shelf-life whether you are a player, manager, coach, director or administrator. The secret is knowing when that shelf-life is up - and I've reached that point. It's time to let someone else have a go. The extra time final whistle has blown for me.

Finally, in football, as in life, don't ever forget all you need is "Respect, Justice and Professionalism". One thing I've learnt is that along with honesty, it's all you need to get through life. If you lose it, then you've lost everything, but if you manage to keep those values close, then you will never, ever go wrong and would have lived a happy content life.

INDEX